Linguistic evolution

$495

CAMBRIDGE STUDIES IN LINGUISTICS

General Editors · W. SIDNEY ALLEN · EUGENIE J. A. HENDERSON · FRED W. HOUSEHOLDER · JOHN LYONS · R. B. LE PAGE · F. R. PALMER · J. L. M. TRIM

LINGUISTIC EVOLUTION

WITH SPECIAL REFERENCE TO ENGLISH

M. L. SAMUELS

Professor of English Language
University of Glasgow

CAMBRIDGE UNIVERSITY PRESS

Published by the Syndics of the Cambridge University Press
Bentley House, 200 Euston Road, London NW1 2DB
American Branch: 32 East 57th Street, New York, N.Y.10022

© Cambridge University Press 1972

Library of Congress Catalogue Card Number: 72-176255

ISBNS: 0 521 08385 0 hard covers
       0 521 09913 7 paperback

First published 1972
First paperback edition 1975

First printed in Great Britain by
Alden & Mowbray Ltd
at the Alden Press, Oxford
Reprinted in Great Britain
at the University Printing House, Cambridge
(Brooke Crutchley, University Printer)

Contents

Preface

It is often said nowadays that we have no theory of historical linguistics, or that the existing theories are unworkable (though it should be added that some of such statements are prompted by genuine modesty and by a desire to disclaim the ability to provide a fresh theory). But to the present writer it has often seemed that the objections raised to previous theories are pseudo-objections, and that it is unduly pessimistic to say we have no theory at all. Admittedly, a theory that could predict details would be impossible, since the interpenetration of extra- and intralinguistic factors is largely a matter of chance. But it is possible to form a theory that is somewhat less ambitious – one that will, for example, make general predictions, indicate what kinds of evidence to look for, and suggest how it is to be interpreted. The present book results from an attempt to provide a theory of this latter kind. Since it uses previous theories as its starting point, it makes no claim to provide either a revolutionary clean sweep or a panacea; but the resulting principles will, it is hoped, give a fair reflection of the 'why' as well as of the 'how' of linguistic change.

In chapter 2, the examples used are for the most part familiar ones from the better-known European languages. It would have been possible to add others from African and American-Indian languages, the study of which has advanced so greatly since 1945; but this might have run the risk of obscurity for all but specialists in those particular languages. Again, while a book of this scope cannot include examples of all the situations and processes that could arise, it is my hope that the principles outlined can be either applied or adapted to special cases in lesser-known languages.

It may be felt by some readers that this book could have been better expressed in generative terms. My reasons for not doing so refer to generative phonology rather than to transformational grammar proper, and they are twofold. Firstly, to have used it at the stage to which it had developed from 1962 to 1968 would have obscured, rather than clarified, my argument. Secondly, as a procedure it seems to be less concerned with the *causes* of linguistic changes than with their description. Indeed, in 1968 P. M. Postal could still write 'there is no more reason for languages to change than there is for automobiles to add fins one year and remove them the next, for jackets to have three buttons one year and two the next'.[1] Only recently have there been

---

[1] *Aspects of Phonological Theory* (New York, 1968) 283.

signs that generative phonology is being adapted to fit the facts of heterogeneity in both time and space.[1]

It is perhaps natural that, in attempting to bring order to a difficult subject, an author may give the impression of oversimplifying and minimising outstanding problems. I have tried in this book to place into perspective those aspects of the subject that I regard as most relevant; but I am only too aware that some problems are unanswerable, and that our tentative answers to others may be suddenly reversed by the accession of new evidence. The very nature of the subject demands continual caveats and qualifications; if I have occasionally omitted them, I can only plead the exigencies of attempting to present an ordered and coherent argument.

The text of this book was largely completed by 1970, and I was therefore unable to take account of B. M. H. Strang's important *History of English* which appeared in that year.

Finally, I should like to record my indebtedness to W. S. Allen, L. W. Collier, and R. B. Le Page for helpful comments and corrections. For the shortcomings that remain, the responsibility is wholly my own.

University of Glasgow   M. L. S.
   June 1972

1 E.g. in B. E. Newton's recent 'Ordering Paradoxes in Phonology', *Journal of Linguistics* 7 (1971) 31–53; and in publications for the Project on Linguistic Analysis led by W. S-Y. Wang of the University of California at Berkeley.

NOTE TO SECOND IMPRESSION

My thanks are due to E. J. Dobson for drawing my attention to his article now referred to on p. 36. According to his view, example (v) on that page would belong rather with the examples that precede it, and would therefore need to be replaced by a further example of the type given on p. 125. On pages 40 and 158 there are corrections of the two formal errors noted by A. J. Bliss in his review in *Notes and Queries* (1974).

June 1974   M.L.S.

Abbreviations

(a) Books and periodicals

Books referred to in footnotes by name of author only are listed in the Bibliography on pp. 182–86. If more than one work for a single author is listed, the reference includes the date of publication. The following other abbreviations are used:

AL	*Archivum Linguisticum*
EAGS	*English and Germanic Studies*
EETS OS	Early English Text Society, Original Series
ES	*English Studies*
JEGPh	*Journal of English and Germanic Philology*
OED	Oxford English Dictionary
PMLA	*Publications of the Modern Language Association of America*
RES	*Review of English Studies*
TPS	*Transactions of the Philological Society*

(b) Languages and dialects

E.	English	MHG	Middle High German
EMnE	Early Modern English	Mn	Modern
Fr.	French	OE	Old English
G.	German	OFr.	Old French
Gk.	Greek	OHG	Old High German
Gmc.	Germanic	ON	Old Norse
Goth.	Gothic	ONhb.	Old Northumbrian
IE	Indo-European	RP	Received Pronunciation
It.	Italian	Sc.	Scots, Scottish
L.	Latin	Skt.	Sanskrit
ME	Middle English	Sp.	Spanish

1 *Introduction*

1.1 Change and evolution

The title of this book ('Linguistic Evolution') was chosen in preference to 'Linguistic Change' although it is about linguistic change. That is because its purpose is to attempt an examination of the large complex of different factors involved, and the title 'Linguistic Change' might have entailed an over-simplification. Nevertheless 'evolution' is itself open to the misunderstanding that some sort of progress is implied, that a clearer or more effective means of communication has been achieved as a result of it. That meaning of 'evolution' is not intended here. We are not concerned here with the prehistoric origins of human language, and, as has often been pointed out, there is today no such thing as a 'primitive' language; every language is of approximately equal value *for the purposes for which it has evolved*, whether it belongs to an advanced or a primitive culture. For English, this can be shown, among other ways, by the fact that in earlier stages certain grammatical distinctions could be made that can no longer be made today (see 4.1 below).

In what sense, then, can a language be said to 'evolve'? We must recognise, firstly, that there is no inevitable one-for-one correspondence between a language and the culture it serves, and that the language need not be a precise mirror of the culture as it exists at any given time. Indeed, the so-called Whorfian hypothesis leaves open the possibility that an individual language, so far from merely accommodating or mirroring a culture's channels of thought, may to some extent even guide and control them, and so, no doubt, in many minor ways, it does. Viewed historically, however, it seems likely that those features in which language today apparently influences culture are relics in the language from a previous stage of the culture. For example, much is made of the Scandinavian terms of relationship, which distinguish automatically, at word-level, between grandparents, according to whether they are on the father's or the mother's side, and so also with uncles and aunts. Yet sociologists are not aware of any striking differences in the *actual* relationships in Scandinavia compared with those of speakers of other Germanic languages. Certainly, they were of special importance in all Germanic-speaking societies 1500 years ago, and their importance may have survived longer in Scandinavia than elsewhere; but today, the survival of the relevant linguistic terms does not seem to have ensured the survival of the corresponding modes of thought.

On the one hand, therefore, language must keep pace with the culture, progress in knowledge, and changing fashions in the society it serves; but on the other, it may retain many outdated features that are relics of past stages of the culture. There is thus a considerable margin of tolerance to both its contents and its limits.

But there are many changes in language that are not obviously the result of such extralinguistic factors. They may have been triggered by these factors, but to what extent and in what ways is not always clear, and the possibility remains that they arise internally for no other reason than that language, as a tool in constant use is (a) liable to constant fluctuation, and/or (b) in need of constant 'repair' or 'renewal'. The result of changes due to such (apparently) intralinguistic factors parallels those that result from extralinguistic: a series of outdated forms that, from the modern point of view, are 'anomalous'. For example, the alternation corresponding to *stand – stood* was regular in the Indo-European system, and so with that corresponding to *seek – sought* in Primitive Germanic, and with that corresponding to *feel – felt* in Old English. Today, when the only productive alternation is that seen in *move – moved*, all these relics of previous systems are more or less anomalous and therefore lessen the efficiency of the modern system. According to Professor A. Martinet, they are due to forces of conservatism and 'inertia', to which are continually opposed the pressures that work towards clearer communication. If that is a fair statement of the position, it would appear, on the one hand, that both externally and internally in language development an equilibrium must be maintained between the old and the new, between the inherited forms and the expressive needs of the present; but at the same time, that the margin of tolerance and choice in the maintenance of that equilibrium is probably fairly wide, except, that is, for certain special points of pressure that vary in each era. It is in that sense that 'evolution' is intended here.

1.2   'Causation'

How far is it either permissible or useful to speak of 'causation' in linguistic change? Some scholars have objected that changes are inevitable and wholly to be expected, and that we should therefore not seek causes or ask 'why', but only investigate the processes and ask 'how'.[1] If the suggestion made above is correct, that the changes are (a) partly to be expected because language is a tool used by a continually changing society, but also (b) partly unpredictable because there are wide limits of tolerance for the direction of change, it then follows that we are attempting both: we are enquiring, firstly, under what conditions the expected changes take place, and secondly, what factors condition the unpredictable changes.

[1] Spence p. 27; cf. Jakobson p. 651 on 'mutability as a constant essential component of any phonetic system'.

There is no logical objection to the term 'cause', but it has the disadvantage that it still carries with it the connotation of a single, indivisible cause. If, therefore, 'cause' is to be preferred stylistically to the more clumsy 'conditioning factor', that connotation must be discounted: it will be one of the main purposes of this book to show that, although one factor may often outweigh others in importance, an *insistence* on a single cause – what Jespersen called 'the all-or-nothing fallacy'[1] – has been, in the past, one of the main drawbacks to progress in diachronic linguistics. In both pure and applied science, the principle of multiple conditioning is a commonplace. Yet in the study of linguistic change it has been treated with suspicion; for long, the linguist who suggested a combination of causes operating in the past was accused of ambivalence. It is only more recently that the controlled study of modern usage has shown that such explanations are nearer the truth than those propounding a single, indivisible cause. In a pioneering article of 1957,[2] Professor Randolph Quirk demonstrated, from a frequency survey, the factors that influence a speaker in his choice between the relative pronouns *which* and *that*, e.g. position in the clause, length of clause, subject or object function, nature of antecedent; and a remarkable finding, supported by his figures, was that factors operating in combination are more potent than those operating singly. It would be unwise, therefore, to assume that a principle that applies to linguistic change today could not have applied to that of the past; and since, as will be shown later, every linguistic change involves at least some degree of choice, the probability of multiple conditioning must constantly be borne in mind.

By the same token, we must not start with preconceptions that parts of the linguistic process are more important than others, and that these must be given priority in the study of change. For some, at present, phonology is less important than grammar or lexis, being merely 'an input–output device that accepts a terminal string with a labelled bracketing and codes it as a phonetic representation'.[3] For others it is grammar that is simpler and less important, being merely a programming device for handling individual items in phonemic shape selected from a lexically based memory store.[4] But for diachronic purposes it would be wholly misleading to assume any such primacies. Though we know little enough about the brain, we do know that it has capacity to handle complexities at *every* level of the linguistic process. There is, therefore, no reason why changes associated with a particular level should be more or less complex than others: we must start by expecting them to have

---

[1] Jespersen (1922) 262.
[2] Quirk (1957), and (1968) 94–108.
[3] N. Chomsky, quoted by E. C. Trager in *Papers in Honor of Leon Dostert*, ed. W. M. Austin (The Hague, 1967) 159.
[4] R. C. Oldfield in *Psycholinguistics Papers*, ed. J. Lyons and R. J. Wales (Edinburgh, 1966) 23.

equal importance and complexity. If the evidence of linguistic evolution suggests otherwise, then that evidence, too, may be used for elucidating the basic
processes of language and thought.

1.3   The evidence

The substance of language, from a descriptive point of view, exists in two
equally valid and autonomous shapes – spoken and written. As a code, each
exists in its own right, and there has been justifiable insistence, in recent
decades, that graphetics and graphemics must in the first instance be studied
separately, before their relationship with phonetics and phonemics can be
considered. This according of equal status to the written language is not to
deny that it is ultimately derived from, and dependent on, the spoken language; but it is necessary, if only to disprove the naive speaker's notion that
the written language is a mirror-image of what he speaks (or vice versa), or
that it is based on contemporary spoken language, and not the spoken language
of various periods in the past.

Having granted that for synchronic purposes the two must be carefully
distinguished, we find that for diachronic purposes our choice of evidence is
far more limited: we must for the most part reconstruct from written records,
bearing in mind continually the differences that exist today between spoken
and written media. Least difficulty arises in the study of the spoken language
of the immediate past, which can be based on comparisons of the speech of
older and younger generations; and even for past periods, a certain minimum
can be reconstructed, by comparative method, from the present spoken forms
of cognate dialects and languages. But for the rest, our only source of detailed
knowledge is from written records, and the disadvantages of these are well
known. A very small proportion of them – for some periods only – contain
useful observations on the spoken language by grammarians, orthoepists,
phoneticians and certain others, e.g. a literary writer like Swift with an interest
in language; but, apart from the sometimes questionable evidence of rhymes,
the vast majority of written records from the past provide no evidence for the
spoken language beyond what can be deduced from the establishment of the
usual correlations of graphemes with segmental phonemes. To hypothesise
further, various procedures are adopted. For example, it is necessary to compare, if possible, specimens from the same dialect and period that differ in
style, in order to establish which features are more likely to occur in informal
style and may therefore be assumed to have been commoner still in the spoken
language. Deviations from the normal written language that seem to arise
from carelessness or illiteracy may provide similar hints. Throughout, features
of the writings that are obviously due to changing literary fashions and

affectations of style must in the first stages be discounted, and the probable degree of archaism in the written language must be assessed.

Even so, we shall know nothing of the suprasegmental features of stress and intonation. A few hints can be gathered from verse structure, but the main evidence is indirect, consisting of those variations and changes of segmental phonemes that seem best explained as due to a weakening of stress in some positions. Here, even more than elsewhere, we are extrapolating from known distributions in languages spoken today.

A further complication is that, for preliterate periods, we must reckon without any written language at all, even though the language survives in written form from an early date. In other words, we have to envisage that a language that had till then, or till an indeterminate time before then, developed as a spoken language only, without conservative influences from the written language, was then first committed to written form; we must estimate the degree of stylisation that was first adopted, and which may, for all we know, have created an immediate gulf between the two media.

In practice, therefore, there is little chance of keeping the two media distinct. But even if that were possible, it is by no means certain that it would be methodologically desirable. Though there are many differences of convention, the two media both expound what is essentially 'the same language'; and although, for the purpose of describing them at a given point of time they must be kept separate, it may be that for studying their development over a period of time, the interactions between the two media are just as important as their developments as entities. Certainly there is a separate continuity of change and development within each medium; but, unless the written language is of the ideographic or logographic type, the two must keep in step, for, if the level of correspondences between them drops, the written language becomes an uneconomic medium, used only by those few in the community who can afford the time to master it. Yet the artificial regulation of orthographies takes place comparatively rarely; the similarity of the two media is preserved by normal interactions, of which the more typical are shown in fig. 1. The broken lines A, A represent continual mutual interactions, consisting mainly of (i) conservative influence of the written language, inhibiting change in the spoken, (ii) exact written representation of new lexical intake into the spoken language, and its converse (iii) exact spoken representation of new lexical intake into the written language.

The full line B represents adjustments in the written language made later than the corresponding changes (e.g. phonemic) in the spoken. The full line C represents the influence of conservative spellings on the spoken language, resulting in 'spelling pronunciations' which may or may not reproduce an earlier spoken form: e.g. /fɔːrhɛd/ is produced afresh from the spelling *forehead*, and replaces /fɒrɪd/, the reflex of an earlier pronunciation which had

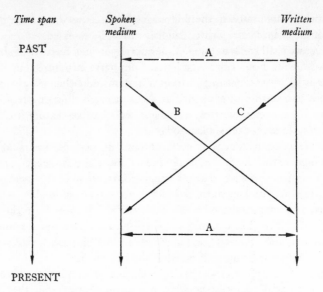

Fig. 1. Interactions between written and spoken media

been closer to the spelling, though not necessarily the same as the new pronunciation.

The scope and types of interaction that have to be taken into account are certain to be much wider and more complex than can be expressed diagrammatically. For example, prescriptivity in grammar acts in part directly from schoolteacher to children, but also indirectly through the written language (cf. 6.6, p. 110). A different kind of complexity occurs where there is a wide gulf between the classical and modern forms of a language (as in the case of Sinhalese): the literary form may influence only the formal register of the spoken language, not the colloquial. For our present purpose, it must suffice to assume that (*a*) a majority of linguistic changes arise in the spoken language, and may or may not ultimately spread to the written medium; (*b*) certain (though fewer) changes originate in the written language, and may or may not spread to the spoken medium; and (*c*) the main influence of the written language is a conservative one – it acts as a brake, inhibiting the general acceptance of many changes that arise in the spoken language.

In subsequent chapters it will be mainly the spoken language that is under discussion; and if the evidence for it consists of written records, they are used subject to the provisos stated above.

1.4   Basic distinctions and approach

The main distinction between internal (intralinguistic) and external (extralinguistic) factors has been referred to above. But there is another distinction that is liable to be confused with it if it is not carefully defined – that between *intrasystemic* and *extrasystemic*. The term system is discussed further in 3.1 and 6.7 (p. 129), but we may start by defining intrasystemic factors as those that operate within a single linguistic system, whether it is regarded as belonging to a small group (subdialect) or to a larger area that is less than that covered by a language (dialect), or to the total of these (the language itself); and extrasystemic factors as those that influence a system from outside it as a result of contact with another system, which may be that of another dialect or subdialect of the same language, or belong to an entirely different language.

The confusion between the two sets of terms arises mainly because, even though systems refer only to linguistic systems, everything that is extra-linguistic must also, in a strictly literal sense, be extrasystemic (this difficulty does not arise with the term intrasystemic). But this overlap is of no use to our investigation, and will be excluded by restricting the term extrasystemic to refer to intralinguistic only, as follows:

Intralinguistic	$\begin{cases} \text{Intrasystemic} \\ \text{Extrasystemic[1] (linguistic sense only)} \end{cases}$
Extralinguistic	$\left[\begin{array}{c} \text{Extrasystemic[2] (non-linguistic sense,} \\ \text{here not used)} \end{array} \right.$

This restriction enables us to separate the two sets, but, even so, we must expect them to co-occur in varying proportions according to situation, as in the following examples:

Example 1. An assimilatory change (e.g. /lɛŋθ/ > /lɛnθ/) arises independently in one community, and spreads to a neighbouring community: the origin of the change is both intralinguistic and intrasystemic, but its spread – viewed from within the second (receiving) system – is extrasystemic.

Example 2. A name is coined for a new invention (e.g. *typewriter, ballpoint*). The origin is extralinguistic, but the coinage is made from intrasystemic sources. If the invention is then introduced to a neighbouring community under the same name an extralinguistic factor (introduction of the invention) is still present, but the introduction of its name constitutes an extrasystemic but intralinguistic influence on the receiving system.

Example 3. The rise of a new standard language is extralinguistic, since a certain degree of movement or interchange in the population is a prerequisite. But the contact of different dialects that produces the standard is itself intralinguistic, and the process can be studied either intrasystemically, with attention focussed on the single – though as yet not homogeneous – system of the rising standard, or extrasystemically, with emphasis on the various influences of the contributing dialects.

In what follows, the distinction between extra- and intralinguistic will usually be assumed as axiomatic, but that between extra- and intrasystemic will constitute one of the main divisions of approach. In chapters 2–5 the causes of change are viewed as operating within a single system, while the extrasystemic aspect is reserved for chapter 6. The other main division of approach is between (a) *parole*-based variation, i.e. sources of variation at the level of idiolect and (b) functional pressure operating at the level of system. Parole-based variation will often be referred to as 'mechanical', but will include all variants, whether arbitrary or motivated, and irrespective of whether they are eventually adopted into the system or not; they will be treated as 'intrasystemic', but only in the broad sense that they occur in the speech of the individual users of a system. The sources of variation will be discussed in chapters 2 and 4, and functional pressure in chapters 3 and 5; but a number of problems that remain unresolved in these chapters will be subsumed in the latter half of chapter 6. In chapters 7 and 8, an attempt is made to formulate a theory of linguistic change and a method for studying all aspects of it simultaneously.

2 Variation in the spoken chain

2.1 Introductory

Human language is extremely highly developed compared with that of animals, and indeed it is probably the main reason for the development of the human brain;[1] but that does not mean that it is mechanically the best and most efficient means of communication that could be devised. The arbitrariness of its chosen combinations of sounds, the necessity of producing them consecutively with organs that were not originally evolved for the purpose, the fluidity of the word-concept spectrum – these are all typical disadvantages that might be held to support the old popular idea that languages naturally 'degenerate'. But that is now outdated, and it is recognised that all types of language are equally valid as communication, provided that they are used in their appropriate place or social milieu (*dialects*), or for the appropriate purpose (*registers*: cf. 6.2). The modern view carries with it the assumption that, in any of these types of a language, potential breakdown in communication is constantly and automatically remedied. It follows that, in any investigation of linguistic change, the first question to be asked is: are linguistic changes purely mechanical in origin, arising from the very nature of the substance of the spoken chain? As has often been noted,[2] success in performing acts of communication varies greatly, and, overall, comparatively few 'bull's-eyes' are scored. This is possible because (*a*) context and situation, and (*b*) the redundancy inherent in all linguistic systems, together provide a wide margin of tolerance for the understanding of actual, as distinct from ideal, utterances or writings. For example, the realisations of a single phoneme /t/ in speech might include not only [tʰ, tˢ, tᶿ] but also [p] and [k] without breakdown in communication; or the realisations of written *t* might be much nearer certain forms of *l* or *r* and still be understood as the writer intended. Such a margin of tolerance is by no means limited to sounds (phones) or letters (graphs); it applies equally well to grammar and lexis, where the choice of a word or construction may not be sufficiently accurate for the context, or may include, e.g., solecisms or inappropriate metaphors.

The number of variants (phonetic, grammatical or lexical) that are continually produced thus is vast, and it contains the 'raw material' of all linguistic

---

[1] At least, this seems to be the more likely of the two possible deductions that one can make from the fact that both language and a developed brain coincide in man alone.
[2] Paul p. 43; Hockett p. 440.

change. As regards the step from variant to change, we may adopt, for the present, a simple formula: the variant is misunderstood as an acceptable form (or reinterpreted) by the hearer, and, when this has happened often enough and been subsequently imitated, it ceases to be merely part of *parole* (sporadic usage in the speech of individuals) and is accepted into *langue* (the language, either in abstract or as codified).

But are the variants any more than the raw material of change? Can any universals be detected that would account for linguistic change as due solely to the tolerated margin of aberration? The remainder of this chapter will deal with the phonetic aspect of this problem, the grammatical and lexical aspects being postponed to chapter 4.

2.2   Conditioned phonetic change: evidence

The phonetic study of modern speech shows widespread use of variants according to context, e.g. at word-boundaries, as in /gʊg gɜl/ 'good girl', /tɛm paʊndz/ 'ten pounds', /hæʒ ʃi/ 'has she'; within the word, as in /əʊpm/ 'open', /lɛnθ/ 'length'; or in unstressed position, as in /ʃəd/ 'should', /hiːd/ 'he would' or 'he had', as well as in the orthographically established *he'd, shan't, won't, can't*, etc. In all such cases, it is evident that short cuts in articulation have been taken: those variants that show phonetically irreversible changes towards simplification are those used in colloquial (i.e. 'less careful') register, while variants not showing such changes are those used in formal register (besides the general distinction of formal–colloquial, other oppositions have been suggested which may or may not co-occur but can produce the same result: forceful–relaxed, careful–slurred, decreased tempo–increased tempo, lento-style–allegro-style). The existence of the written language is a strong influence towards the preservation of formal variants, but that does not alter the basic probability that the synchronic distinction 'careful–careless' reflects a diachronic process that stems from ease of articulation ('the principle of least effort').

Ever since Saussure's insistence that the diachronic and synchronic planes be kept separate, many linguists have been reluctant to extrapolate from synchronic evidence in this way, but it is not easy to see why. The principle of least effort has been amply demonstrated; its most obvious manifestation is that shorter linguistic forms are preferred to longer ones, and that those words which, by formative accident, are inconveniently long for frequent use (*telephone, omnibus, underground*) are subsequently replaced by shorter forms (*phone, bus, tube*).

It may be objected that the existence of two variants today provides no proof of change in the past; that all we know is that the same individual says

/gəʊɪŋ tə gəʊ/ in formal register but /gənə gəʊ/ in colloquial register, and that the precise diachronic link between the two escapes us. It is true that we are unable to tell whether a given form continually undergoes fresh and repeated reduction by each new user, or whether it is a repetition of the same form learned from others. But this argument is relevant only to the *chronology* of the change. For example, even where there is historical evidence for full and reduced variants in the same text (as in Shakespeare's *Ile/I will/*, *Ild/I would*), the reduced forms may have existed much earlier in the spoken language, the only limit here being provided by the Southern ME *ich*, which combined in corresponding but quite different contractions *ichil* and *icholde*. Apart from such uncertainties of chronology, the fact remains that the only possible etymologies for the two variants leave us with no alternative but to assume that one variant has 'come from' the other; and the assumption is confirmed by the overall absence of other variants to disprove it.

Again, if it is objected that the process of change from one form to another in the language as a whole cannot be treated as parallel to a pair of register-variants today, we may answer that the process assumed for the past *is* parallel – that assimilated or contracted forms existed at first as colloquial register-variants beside the full forms, but subsequently spread beyond colloquial register. This problem will be discussed more fully in connection with extrasystemic influences (ch. 6). For the present, we are restricting the argument to those forms or variants in a single system for which reasonably certain etymologies can be deduced from forms in a closely related antecedent system. On that basis alone, we may agree with E. Coseriu that the Saussurean dichotomy has long been interpreted too rigidly: the language itself is continually changing, and it is only synchronic *descriptions* of it that are static and give us, as it were, a still photograph of the moving object.[1]

In principle, therefore, and subject to further conditions that will appear in chapter 6, it is reasonable to assume that the same process, prompted by ease of articulation, is to be seen (*a*) in certain changes evidenced only in successive stages of a language and shown, e.g., in a formula like *eall swa > al swo > also > alse > als > as*, and (*b*) in contemporary variants like *cannot–can't* that belong respectively to 'careful' and 'careless' varieties of language.

Finally, it should be noted that variants arise *in spite of* the fact that every speaker can check or 'monitor' his output from the feedback through his hearing mechanism, i.e. there is less care in checking as well as in articulation. Whether this fact lends support to the theory that most phonetic variants arise in childhood, when monitoring feedback has not yet been perfected, must at present remain an open question (cf. 6.7); but it confirms that, for studying the origin of variants, articulatory criteria take precedence over acoustic (cf. 3.2).

[1] Spence p. 24.

2.3　Conditioned phonetic change: extent

The relation of conditioned change to the principle of least effort has been discussed at some length because the so-called 'ease-theory' of linguistic change has so often been questioned in the past. Obviously it cannot provide an explanation for all change; but its part is by no means negligible, as may be seen from the following outline of the main types of conditioned change.[1] (The examples that will be given are of changes that could take place within a single system as a result of inertia, but this is not to deny that the same changes could take place from extrasystemic contact simply because the structure of the receiving language does not contain certain sequences.)

(i) *Assimilatory phenomena*

The articulation of a segment is brought nearer to that of those adjoining it. The more important types are:

(a) Regressive assimilation of consonants, as in L. *adcedere > accedere, sec + mentum > segmentum*, **scribtum > scriptum >* It. *scritto*, OE *heahre > hearre, cyþde > cydde, wifman > wimman, æmete > ant*, E. dial. *lopster* 'lobster', /dlʊv/ 'glove', /tloːz/ 'clothes', /brɛtθ/ 'breadth', Sc. dial. /tneɪf/ 'knife'.

(b) Progressive assimilation of consonants, as in OE **bitþ > bitt* 'bites', *þisre > þisse*, ON **gulþ > gull* 'gold', OE *eln > ell*, ME *mylne > mill*, ME *wiltu* 'wilt thou'; cf. /tj/ > /tʃ/ in *feature, nature*, /dj/ > /dʒ/ in *did you?*

(c) Influence of consonants on vowels, e.g. of /w/ in OE *sweord > swurd, weoruld > woruld, wille > wylle* (ME *wol*, cf. *will–won't*), ME *wimman > woman*, MnE *want, swan, quality*, E. dial. /twɔʊv/ 'twelve', cf. G. *zwölf < MHG zwelf*; of /l/ in /tʃʊldrən/ 'children'; of /r/ in ME *kerve > carve, sterre > star*, MnE *burn, bird, earth*.

(d) Influence of vowels on consonants, e.g. palatalisation of /k, g/ in L. *caelum >* Fr. *ciel, centum > cent, canem > chien, cantare > chanter, causa > chose, argentum > argent*; E. *chin, cheese* (cf. G. *Kinn, Käse*), *yellow, yield* (cf. G. *gelb, gelten*).

(e) Voicing of intervocalic consonants (i.e. voicing ceases to be interrupted), e.g. American English [d] in *butter, sitting*; Latin intervocalic /p, t, k/ as in *ripa, vita, mutare, pacare, saponem* voiced to /b, d, g/ in the early western

---

[1] The terms 'conditioned' and 'isolative' are retained here. The introduction of distinctive feature analysis (and of prosodic analysis in the Firthian sense) has tended to blur the distinction between the two, and it is not used here as one that can be regarded as clear-cut throughout. Nevertheless, the distinction between features that belong to whole clauses and those that are limited to segments or syllables (or occasionally sequences of syllables within a word) remains an important one for the tracing of historical developments, and, as will be suggested below, bears a close distributional relationship to the traditional distinction between 'isolative' and 'conditioned'.

Romance languages, and to some extent in Italian (e.g. *pagare*). Cf. (*f*) below.

(*f*) Loss of plosion in intervocalic consonants, so that the flow of breath continues through three segments: Western Romance /b, d, g/ (as in (*e*) above)>/β, ð, ɣ/, preserved in Spanish and Portuguese (*riba, vida, mudar, pagar*, Sp. *jabon*, Port. *sabão*) but with loss or further change in French to *rive, vie, muer, payer, savon*. Cf. ME *fader, hider, togedere*>*father, hither, together*. 'Lenition' of plosives between voiced segments in Celtic may also be classified here, though it is more extensive in that it includes 'initial mutation' conditioned by a preceding word-ending (cf. (*k*) below).[1]

(*g*) Replacement of non-initial /t/, and to some extent of /p, k/, by [ʔ] (i.e. plosion is preserved, but is performed by the vocal cords themselves, not by tongue or lips): regional and colloquial English, not only intervocalically, as in [bʌʔə] 'butter' [kɛʔəl] 'kettle', but also before another consonant, as in [kʌʔfʊl] 'cupful', [fʊʔbɔːl] 'football', and finally, as in [ʌʔ] 'up', [bʊʔ] 'book'.

(*h*) Unvoicing of final consonants (i.e. voicing is not maintained till the end of the word, especially before a pause): ME (W. Midl.) *hont* 'hand', *lomp* 'lamb', E. dial. /nʌθɪŋk/ 'nothing'; /-p, -t, -k/ in G. *Weib, Lied, Tag*, etc.

(*i*) Vocalisation of consonants, especially of [ɫ] to [o] or [ʊ] as in [fiːʊd] 'field', [mɪʊk] 'milk'. Cf. L. *alterum*>Fr. *autre, parabola*>**parawla*>*parole*, OE *dæg*>*day, dragan*>*draw, hafoc*>*hawk*, Sc. dial. /bɔ/ 'ball', /fu/ 'full'.

(*j*) New articulation resulting from fusion, as in OE **bīdþ*>*bītt* 'awaits'. Cf. /sj/>/ʃ/ as in ME *nacioun*, MnE /neɪʃən/, and /zj/>/ʒ/, as in ME *visioun*, MnE /vɪʒən/.

(*k*) Alternation of forms resulting from different assimilations at word-boundaries ('sandhi'), e.g. ME (*Ancrene Riwle*, Nero MS) *ðe ualse uikelare* but *wurst fikelare, one ureond* but *his freond*. Initial consonant alternations of this type are a prominent feature of the Celtic languages, and include nasalisation and lengthening (gemination) that result from assimilation with the consonants that originally ended the preceding word, as well as 'lenition' (cf. (*f*) above).

(*l*) Alternation of forms according to well-defined variations of clause-stress, e.g. MnE /haz, həz, (ə)z/ 'has', /and, (ə)nd, (ə)n/ 'and' (cf. (ii) below, and also 5.5 for discussion of reduction in weakly stressed positions); and alternation that results from regular variation of word-stress, e.g. /rɛb(ə)l/ noun ~ /rɪˈbɛl/ verb 'rebel' (cf. 'Verner's Law', 3.5 below).

(ii) *Simplification by loss of segments*

Decrease in the length of words due to the loss of one or more segments is

---

[1] The term 'lenition' is used here to refer to the changes that took place in prehistoric Celtic before the loss of endings, and not to the surviving morphophonemic alternations.

often closely related to assimilation, e.g. the omission of /k/ in L. *pasc+tor>* *pastor*, *quinctus>quintus* leaves the purely dental–alveolar sequences /st, nt/; or loss may provide the conditions for a subsequent assimilation, as in OE *æmete>* ME *amte>ant*. The loss of vowels is from syllables with least stress in the word or clause. It is a succession of such losses of both vowels and consonants that is mainly to account for changes like L. *testimonium>* Fr. *témoin*, L. *consobrinum>* Fr. *cousin*, IE */bherɔnɔm/>* E. *bear* (cf. Skt. *bharaṇam*). The principal types are:

(a) Loss of intervocalic consonant with contraction of vowels, as in Gmc. */sexwan/>* OE *sēon* 'see' (cf. Goth. *saihʳan*, OHG *sehan*), L. *vita>* OFr. *vidhe>* Fr. *vie*, *pavorem>peur*, *securum>sûr*, Mn Sc. /dil/ 'devil'.

(b) Loss of medial vowel (syncope), as in L. *homines>* Fr. *hommes*, *bonitatem>bonté*, *anima>âme*, *tabula>table*, *manducare>manger*, *calidum>* It. *caldo*, OE *hatte* (cf. Goth. *háitada*), *heht* (cf. Goth. *haiháit*), *hierde* (cf. Goth. *hausida*), *ænlipig>ælpig>* ME *alpi* 'single'; cf. MnE *business*, *evening*, *every*, *ordinary*, *Wednesday*, *Salisbury*.

(c) Simplification of consonant clusters, as in L. *gnatus>natus*, */dɪdksko/>* disco, *testa>* Fr. *tête*, *patrem>père*, *rubeum>*/robju/>*rouge*, OE *cwipst>* *cwist* '(thou) sayest', *betst>best*, *godspell>gospel*, *hlæfdige>lady*, *hwylc>* *which*, ME *swuch>such*, *laund>lawn*, MnE *know*, *gnaw*, *write*, *right*, *bought*, *castle*, *climb*, *lamb*, E. dial. /o:l/ 'old', /tʃaɪl/ 'child', Sc. dial. /fak/ 'fact'; and by combination with (b) above, L. *dubitare>* Fr. *douter*, *civitatem>cité*, OE *heafod>* ME *heued* (*hefd*)*>head*, *hlaford>lord*, *macode>made*, *nawiht>* ME *naʒt*, *noʒt*, *not*.

(d) Loss of initial and final unstressed vowels (apocope): Gmc. nom. sg. masc. */-az/* (IE */-ɔs/*), preserved in Finnish loanword *kuningas* and Runic *stainaR*, but reduced in Goth. *dags*, ON *dagr* and lost in OE *dæg*; L. *murus*, *-um>* It. Sp. *muro*, but OFr. *murs*, *mur*; ON *gnógr*, *glikr* (cf. OE *genoh*, *gelic*), MHG *gelouben>glauben*, *beliben>bleiben*, E. dial. /gri:/ 'agree', /bli:v/ 'believe', /nʌf/ 'enough', /lɛvn/ 'eleven'.

(iii) *Addition of segments or glides*

'Addition' of substance would not at first sight appear to involve economy of effort. Yet the occurrences (although of different types and origins) have one feature in common – that they assist in smoothness of transition between segments or words:

(a) The insertion of a glide-vowel between the two consonants of a cluster is parallel and alternative to assimilation or reduction of the consonants, as may be seen by comparing /kəneɪ/ 'knee' in S. Scottish dialect with /tni/ (obsolete) and /tneɪf/ in E. Scottish. The insertion of the glide enables the inherited features of the main allophones of the consonants to be preserved instead of being adapted or lost. Cf. Sc. dial. /wəreɪt/ 'write', E. dial. /fɪləm, vɪləm/ 'film', /kɔrən/ 'corn'. The quality of the glide itself may, however, be determined by features elsewhere in the word, as in OE nom. sg. *burg* > *burug* but dat. sg. *byrg* > *byrig*, ONhb. *wyrihta* but *worohton*, *perh* > *perih* but ME *purh* > *puruh* (cf. (vi) (*a*) below).

(*b*) A similar process is to be seen in the conditioned diphthongs that arise in the sequence VC, e.g. the essential features of front [æ] and back [ɫ] in early OE */æld/ 'old' were preserved in Southern OE *eald*, but in Northern OE *ald* */æ/ was retracted to [ɑ] by assimilation to [ɫ]; cf. OE */xertæ/ > *heorte* (conditioned diphthong), and ME *hert(e)* > *heart* (assimilation of vowel). Other examples are OE */fex/ > *feoh*, ME *sah* > *sauʒ* 'saw', *ehte* > *eight*, E. dial. /fleɪʃ/ 'flesh', /aɪʃ/ 'ash'.

(*c*) A plosive is often inserted into consonant clusters that demand complex transitions, notably those containing /m, n, l, r/: Gk. ἀνήρ nom. but ἀνδρός gen., L. *em(p)tum*, *camera* > Fr. *chambre*, *simulare* > *sembler*, *pulverem* > *pol(d)re* > *poudre*, *tenerum* > *tendre*, OE *æmtig* > *empty*, *punor* > *thunder*, ME *nymel* > *nimble*. In some cases this change is due to faulty coordination of the articulators: in clusters starting with [m, n], the plosives [b, d] are automatically produced if, in anticipation of the next consonant, the nasal passage is closed too soon. In other cases it may be due to misinterpretation by the hearer of the particular allophones used, e.g. a strongly trilled [r] after [l, n] may be interpreted as [dr].

(*d*) Linking in hiatus is in many cases automatic, e.g. rounded or high-front vowels and diphthongs in English are followed by the corresponding consonantal glides [j, w] before another vowel, as in [gəʊʷɒn] 'go on!', [hiʲɪz] 'he is', [kraɪʲaʊt] 'cry out'; and this explains the retention of the fuller forms for *to* and *the* in hiatus, e.g. [tʊʷʌs] 'to us', [ðiʲɑːt] 'the art', compared with [tə, ðə] before consonants.

Typical hiatus-links in English, French and German are not, strictly speaking, 'added', since they survive from older forms, e.g. *a(n)*, /r/ in *sore arm* but not in *sore foot*, Fr. /n, t, z/ in *un homme, a-t-il, mes enfants*. But they may be regarded as additions when extended to contexts where they are not historical, as with 'intrusive' /r/ in /lɔːrənɔːdə/ 'law and order', Bavarian dial. /vierɪ/ = *wie ich*, /n/ in ME *he hafden al* sg. 'he had all' (Laʒamon's *Brut* A), Swiss dial. /voːnɪ/ = *wo ich*.

(iv) *Distance assimilation (vowel harmony)*

This change comprises the extension of a distinctive feature (front or back quality of a vowel) to the vowels of other syllables in a word. Some doubt attaches to whether the feature spreads through intervening consonants (in which case the change is a combination of the assimilations in 1(*c*) and (*d*) above) or whether the change is psychological, resulting from a simplificatory habit ('rule') adopted in the coordinating mechanism; probably either or both factors may apply in different languages.[1] In some languages the change is merely occasional, e.g. L. *ne hilum*>*nihil*, OE *finger* but *hungor*, *dæges* but *dagas*; but in others, especially Turkish, it is a prominent structural feature. A related change in Germanic, umlaut (mutation), evidently has word-stress as a conditioning factor, since it takes place only in stressed vowels when followed by unstressed /ɪ, j, ʊ/ in the next syllable. This to some extent differentiates the Germanic mutations as a special type, since it must be partly because of the weakening of the unstressed syllables that their most prominent mark is anticipated and added to the preceding syllable, e.g. Gmc. */foːt~foːtiz/ eventually yields *foot–feet*, cf. */land~landu/>ON *land–lǫnd*.

(v) *Dissimilation*

Dissimilation of adjoining consonants is parallel to (ia, ib) and (iiia) above in that it provides a simpler articulation, but nearer to (iiia) in that it preserves, to a greater extent than assimilation, the distinctive features of the cluster as a whole. Thus in OE *cies(i)þ*>*ciest* '(he) chooses', one of the two fricatives is dissimilated to a plosive, and likewise in OE *þeofþ*>*theft*, *hehþu*>*height* *gesihþ*>*sight*.

Dissimilation of non-contiguous consonants results less from the articulation itself than from difficulty in coordinating it. In most languages simple reduplications constituting the whole word seem to cause no difficulty, and indeed are sometimes created by the minor change known as distance assimilation, e.g. OFr. *cerchier*>*chercher*. But when the repeated consonants occur at arbitrary, irregular intervals among other consonants in the same word (as in tongue-twisters over the space of several words), one instance of the repeated consonant is often replaced by another that is similar in articulation, notably /l/ by /r/, as in L. *Mercurii dies*>It. *mercoledì*, *peregrinus*>*pellegrino*, *arborem*>Sp. *arbol*, Fr. dial. *albre*. Cf. L. *caeluleus*>*caeruleus*, *singulalis*> *singularis*, *medidie*>*meridie*, OE reduplicated pret. *leolt*>*leort* (Goth. *lailot*), Gk. *θιθημι*>τίθημι, *φεφευγα*>πέφευγα, E. dial. *frail* = Std. E. *flail*.

(vi) *Minor confusions*

(a) Confusion in the ordering of segments (metathesis) is of two types.

---

[1] In descriptive analysis, such situations are simply treated as the extension, over a number of segments, of a distinctive feature (or prosody in the Firthian sense) like palatalisation or nasalisation. But since the ultimate origins of these features are single segments, e.g. /j, n/ (whether lost or preserved), it is preferable for historical purposes to retain a segmental treatment throughout.

Firstly, the order of /r/ and a vowel may be reversed, as in L. *turbulare*>Fr. *troubler*, OE *þridda*>*third*, OE *þurh*>*through*, Sc. dial. /mɔdrən/ 'modern'; this may amount to no more than insertion of a glide-vowel and misinterpretation of the stress (OE *worhte*>*worohte*>*wrohte* 'wrought', *þurh*>*þuruh*> ME *þorouʒ*>*through*). Secondly, the order of two adjoining consonants may be reversed. In some cases this may be due to preference for a sequence that is commoner in the language, e.g. Gk. *τιτκῳ>τικτω, L. *vepsa*>*vespa* (and conversely, English dialects with /wɔps/ as their original form for 'wasp' may also show /krɪps/ 'crisp', /klaps/ 'clasp'); cf. also OE *ascian*>*axian*, *fiscas*>*fixas*, at a period when /sk/ was losing in distribution to /ʃ/ (3.6). But forms like L. *ascia* 'axe', *viscum* 'mistletoe' (cf. Gk. ἰξός) cannot be explained thus; it is possible that, at some time in the history of Latin, /sk, ks/ were especially liable to confusion since, as a result of normal phonetic processes, they were coming to be combined in the same paradigm (*misceo, mixtum*).

(*b*) Conflation of repeated sequences (haplology, as in L. *nutri-trix*> *nutrix*) is sometimes described as a short cut in which the first /tr/ is mistaken for the second in articulation, but the process may be more complex. To judge from British habits of articulating words like *temporary, veterinary*, there exist both hesitation and slurring in attempts to pronounce both syllables; then, in order to avoid this, speakers settle for /tɛmpərɪ, vɛtɪnrɪ/, and a convention gradually arises that the shortened forms will serve. The change is to some extent an alternative to dissimilation, since it eliminates repetition of a segment.

The above short survey under headings (i) to (vi) could not include all the subtypes and variations of conditioned change to be found in different languages (some further examples will occur in later chapters); but it is intended as a representative selection from the main types. In a majority of these, ease of articulation is prominent as a prime source of variation, while the remainder appear to have a close connection with attempts to ease difficulties in coordinating the articulation of complex forms. These factors, combined with those of faulty transmission and/or interpretation, are sufficient to account for the origin of conditioned phonetic variants, and it can hardly be claimed that this type of change constitutes a problem in the history of language. With the obvious exception of straightforward addition to the lexis for the naming of new objects, it is the most easily explained type of linguistic change; in view of the nature of language and its transmission, it is wholly to be expected, and, indeed, its absence would be more difficult to explain than its presence.

An objection frequently raised[1] to the above explanation is that, if such changes are so simple, they should appear in all languages and dialects to a full and equal extent, and not in varying proportions in each. The answer to

[1] Most recently by King p. 189.

this will be given more fully in the remainder of this chapter and in chapters 5 and 6, but a few general points may be anticipated here. Firstly, there must be a limit to the rate and quantity of assimilations, contractions and other rearrangements that is tolerable in a single dialect if intelligibility is to be maintained, so that, even if a large proportion of them are continually occurring in certain colloquial styles, only a small proportion could be in process of acceptance into other styles at any given time. Secondly, the fact that their incidence differs according to language and dialect follows from the very nature of dialects, which owe their existence to development in part-isolation (6.2): in each dialect, there are differences in the basis of articulation (2.4), in the effects of suprasegmental features on the spoken chain (2.5), in the forms that are socially accepted or rejected as status-markers (6.5), or selected for functional utility (5.2), or merely redistributed at random (2.7, 6.7). Since all these factors have relevance for the subject as a whole and not merely for conditioned phonetic change, they are dealt with in turn in later chapters. For the present, we may conclude that conditioned phonetic change, though it covers a wide sphere and has many repercussions on other spheres, is not difficult to explain either as regards basic causes or varying incidence. It has been dealt with first so that it can, as it were, be taken for granted and not allowed to complicate discussion of the more difficult problems that remain.

2.4   Isolative phonetic change: introductory

The main problem of phonetic change arises from 'spontaneous' (isolative) changes in which a phoneme changes in all, or nearly all, of its occurrences irrespective of environment, as in OE *hām, stān, hlāf > home, stone, loaf*. The neogrammarians of the last century tabulated such changes in great detail, but they were mainly concerned to observe correspondences between different stages of a language, and to formulate 'laws' for the changes. The phonetic grounds for them were never specified beyond what H. Paul summarised as 'displacement of the motory sensation[1]'. Individual changes might be attributed to 'raising of the tongue', 'lip-rounding', etc., and a battery of metaphorical terms like *Aufhellung* and *Brechung* was evolved which helped to hypostatise them, for a number of generations, as so well based as to need no further explanation. Later, we find terms like 'trend' or 'drift' of a language, which no more explain the changes than did 'the genius of the language' in the eighteenth century. It is small wonder, then, that modern scholars have turned from a purely mechanical approach and explored other possibilities – the requirements of the language system, the influence of substrata or of neighbouring languages, or the social origins of change of fashion. Before

[1] Paul ch. II.

proceeding to these, we must assess how far purely phonetic factors can explain the origins of 'spontaneous' sound-change.

Firstly, the boundary between those failures in performance that are purely accidental and those that are not is by no means clear-cut. The number of speakers with genuine speech defects like cleft palate or hare lip is comparatively small, but they engage in as much speech activity as others, and their speech reinforces tendencies already existing in other speakers, such as the substitution of a glottal plosive for other plosives, or of a voiceless lateral fricative for [s]. If such influences cannot be regarded as more than marginal, others are stronger. For example, the extraction of all teeth and the wearing of full sets of dentures (often of poor fit) from an early age were at one time common practice in certain sections of the Glasgow population: in these sections, even in speakers still possessing all their own teeth, the distinction between /s/ and /ʃ/ is less clear than elsewhere, and it is probably only preserved at all under influence of the standard language.[1] This is a special case because there is direct interference with the speech mechanism, but the influence of paralinguistic features, such as the voice qualities typical of different regions, is much wider. It has been suggested that the prevalence of adenoids in Liverpool speakers has been responsible not only for the local voice quality but for changes in the phonetic system of the dialect.[2] It is probably reasonable to assume that inherited (i.e. environmentally transmitted or 'learnt') features of voice quality are the indirect causes of linguistic change in many regions; and although it has yet to be shown that they could affect whole languages, they cannot be ignored in dialect research.

With voice quality must be considered another phonetic feature that is environmentally inherited and is still more likely to affect the development of a language. It is what has been variously termed its 'basis of articulation' or 'articulatory setting', and refers to the configuration of the movable speech organs typical of a given language. It was once thought[3] that this was purely a 'rest-position' (G. *Ruhelage*) which was connected in some vague way with national or regional habits of both physique and temperament; but it has now been shown[4] to be a special setting that is adopted whenever speech is in progress, differing from a rest position and including numerous adjustments of muscular tensions throughout the speech organs. According to this latter view, the setting is that which is ideal for the pronunciation of all the sounds in a given language, especially its commonest sounds; but this assumption would be extremely difficult to prove, for, when one considers how great is

[1] Confusion of /s/ and /ʃ/ without any special phonetic abnormality might be attributed to contact with Gaelic, but in the Glasgow area the sound in question is much nearer to the voiceless lateral fricative typical of a speech disorder.
[2] Abercrombie (1967) 94–5.
[3] Sievers (1894) 55–7, 272; Heffner pp. 98–9.
[4] B. Honikman, 'Articulatory Settings', in Abercrombie (1964) 73–84.

the range of allophonic choice available in any language, it is hard to see why the setting should be determined by the particular allophones in use. One might equally well assume that it was determined by the sounds used at various times in the past history of the language, and that it now determines, and is not determined by, the allophones actually selected.

Whatever the precise origins of articulatory settings, they vary greatly from language to language. The position of the tongue may vary from high and front to low and retracted, the lips may be rounded, neutral or spread, and the jaws may vary in degree of aperture (the nature of the variation may be seen most clearly by comparing the hesitation-phenomena of various languages, e.g. English /əm/ or /ɜ/, Scots /eː(ə)/, Norwegian /ø/, Russian /ḿ/). It follows that articulatory movements must vary in each language, not only for the obvious fact that the phones themselves differ, but because the starting and finishing points of the articulators are different. It is likely, therefore, that when changes take place, there will be an inbuilt preference for fronting in some languages, for raising in others, and in yet others for rounding or retraction. The subject has not been extensively studied, but the possibility remains that the direction of sound-change may be determined by a feature which, though perhaps partly functional in origin, is environmentally transmitted in each language, i.e. it is automatically learnt by imitation in childhood.

The factors just outlined have relevance for all phonetic change, whether isolative or conditioned. But a certain minority of isolative changes are similar to conditioned change in that they require little explanation beyond that of economy of effort. They are those that involve (a) the loss of a distinctive feature from a phoneme in all, or most, of its contexts, e.g. the loss of fricativity in the change of prehistoric Gk. /s/ to /h/, or of Gmc. (especially initial) /x/ to /h/; or (b) ultimate loss of all distinctive features resulting in complete loss of a phoneme, e.g. of IE /p/ in Celtic, IE /w/ in Gk.; or (c) the simplification of a complex articulation, e.g. /ã/ > /a/, Gmc. /aɪ/ > OE /aː/, Gmc. /xʷ/ > OE /hw/ > MnE /w/, sometimes by prior assimilation of one element to another, e.g. /aɪ/ > /eː/, /au/ > /ɔː, oː/, both of which are common changes, as may be seen from later Latin, Old Saxon, and Early Modern English. (These latter monophthongisations may have close systemic connection with the opposite process of 'spontaneous' diphthongisation (cf. 2.5, 3.3), but the origin of variation is different in each case.)

The distribution of such simplifications is not always complete, and to that extent they resemble conditioned changes; but since there is no obvious conditioning factor, it is methodologically preferable to class them with the residue (i.e. with all the isolative changes requiring explanation). The history of some of them (e.g. /hw/ > /w/, 6.7; /x/ > /h/, 8.3) shows that the feature was lost first in some contexts only, and its loss was then gradually generalised. It suggests that isolative change may have the same origins as conditioned change, but that, for reasons that are not immediately obvious, it is extended to include all contexts. We shall return to this possibility at the end of this chapter.

2.5 Isolative change: principal mechanism

The majority of variants of segmental phonemes, in so far as they are not conditioned by contiguous segments (2.3) or by well-defined alternations of suprasegmentals (p. 13), arise under the influence of those suprasegmental features whose incidence is not constant but varies according to both context and situation: stress and intensity, pitch and intonation, tempo, quantity and rhythmic pattern.[1] For our present purpose we need not define whether these belong to one or more of paralanguage, phonetics or phonology. The point is that, whereas in 2.2 above only *one* extreme in the range of register-variations was adduced to account for 'careless' (e.g. unstressed, relaxed or slurred) variants, here, in looking for the sources of isolative changes, *both* extremes must be considered, i.e. we must also include variants arising in 'careful', 'forceful' or 'committed' styles.

To consider vowels first, there is evidence to suggest that the stressed variants found in more forceful styles may show a *higher* or *more fronted* tongue-position, whereas the less stressed variants of relaxed styles may show *lower*, *more centralised* or *retracted* tongue-positions. The evidence for this claim is circumstantial but can hardly be ignored. Firstly, such a distribution of variants has been often observed, e.g. in the London dialect:

I'm 'going down the 'road: [daʊn].
Get 'down!: [dæʊn].

A similar distribution of [ɛ] and [iɛ] has been observed in Sicilian dialects.[2] If it is objected that such variants could have arisen in a quite different way, and have been merely selected to carry the distinction, there is a long-standing corpus of experimental evidence which shows a close correlation of the increased muscular energies required for (*a*) greater stress, and (*b*) vowels with higher and more fronted tongue-positions.[3]

The reverse process – the use of a lowered variant as a result of decreased

---

[1] Included here are all prosodic and paralinguistic features except the few already specified as 'well-defined alternations' on p. 13 above. Such exceptions do not differ in principle from the rest; they happen merely to yield such pronounced and much-used contrasts as to condition doublets from originally single segmental sequences.

[2] Schmitt pp. 68ff.

[3] Dieth p. 83, with references there quoted; Ladefoged ch. 1. The experimental evidence does not of itself prove the point in question, but it is significant when taken together with the evidence of stress-variants.

muscular energy – may be deduced from a comparison of the diaphones of certain English diphthongs. The vowel of *made* or *say* is today realised variously as [eɪ] (RP), [eˑ] (Scots), [ɛ:,ɛə] (Yorks.), [ɛɪ] (London and some types of RP), [æɪ, aɪ] (Cockney). The evidence of seventeenth- and eighteenth-century writers on pronunciation indicates that the main Southern reflexes descend from a sound no lower than mid-front [ę:]. As the accompanying sonagrams[1] show, the present diphthong [ɛɪ] does, *at one point of its span*, achieve the same acoustic effect as the monophthong [e:]. The origin of [ɛɪ, æɪ, aɪ] is therefore likely to have been relaxed style, in which the speaker began at a lower tongue-height than that needed for [e:], but then compensated by raising the tongue to a height greater than that required initially. An analogy, which both illustrates the process and suggests that relaxed style is the origin, is to be found in a certain type of languid crooning (or incompetent singing, as professionals might regard it) in which the performer never hits the higher notes at the point of expectation, but starts them lower and climbs up to them *glissando*. Other diphthongs of this origin are to be seen in Cockney [səɪ] 'see' and [fəʊd] 'food': the original vowels [i:, u:] were begun from lower and more central positions (at first [ɪ, ʊ], then [ə]) and their quality was reached only towards the end of the articulation. The same could be said of Cockney [gʌʊ] 'go' and probably of RP [gəʊ], which both show lowering and centralisation of the first element of [oʊ].

Such cases suggest that if the whole range of suprasegmental features is taken into account, the initial occurrence (if no more) of most new vocalic and diphthongal variants could be explained. The combinations in which such features can occur are many and complex; indeed, stress alone implies a combination of muscular energy which can manifest itself at various points on any or all of the scales of quantity, loudness and softness, tenseness and laxness, high and low pitch, and rising and falling patterns of intonation. In the past, certain phoneticians[2] have suggested that it is *varying* combinations of such features that produce different types of vocalic and diphthongal change. These suggestions have been largely ignored in recent decades, as is shown by an authoritative statement like Bloomfield's 'no permanent factor ... can account for specific changes which occur at one time and place and not at another'.[3] But the validity of such a negative approach depends on how much is being asked of the 'permanent factors'. The influence of suprasegmental features probably does account for a majority of variants that exist in the spoken chain, but not for the selection of one variant or another at a given point in the history of a dialect, and its generalisation to all contexts of the phoneme. It was thus the claim that this factor provided the whole cause for

---

[1] My thanks are due to Dr A. Classe for his kindness in supplying me with these.
[2] E.g. Fouché (1927), Schmitt (1931).
[3] Bloomfield p. 386.

'He made haste to say'

(i) Scots

(ii) English

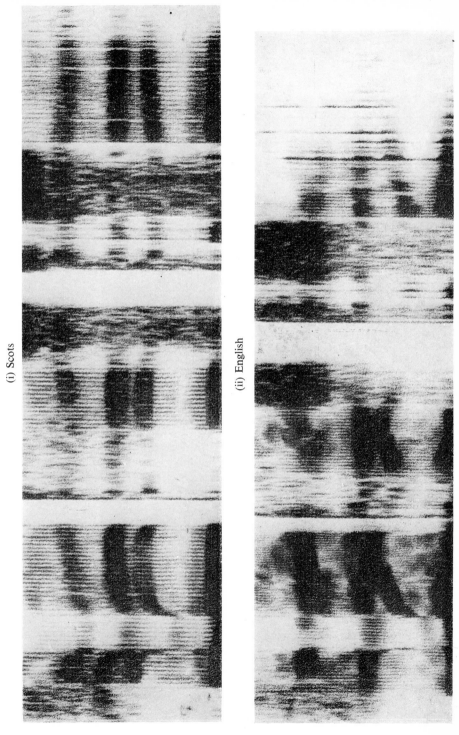

change that gave rise to suspicion; if it is viewed as the mere origin of variation, there are no grounds for rejecting it. Where subsequent developments confirm the possibility, we do not deny it: the distinction between *holy* and *holiday* shows what was at one time a complex distinction between configurations of stress, rhythm, tempo and quantity which happens to have been preserved and emphasised for us by subsequent divergent development. In particular, the effect of suprasegmental features on the phonetic shape of diphthongs was established long ago by Duraffour for the Provençal dialects;[1] it is borne out by a pair like [gúəd] 'good' but [gwódlək] in Frisian dialects;[2] and it is possible to find similar fluctuations in some types of English, e.g.

(a) *I can't 'pay* (deliberate statement with falling intonation): [pe¹].

(b) *You can't 'pay?* (surprised or outraged question with rising intonation): [pei].

It may be objected that the variety of isolative changes is so great that it is impracticable to attempt an account of their origin from suprasegmental influences; and, in view of our lack of detailed evidence on the subject, the objection has some cogency. However, it is possible, partly by the reverse process of deducing what kinds of suprasegmental a given variant would best fit, to arrive at a tentative, hypothetical scheme, the object of which is to show merely how different combinations of suprasegmentals might be expected to produce the commonest types of variants to be found both in past records and in modern dialects.

A. *Long vowels and diphthongs*

1. Forceful style, greater stress, with
   (a) level or rising intonation: raising, e.g. [e:] > [i:], [aʊ] > [æʊ]; fronting, e.g. [ɑ:] > [æ:], [u:] > [y:], [ɑʊ] > [øy].
   (b) falling intonation: centring diphthongisation, with the first element higher than the original vowel, e.g. [e:] > [iə], [o:] > [uɔ, uə].
2. Relaxed style, less stress, with
   (a) level or rising intonation: [i:] > [əɪ], [u:] > [əʊ].
   (b) falling intonation: centring diphthongisation without raising of the first element, e.g. [ɛ:] > [ɛə].

B. *Short vowels*

These are less capable of showing the effects of one of the elements of increased

---

1 Duraffour (1932), especially p. 66.
2 Frings pp. 25–6 and references there quoted; J. M. N. Kapteyn in W. Steller (ed.), *Festschrift T. Siebs* (Breslau, 1933) 152ff; and for parallels from Sicilian and Russian, Schmitt pp. 68ff.

B

stress – muscular tension. Increased stress may be manifested by lengthening of the syllable, either by lengthening of the vowel itself,[1] or by doubling of the following consonant[2] (cf. 3.10). Under conditions of less stress, lowering and centralisation may occur, e.g. [ɪ] > [ə], [ʊ] > [ə, ʌ] (but cf. 3.9). The above scheme includes only the main suprasegmental features. It does not include a distinction like *clipped–drawled*,[3] though these features are probably responsible for further variants. Certain types of RP that are characterised by drawling show diphthongised forms like [bæᵊd] 'bad', and it can hardly be a coincidence that diphthongisation of short vowels has gone still further in those United States dialects that are described as having a 'Southern drawl'. At the other extreme, 'clipped' pronunciations may account for shortened variants, and these may arise in great numbers when there is a change in the rhythm of the language, e.g. from stress-timed to syllable-timed. In the latter type of rhythm there is a tendency to level the quantity of each syllable, and this may account for the stress-shift in diphthongs in later Old and Middle French, e.g. /roi/ > /rwe/. A similar change, though less radical, presumably underlies the change of early ON [bɛᵃrɣɑ] > *bjarga*, [hɛᵃlpɑ] > *hjalpa* (later *hjálpa*); and a parallel has occasionally occurred in English when a short variant of a diphthongised vowel has come to stand in unstressed position, as in /wʌn/ 'one', Sc. /eːn/ > /jɪn/.

As regards variations of consonants, the directions likely to be taken in isolative change are (apart from the simplifications mentioned in 2.4) more limited than for vowels, since their articulations depend on discrete positions like dental or velar, not on a continuum of tongue-positions as in the case of vowels (though, within groups of closely related consonants, it is not hard to see why there can be interchange between, say, [ɣ] and [R], or between [v], [w] and [β]). It is possible, too, that the effects of suprasegmental variation are less on consonants, which occur at syllable boundaries, than on vowels, which occur at the peak of the syllable. But even so, the effects of the forceful/relaxed distinction must still be reckoned with, especially on the coordination of articulatory movements required for plosives. In relaxed articulation, if the active articulator of the plosion (lip, tongue or velum) is not withdrawn soon enough for a clear-cut plosion, the result is affrication: since the articulator is still in its original position after plosion has started, friction intervenes between plosion and the vowel that follows, so that alveolar [t] is realised as [tˢ], dental [t] as [tᶿ], [p] as [pᶲ] and [k] as [kˣ]. Conversely, in certain types of forceful articulation, the onset of voice after plosion may be delayed *without* fricative interference, so that [p, t, k] are realised as aspirated [pʰ, tʰ, kʰ].

---

[1] See especially Laziczius pp. 38–63.
[2] Cf. B. E. Newton, 'Spontaneous Gemination in Cypriot Greek', *Lingua* 20 (1968) 15–57 and references there quoted.
[3] For the great variety of contexts in which these and other prosodic features are found in Modern English, see Crystal pp. 300–8.

One of the best known of irreversible consonant-changes is that of voiceless plosives to fricatives or affricates, as in IE [p, t, k] > Gmc. [f, θ, x], Ancient Gk. [ph, th, kh] > Mn Gk. [f, θ, x], OHG [p, t, k] > [pf, ts, kx]. In all these, without postulating affrication or aspiration as the causes, we may at least regard them as the sources of variation.[1]

2.6 A problem: preliminary statement

One of the problems that lie at the root of this enquiry may now be stated in preliminary fashion. If an isolative change such as the raising of vowels is due – even only initially – to the influence of suprasegmental features, why is it that this conditioning factor does not apply equally to *all* vowels, and what relation has it to mergers and circular shifts? In the case of the latter, it may be objected that variants of *opposite* origins have to be assumed for different parts of the shift, e.g. for the Great Vowel Shift, forceful-style variants for the changes /e:/ > /i:/, /a:/ > /e:/, /ɛ:/ > /e:/, /o:/ > /u:/ and /ɔ:/ > /o:/, but relaxed-style variants for the diphthongisations /i:/ > /aɪ/, /u:/ > /aʊ/. This apparent contradiction is, however, only superficial. All linguistic change entails a process of selection (7.2), and all the variants are of mechanical origin and are continually and automatically present in the spoken chain. Moreover, the combination of variants that originally belonged to different registers (or dialects) into a single register is, as we shall see, the basis of grammatical restructuring, and may therefore reasonably be assumed for phonology also.

The more basic problem that remains is: why do forceful-style variants preponderate at different times and places in linguistic history, and why are redistributions of the type just mentioned a necessary consequence of such imbalances? Answers to this problem will be attempted in 3.7 and in chapter 6.

2.7 Conditioned and isolative change

We have seen that the variants contributing to both conditioned and isolative change can be termed broadly 'stylistic' in origin. In conditioned change, those typical of relaxed style are uppermost, i.e. the effects of ease in articulation are prominent; in isolative change, the variants may be those typical of *either* relaxed *or* forceful style, i.e. both ease and greater intensity of articulation have to be taken into account. Furthermore, there is a close relation in origin between the two types. In conditioned change, the variants arise (i) from

---

[1] The Celtic lenitions (2.3) are sometimes classed with these changes on the ground that they include the parallel result [p, t, k] > [f, θ, x]; but they always involve a split which was conditioned by the alternation of forceful and relaxed articulations according to phonetic context, and not by stylistically induced suprasegmentals.

assimilation or other adaptation of contiguous segments, (ii) from easing the coordination of a whole succession of segments, and (iii) more rarely, from assimilation of segments to certain well-defined alternations of suprasegmentals, such as those of word-stress in 'Verner's Law' (3.5). In isolative change, too, the segments in question are assimilated or adapted, but in this case to suprasegmentals that are less predictable in distribution: those that may accompany different registers, prosodies, paralinguistic features and the like (2.4–5).

But if the two types are as closely related as this, why is there such a difference in their distribution? Why do conditioned variants remain limited to certain contexts, whereas isolative change, although similarly limited in origin, is extended to all contexts of the phoneme? A clue is provided by the difference in the types and distributions of assimilation that have just been referred to. In conditioned change, various allophones can remain widely dispersed because the conditioning is overt (i.e. the distribution can be imitated and learnt); but in isolative change the conditioning is covert – the distribution in which the whole range of register-variants can occur is not obvious. If the conditioning factor can be perceived and learnt, the variants can survive, irrespective of whether the distributions remain purely allophonic or are in time reallocated to different phonemes (3.5–6). But the harder the conditioning factor is to perceive, the less chance there is of this, and the result will be that, of two covertly conditioned variants, one is generalised at the expense of the other: if the newer form is preferred, isolative change takes place; if the older form is preferred, there is no change at all. (The notion that a child learns the overt distinctions by 'rule', but that there is no rule that could be formulated for covert and more fluid distributions, would no doubt be another way of putting the matter; but it is by no means a *sine qua non* for the description of the overall historical process.)

The above explanation is aimed at the two extremes – change that is obviously conditioned, and change which, to judge from evidence available, affects a majority of the instances of a given phoneme more or less simultaneously. But there are other types that may be regarded as midway between these two extremes. As already suggested above (p. 20f), simplificatory changes are more likely to have taken place gradually, context by context (see further pp. 120–3 and 8.3). A similar gradual spread may apply to any conditioned change if the conditions are successively widened, or simply because a new generation misunderstands the previous distribution and extends it to contexts where no conditioning applies[1] (cf. p. 124f below). Furthermore, the rise of suprasegmentally conditioned doublets is well attested, and preferences for one

---

[1] Especially in cases of isolative change which show an unusual direction, it is necessary to explore the possibility that they might conceal a long process of spread from an originally limited conditioning to other relevant parts of the lexis. Cf. the term

or other of the two forms may take time to become established, affecting different parts of the lexis in different ways. For example, the present distribution of the types *flood, mood* and *good* reflects changes of quantity at different periods, and results from selections – whether arbitrary or motivated – that were independent of the original conditioning factors (cf. pp. 35 and 125).

To sum up thus far: variation of mechanical origin in the spoken chain provides a sufficient explanation for conditioned phonetic change; it will also explain the origins of isolative change, but the question of its relative importance for the process and incidence of isolative change as a whole is left open for the present, and will be resumed in chapters 3, 6 and 7.

'lexical diffusion' proposed by Wang pp. 12–18.
Other unexpected changes may be open to similar explanations. For example, the change of initial *gr-* to *r-* in South Italian dialects (e.g. *ranne* = *grande*) is unlikely to be a straightforward simplification since that would imply an unusually low standard of what is 'hard to pronounce'; more probably, therefore, it is an extension from another change normal in the same dialects, in which *gl-* > [ʎ].

3 System: the phoneme

3.1 System and substance

Hitherto we have been concerned with sources of variation in the substance of the spoken chain, but only a minority of such variations could be said to aid communication; some may ultimately do so, but the majority when first used are a hindrance, or at best are neutral. The essential complement of the substance of communication is the system: this requires stability of functional units which are discrete in form yet overlap sufficiently in function to provide a margin of redundancy.

The dichotomy of 'form' and 'function' is one that is taken for granted in descriptive linguistics: in any living language, it is open to observation what precise functions are borne by any given phoneme or morpheme, and the problem is no more than one of accurate description. But to anyone looking for the causes of change, it is by no means always clear whether a change takes place primarily because a function in the system is not being performed efficiently (i.e. adequately for 'expressive needs'), or because of any of the mechanical reasons outlined in chapter 2. Indeed, Saussure went so far as to deny that a history of functions (i.e. of systems as distinct from forms) is possible at all; for him, system was a synchronic manifestation only.[1] Since Saussure there has been continual controversy: some have supported a mechanical solution, others a functional one (and yet others have denied the possibility of discovering any solution at all). The precise boundary-line escapes us, mainly because we have no means of telling which of the two, form or function, occupies more importance in the brain-process of the speaker or writer. It is true that we can tell what happens in cases of slow, *conscious* selection from a number of alternative means of expression. But the process of selection is usually unconscious. Does it involve merely fitting a ready-made stretch of the inherited spoken chain, recalled from memory, to a given situation? If so, the mechanical factors in change would appear more important. Or is there fresh selection of each functional element in the utterance? In that case, the functional factor would outweigh the mechanical. These are questions for which the psycholinguist has not yet provided an answer, and perhaps no answer is possible. From a subjective viewpoint, it might be surmised that, since many tactless or otherwise inapposite utterances turn out, in

---

[1] Saussure (1960) 81.

retrospect, to have been uses of previously learnt stretches of the spoken chain that simply did not fit the situation, our overall use of the 'form-directed' spoken chain is greater than we might think, and in any event greater than the conventionalities of cliché and phatic communion to which it is often restricted. Information theory has shown that all common collocations, being predictable, are more easily understood than rare collocations; and since the same presumably applies to the speaker's selection of them from the memory-store, their use is but another demonstration of the principle of least effort. On the other hand, a brain that is alerted to the danger of inapposite utterance will presumably 'check' the functional value of the units it selects. It depends, therefore, on the degree of alertness, whether an utterance is to be classed as 'form-directed' or 'function-directed'; naturally there are borderline cases, but it is probably wrong to assume that utterance normally results from a conflict, within the brain, between the need for intelligibility and the tendency to rely on stretches of actual or embryo cliché. In the genesis of a single utterance, one or other factor will have the upper hand (which one depends on the speakers and the situation); but there is no way of gauging from individual utterances the relative importance of each factor for the processes of change. But although the two factors cannot be separated at the level of idiolect, it is reasonable to suppose that the total utterances of a community will fall mainly into one or the other of the two types – 'form-directed' and 'function-directed'. Both types belong to the same language, and neither (except in extreme cases of cliché or innovation) is overtly distinguishable; they are interdependent and interact, and neither would exist or be understood without the other. It follows that, for the study of change, both types must in the first instance be accorded equal consideration (cf. 7.1–2).

Since the functional unit of the phonological system, the phoneme, is not in itself (except as specified in 3.10) a unit that carries meaning, it differs from the functional unit of the grammatical and lexical systems, the morpheme. Consequently each must be discussed separately, and the remainder of this chapter will be restricted to the phonological system, the grammatical and lexical systems being deferred to chapters 4 and 5.

3.2 The phoneme

The term 'phoneme' is understood here in the conventional sense, i.e. that which is currently dubbed pejoratively by its opponents as 'taxonomic' and 'autonomous'. Ample reasons have been given by other writers for not accepting the Chomsky–Halle 'systematic' phoneme.[1] Two of the principles adopted by this school may be noted here as especially unsuitable for historical

---

[1] See especially Householder (1965) and references quoted by C. F. Hockett, *The State of the Art* (The Hague, 1967) 3.

study. Firstly, although it is indeed highly desirable that phonology and morphology should be considered together (cf. 7.2), this does not mean that the two must be forcibly and artificially yoked throughout. The view that rules remain in the language for just so long as they are morphophonemically relevant is misleading in that it excludes a far more probable alternative – that much morphophonemic alternation is, in origin at least, sheer coincidence. For example, *crime–criminal* is only one case among many like *rhyme–rim, pine–pin, slime–slim*. All have developed in the same way and for the same reasons, and it is wholly unreasonable to suppose that the learner regards the difference between /aɪ/ and /ɪ/ as of a different order in *crime–criminal*, or that he needs a 'rule to transform the underlying systematic phoneme /ī/' for such correlations only.

Secondly, the principle that 'given two distinct phonological representations, their phonetic representations are not necessarily contrastive' ignores an important difference between phonology and grammar, that the former is mainly arbitrary, the latter motivated. Generative phonology insists on equating them: just as syntactic homonymity is tolerated in *Flying planes can be dangerous*, and the ambiguity is 'resolved by the underlying rules', so with phonological homonymy. But this is simply not the case; syntactic homonymities are minor pressure-points that result from small areas of overlap between two grammatical constructions, and they can always be avoided by the selection of alternative constructions. In phonology, by contrast, arbitrary homonymous forms can be learnt, but, if there is a large overlap in their privilege of occurrence, the inconvenience proves more than a match for the 'underlying rules'. In other words, if every speaker knows how to separate, by rule, non-contrastive phonetic representations, why is it that homonymy has the effects that linguistic geography proves it to have (5.2)? Evidently the 'systematic phoneme' raises more problems than it solves.

For studying the historical development of the conventional phoneme, five main areas will be considered here: (i) its distinctiveness or 'differentness' from the other phonemes in the system, measured by the suitability of the oppositions by which its distinctive features exist and are maintained; (ii) its distribution in the system of grammar and lexis; (iii) the energy required for the pronunciation of its combination of distinctive features, and the possibility of economy of energy by omitting one or more of them; (iv) its sonority or 'carrying power'; and (v) its phonaesthetic or 'expressive' properties. Of these five, the first is the most important and will be given greatest weight in the discussion that follows.

Although distinctive features must have some basis in phonic substance, they operate essentially at the level of system, i.e. they are expected in certain combinations and contexts in each language, and may be interpreted as present even though they are absent from, or inaccurately represented in, the substance. But since they are abstract, they can be described only in the terms that correspond at the level of phonic substance. As regards the current controversy as to whether articulatory or acoustic evidence is to be preferred, the study of change evidently demands both: the production of new variants is mainly articulatory in nature, their spread and imitation mainly acoustic, and both are continually coordinated by the process of monitoring. But for the description of change, articulatory evidence provides more detailed distinctions;[1] and articulatory terms are usually more explicit, e.g. 'loss of plosion' or 'replacement of plosion by fricativity' tells us more about the nature of the main change in L. *saponem* > Fr. *savon* than '[+continuant]'. Furthermore, there is as yet little agreement on the acoustic terms to be used: for the change just mentioned, some would include [+strident], others not.

As in chapter 2, therefore, we shall continue to use articulatory terms, with the proviso that they presuppose the corresponding acoustic terms wherever relevant.

3.3 Phonological space

Each phoneme, ideally, must remain at a point of full, if not always maximum, differentiation from its neighbours in its system (vocalic or consonantal), so that the groups of words in which it occurs remain distinguished and viable. If one phoneme shifts, others will also shift in such a way that the differentiation is preserved ('push-chain mechanism'), while others again will automatically increase their area of possible realisation by moving into the vacated space ('drag-chain mechanism'). Phonemic shifts are therefore often extensive and involve a large part of the vocalic or consonantal systems. But if differentiation is inadequately preserved, two phonemes may merge; there will then be more space for differentiation than before, and a fresh realignment of other phonemes. Conversely, if a new phoneme appears, there will be less space, and a realignment in the opposite direction. These principles of phonological space have been confirmed by the comparison of neighbouring dialects, e.g. Swiss dialects possessing the three phonemes /ɑ:/, /æ:/ and /ɔ:/ use only central allophones of /ɑ:/, whereas those with only the two phonemes /ɑ:/ and /æ:/ have a greater allophonic range for /ɑ:/ and typically show a more retracted vowel.[2]

The amount of space available in any given system is a purely relative matter, since the numbers of phonemes in different languages vary so greatly. But it is reasonable to assume, firstly, that there are established margins of space between the different groups of words distinguished by the phonemes of each language, and that these margins cannot be suddenly de-

[1] Cf. E. C. Fudge, 'The Nature of Phonological Primes', *Journal of Linguistics* 3 (1967) 1–34. [2] Moulton (1962).

creased; and, secondly, since the simplificatory phonetic processes described in 2.3 may have the paradoxical effect of increasing the number of phonemes (e.g. /k/+front vowel>/c/ or /tʃ/, /zj/>/ʒ/), that a principle of economy of units operates to some extent in every system (cf. 5.1).

To this standard theory of phonological space, certain qualifications need to be added. Firstly it is uncertain whether diphthongs should be regarded as constituting a third system, distinct from those of vowels or consonants. They evidently perform the same function as vowels in structure, and in some systems it would be misleading to separate them since they patently complete a vowel-pattern that would otherwise be incomplete. At the same time, the degree of phonetic distinctiveness from neighbouring vowels that is achieved by the gliding property of diphthongs is often greater than might be expected, and they are therefore better regarded as a partly autonomous section of the vowel system as a whole; they possess an extra feature that enables them to remain close to, yet distinct from, vowels in the total vocalic space available, and their function can be important. It is probably for this reason that where, by simplificatory change, diphthongs merge with monophthongs (e.g. OE ēo>ME/e:/, ēa>/ɛ:/) a new series of diphthongs arises, as seen in ME dai, sauʒ (cf. 8.3); or, conversely, where extra diphthongs are created, other diphthongs are monophthongised (cf. 3.8).

Secondly, the operation of push- and drag-chain processes varies somewhat according to whether the system in question is vocalic or consonantal. The spacing of vocalic phonemes is governed mainly by tongue position, so that the whole area of the classic 'vowel-quadrilateral' is available for *gradual* shift, without sudden abandonment of one articulation and adoption of another (cf. 6.7). Obvious distinctive features like the rounding of front vowels are probably the result of secondary complex articulations. The view that vocalic changes are always discrete, and result from rules of the form '→[+tense/lax/ grave/acute, etc.]' is difficult to reconcile with the proved existence of movement in phonological space. Certainly features like tenseness and laxness are important for vowel-change, but their presence does not exclude the possibility that *any* vowel-change can be a gradual one. On the other hand, the articulations of consonants cannot always pass gradually from one position to another, since their differentiation depends on combinations of distinctive features like fricativity vs. plosion, voice vs. voicelessness, velarity vs. labiality. Many of them admit of gradual change, e.g. plosive>fricative, voiced> voiceless; and in other cases gradual change can occur if the transition is bridged by a secondary or adjoining articulation, as in IE *kʷoteros>Gk. πότερος, or Middle Sc. /xwat/>Mn NE Sc. /ɸat/ or /fat/ (even the change of IE *kʷis to Gk. τίς has been plausibly explained via a labiopalatal stage [kɥ], whence subsequently [kj] and [tj]).[1] But a change like that of /θ/ to /f/

[1] Allen (1957–8).

(as in Old French, Cockney English) is less open to such explanations. One can assume that a labialised [θʷ] develops in final position before lip-closure, and is then extended to other positions; but the change is more probably a 'saltatory' one in which a single feature is reinterpreted (dental > labial). However, this involves only a slight alteration in transmission if the other features (fricativity, voicelessness) remain constant.

We may conclude that the great majority of phonetic changes can take place by gradual and imperceptible stages, though they need not necessarily do so (cf. pp. 125–7). Apart, therefore, from the operation of the essential phonemic principle that distinctions are maintained intact, it would be possible to regard multiple shifts as non-systemic. But in the case of merger or the appearance of a new phoneme, there are further considerations.

3.4 Integration

The importance of a phoneme in the system depends on

(i) the number of oppositions it supports, and the frequency of those oppositions in use ('functional yield'), and

(ii) whether or not it fits the symmetry of the phonemic pattern and is therefore 'well integrated' both as a member of its own series and as having correlations in other series.

It is difficult to assess the validity of these two factors in influencing change. It seems likely that if there are few pairs of words in which two neighbouring phonemes are contrasted, there will be nothing to inhibit their merger; whereas, if a merger would create a large number of homonyms in frequent use in the same contexts, the phonemes are more likely to be kept apart. In other words, a large functional yield favours the continuance of a phoneme, a small functional yield renders it liable to merger. This deduction follows from the fact that in general phonemes with small functional yields are rarer and that homonymity is kept within reasonable proportions; but it has not been substantiated in detail, and scholars are not agreed on its relevance for change.[1] Some indications that it plays a part in the selection of variants will be given in 7.3, but, as will appear from the remainder of this chapter, it seems to have less importance than purely mechanical factors.

The criterion of symmetry of pattern is just as hard to establish. It can be argued that many modern phonemic systems are in fact unsymmetrical, though it is then counter-argued that all these are in a transitional state (which

---

[1] A typical argument is that, in languages showing widespread merger, functional yield did not inhibit it, and other remedies had to be found subsequently (e.g. classifiers and explanatory compounds in colloquial Chinese). But to this it can be answered that functional yields do normally inhibit merger, and that it is only in cases of abnormal mechanical pressures towards merger that they fail to do so.

is true of any system), and that there is continual pressure to make them more symmetrical (which is not necessarily true). However, since symmetry of systems is, among known languages, commoner than asymmetry, the criterion probably has some validity, especially if it is regarded as complementary to the principle of functional yield. The MnE phoneme /ʒ/ arose in the fifteenth and sixteenth centuries from the combination /zj/, as in *measure, vision* – a change parallel to /sj/ > /ʃ/, except that /ʃ/ joined an already well-established phoneme. /zj/ might easily have been restored under the influence of the spelling, for even today /ʃ, ʒ/ are in free variation with /sj, zj/ in words like *Asia, azure, Rhodesia,* and Shakespeare's pun (in *Love's Labour's Lost*) on *shooter* and *suitor* no longer holds. Support from French words like *rouge* and *garage* is not great, since the nearest native equivalent in final position, /dʒ/, is often substituted. Its functional yield is negligible: the minimal pairs are obscure and far-fetched (*confusion–Confucian, measure–mesher* 'one who makes meshes'); and its function is otherwise merely a supporting one, as in *vision–fission*. Why, then, is it an established phoneme, and not merely a marginal realisation of /zj/, as [ç] is of /hj/ in *Hugh, huge?* The only possible reason is that all other English fricatives occur in both voiced and voiceless varieties, and that without /ʒ/ there would be a gap opposite /ʃ/, a phoneme with a large functional yield.

Though each on its own might not help, when considered together in this way the two criteria of functional yield and symmetry of pattern can be expected to give some general idea of the systemic pressures working for the preservation of a given phoneme. If merger takes place in spite of them, it can be deduced to be non-systemic in origin.

3.5 Phonemicisation and split

Although the phoneme is the operative unit in communication, its importance in the initiation of change has perhaps been overrated in the past. Mergers take place either through purely phonetic processes, or (conceivably) through lack of support or integration for one or both of the merging phonemes; but the origin of a new phoneme could not be regarded as controlled by functional factors even to that limited extent. It may be introduced from another system (6.5) or it may arise from the combination of two existing phonemes (2.3) or from phonetic divergence (2.3); but there is no way in which a phoneme – perhaps overloaded by previous mergers – can shed or transfer part of its load. From a purely intrasystemic viewpoint, merger is irreversible; the old distribution can be 'borrowed back' from a neighbouring system, but, failing that, the balance can be restored only approximately, and then only if the phonetic prerequisites for a new phoneme are present. If they are not, the necessary regulation must come from other, added remedies: homonyms causing ambiguity are gradually replaced by new forms (5.2), or a new phonemic distribution is borrowed from another dialect (7.3).

The split of one phoneme into two is clearly mechanical in origin: what are at first allophones of a single phoneme are 'phonemicised', or attain the status of separate phonemes.[1] This process is so varied in origin as to appear random, not motivated; it is only at the point when one of a number of possible 'accidents' have taken place that we are in a position to define the two phones in question as no longer in complementary distribution, and therefore, on grounds of distribution as well as of phonetic distinctiveness, as separate phonemes. The variety of these 'accidents' may be seen from the following five examples:

(i) In Old English, the phones that were later denoted by the symbols *æ* and *a* must at first have been in complementary distribution, i.e. [ɑ] before a back vowel in the following syllable, [æ] elsewhere, for that was still their main distribution in the historic period, and they originated from a single phoneme in Germanic. In West Saxon, by morphophonemic analogy, [ɑ] spread to . positions before a front vowel in verbs (e.g. **ic fære* > *ic fare* 'I go') and adjectives (e.g. **glædes* gen. sg. >*glades*) so that it was no longer in complementary distribution with [æ] and distinctions such as *fare* 'I go' ~ *fære* dat. sg. 'journey' came into being. But in Old Northumbrian this particular analogy did not take place, and the phonemicisation is shown by a quite different 'accident' (see (ii) below).

(ii) In Old English and all other early Germanic languages except Gothic, fronted allophones of back vowels developed in the position before /i, i:, j/ in the following syllable (i-umlaut or i-mutation, see p. 16 above). These allophones achieved phonemic status only when the following /ɪ/ or /j/ had either disappeared or changed to /-e/ in some, though not necessarily all, contexts. Thus when the final /ɪ/ of prehistoric OE */foːtɪ/ (= *[føːtɪ]) disappeared, there were two functionally distinct forms /føːt/ (dat. sg.) and /foːt/ (nom. sg.).

In Old Northumbrian it was by this process that the variants [æ] and [ɑ] were phonemicised: Germanic **fallan* 'fall' ~ **falljan* 'cause to fall, fell' was realised in West Saxon as *feallan* ~ *fiellan*, but in Northumbrian as *falla(n)* ~ *fælla(n)*. The minimal pairs distinguishing /æ/ and /ɑ/ are thus of wholly

---

[1] In some cases of split, the original phonetic conditioning becomes concealed by later changes (cf. the differentiation of the types *flood*, *mood*, and *good* from doublets, or possibly even triplets, that survived for a long period with divergent qualitative developments, p. 27 above). Wang (pp. 17 and 21) suggests that the view of split as allophonically conditioned will have to be revised, and there is justification in his view that later redistributions of variants need no longer depend on conditioning. However, there must be *some* source for the original variation, and that is here assumed to be any of the changes enumerated in ch. 2 (whether of segmental or suprasegmental origin), or of the other relevant factors which are discussed in ch. 6 below (e.g. polarisation, substratal influence).

different origin in the two dialects, but the difference can hardly be regarded as other than fortuitous.

(iii) In early Old English, /k/ developed a front allophone [c]. [k] and [c] remained in complementary distribution until *i*-mutation, whereby the sequence [ka-] could yield [ke-] at a time when front allophones of [k] were no longer being developed. Since both [k] and [c] now occurred before front vowels they were no longer in complementary distribution, and hence OE *cennan, cempa, cene* with /k/ but *ceald, ceosan* with /c/.

(iv) In early Germanic, medial and final voiced fricatives were in complementary distribution with voiceless, according to whether they were preceded by a stressed vowel, i.e. [f, θ, x, s] after a stressed vowel, but [β, ð, ɣ, z] when the stress fell elsewhere in the word. But later in Germanic stressing on the root-syllable was generalised, and because of this stress-shift the voiced allophones [β, ð, ɣ, z] were no longer in complementary distribution with [f, θ, x, s]. Hence the alternations associated with 'Verner's Law', e.g. OE *teah* 'he drew' but pl. *tugon, ceas* 'he chose' but pl. *curon* (with /z/ > /r/).

(v) The last example is one that belongs properly to chapter 6, since it results from contact of systems, but it must be mentioned here because of the questions of principle involved. In the late sixteenth century, the reflex of ME /ʊ/ developed an unrounded allophone [ɤ] (later centralised to [ə] and [ʌ]) after consonants other than labial, while [ʊ] remained after labials. At that period, therefore, the vowels of *cut* and *put* differed slightly but were in complementary distribution. But from 1640 onwards, writers on pronunciation show awareness that the two sounds are distinct, and some indicate pronunciations like [pət/pʌt] 'put' and [pəl/pʌl] 'pull', which suggests that [ʊ] and [ə/ʌ] were no longer in complementary distribution. The possibility of contrast has existed since then, as is shown not only by a modern pair like *put* and *putt* but also the interesting distinction made by Elphinston in 1765 between /bʊl/ 'animal' and /bʌl/ 'decree'.[1]

The prerequisite for this phonemicisation is that the same speakers should start to use both variants after labials, but without, as in the previous cases, a further change taking place.[2] In this case, the 'accident' is none other than the mixture itself, which is not so improbable if it is borne in mind that not all dialects possessed both variants. As today, many dialects retained [ʊ] throughout, while others generalised the new [ɤ, ə, ʌ] in all contexts; in that situation, the mixture could take place in various ways: simply as an accident of upbringing or environment, a single speaker might imitate users of [ʊ] for some of his words but users of [ə] for others, with the result that in his idiolect the sounds were in overlapping, not complementary distribution; or the mixture could be due to inconsistent imitation of a prestige dialect, or to the use of both sounds in the same words, at first in different registers, but later without regard

---

[1] Jespersen (1909) 1 ch. XI § 66.
[2] For a different view, see E. J. Dobson, *Brno Studies in English* 8 (1969) 43–8.

to register. This is a simplified, preliminary statement of how such mixture may take place; it will be dealt with further in chapter 6.

It may be seen from the above five examples that the 'accidents' are of very varied kinds: grammatical analogy, loss of a following syllable, another change to an adjoining phoneme, a stress shift, and influence from another system. This suggests that they are not closely connected with the phonetic split, and that the phonemic split itself is primarily mechanical in origin since it results from a combination of mechanical change and coincidence.

Naturally, it is still possible to argue that what appears to us as coincidental is in fact nothing of the sort, and that the functional pressures towards phonemicisation are more important than the mechanical. But here again, if functional criteria are applied there is no consistency from case to case. In example (i) above, the split of Gmc. /a/ to /æ/ and /ɑ/ increased congruity of pattern, for the open series was the only one in which there had been no correlation of length. The imperfect correlation /æ:/∼/ɑ/ in Gmc. had given place in prehistoric OE to /æ:/∼/ɑ:/ (<Gmc. /ɑi/)∼/æ/, which still lacked /ɑ/. The split of /æ/ filled the gap, yielding /æ:/, /æ/∼/ɑ:/, /ɑ/.[1]

The opposite is the case with example (ii) above. The addition of the rounded vowels represented by *y* and *œ* did not increase the symmetry of the system, but they constituted an important marking feature of both the grammatical and derivational systems, and their functional load was large.

In example (v), the split of /ʊ/ to /ʊ/ and /ə/ (later ʌ) satisfied neither criterion, neither pattern congruity nor functional load. The problem is complicated by the fact that, after the period of the original phonetic divergence of [ʊ] and [ə, ʌ], but probably during the period when the phonemic split was occurring, the reduced distribution of [ʊ] was strengthened by another purely mechanical change – the many new shortenings of /u:/ as in RP *book*, *good*. These provide a large proportion of the present yield of /ʊ∼ʌ/, as may be seen from the pairs *book–buck*, *look–luck*, *rook–ruck*, *took–tuck*, *could–cud*, *stood–stud*. The opposition /u:∼ʌ/ also has a large yield, consisting as it does of most of the original yield of ME/u:∼ʊ/ (type *mood–mud*, *shoot–shut*, etc.); but the surviving opposition /u:∼ʊ/ is thus left with only a small yield (*fool–full*, *pool–pull*).

There is, therefore, some doubt whether 'split' can be regarded as functionally motivated at all: provided there is phonological space for it, it may in other respects be of purely mechanical origin. It has even been claimed that the 'accidents' that give rise to the process of phonemicisation are irrelevant,

---

[1] This is not to say that the classical Old English system was wholly symmetrical, for the first elements of the remaining diphthongs were by now all fronted (/æ:ɑ, æɑ/, /e:o, eo/), and this outstanding asymmetry was not resolved until Middle English; but the pattern of non-diphthongal vowels was symmetrical, though the functional yield of the opposition /æ/ ∼ /ɑ/ was never great, and the distinction was itself to disappear in Middle English.

and that phonetic splits of the magnitude of those between EMnE/ʊ/ and /ʌ/ or OE /k/ and /tʃ/ would have taken place without them.[1] In effect, in the case of example (v) such a claim is tantamount to saying that the first speakers who combined /bʊ-/ and /bʌ-/ in one system during the learning process were subconsciously aware of an essential difference between the two: by redistributing the allophones (or diaphones) [ʊ, ʌ] of previous generations, they were utilising a mechanical phonetic divergence that had increased so greatly that it could not fail to be recognised, and the mere recognition of this divergence (especially in a new generation with no preconceptions) *was* phonemicisation.

The origin of this difference of opinion lies in the two different criteria by which a phoneme is defined – distinctive features and contrasting distributions. It is indeed possible to find cases of split which depend on divergence of distinctive features only; the distribution of the two original allophones never in fact overlaps, they remain in complementary distribution even as new phonemes, and no new contrasts come into being (an example is provided by the split of Gmc. /x/ to /h/ and /x/, discussed below in 8.3). But usually, when a phonetic change occurs that is significant enough to give rise to a new phoneme, the phone in question has, purely by virtue of its distribution in structure, certain potentialities for contrast. The 'accidents' that constitute phonemicisation bring about no more than the realisation of those existing potentialities, and their importance in each case is to be judged by the extent of the contrasts thus activated, and by the speed by which this takes place. As was shown in examples (i) and (ii) above, the nature of the accident is not important; provided the potentiality for contrast exists, it is likely to be realised sooner or later, though the accident may be only one of many that could have given the same result; and the greater the potentiality for contrast, the sooner it is likely to be realised, i.e. the more inevitable and less accidental the phonemicisation actually is.

But in some cases of split, phonemicisation could be regarded as more than mere activation of existing potentialities, i.e. as playing some part in the process of split. In example (iii) above, the change of /k/ to /tʃ/ can hardly have been otherwise than via /c/ (a stage most probably to be seen in the runic distinction between front ᚲ and back ᚴ), but there are no indications of a change to [tʃ] until the late-ninth-century reverse spellings *c, cc* for original /tj/, as in *fecc(e)an* 'fetch'. Yet the changes which disturbed the originally complementary distribution of [k] and [c] were undoubtedly before this, and probably completed in all dialects by the eighth century. The most probable interpretation of this sequence is as follows:

(*a*) phonetic divergence to back and front allophones [k, c];

---

[1] Cf. Ladd (1964) 655: 'the variation between the two allophones reached such a degree that they could stand on their own without the support of the conditioning sounds'.

(*b*) disruption of complementary distribution, with phonemicisation to /k/ and /c/;

(*c*) as a result of this phonemicisation, further phonetic divergence ('polarisation' of the existing difference) to /k/ and /tʃ/;

(*d*) increased yield of the new phoneme /tʃ/ by additions from the phonetically close /tj/.

These details suggest that phonetic divergence, though it is the origin, is not necessarily the only factor in the process of phonemic split, since the divergence may increase *after* the contrasts have been actualised. In such cases the two factors, mechanical and functional, may be seen as complementary and as dovetailing to produce an increased momentum of change.

3.6 Phonemicisation: other changes

The view expressed above, that phonemicisation may be assessed quantitatively by the contrasts produced and the speed by which they are produced, is confirmed by its lesser role in other phonemic changes, 'fusion' and 'split plus merger'.

'Fusion', as in /zj/ > /ʒ/ (2.3), occupies a midway place: the contexts are specialised, and there is therefore little chance that contrasts could arise either speedily or in any quantity. The most obvious source of contrast is the restoration of the original sequence under the influence of the spelling, e.g. MnE /vizjəl/ 'visual' compared with /viʒən/ 'vision'. In such cases it is quite possible that the status of the new phoneme should remain no more than marginal, though in the particular case of /ʒ/ there are other reasons for its integration (3.4). The change of /sk/ to /ʃ/ in late OE is less clear. In medial and final position at least, /sk/ would appear to have survived throughout, and /ʃ/ was phonemicised when, through analogical extensions, it came to stand in the same environment as /sk/ in the various inflected forms of words like *frosc* 'frog' and *þerscan* 'thresh'. But in initial position, the native /sk/ probably did not survive, and phonemicisation of /ʃ/ was, strictly speaking, only completed by the very gradual process in which /sk/ was reintroduced from other languages, e.g. *school* (from L.) or *skin* (from ON).

The change often called 'split plus merger' shows phonemicisation at its minimum relevance. Whereas split proper leads to the rise of a new phoneme (with subsequent integration into the system), this change is no more than a redistribution between two existing phonemes: certain allophones of one phoneme are reinterpreted as belonging to another because, by the normal processes of conditioned phonetic change, their distinctive features are now closer to the allophones of the latter than to those of the former. For example, ME /ɑ/ when proceded by /w/ (as in *wash, swan*) but not when followed by a velar (as in *wax, waggon*) was redistributed, at first in dialect but later in

London English, to /o/. From a strictly distributional point of view, such a change, initially at least, was no more than a neutralisation of the opposition between /ɑ/ and /o/: in that context, these two phonemes overlapped in their realisations, much as in Mn G. the realisations of /p, t, k/ and /b, d, g/ can be only /p, t, k/ in final position. Such overlaps may be disturbed by any of the 'accidents' hitherto mentioned: the opposition /wɑ/ ~ /wo/ was reactivated in any system that accepted the analogical preterite form *swam*, and earlier, similar mixtures are evident in ME texts that contain spellings like *swolȝ* 'swallow' or *whot* 'what'. But whether the neutralisation is terminated or not is irrelevant to the transfer itself, which depends purely on phonetic conditioning and the presence of a receiving phoneme with which it can be identified. This can be demonstrated by comparing the status of the palatal reflexes of Gmc. /k/ and /ɣ/ in OE. As shown above (3.4–5) the new phoneme /tʃ/ arose from the split of /k/ and was gradually integrated during the OE period. In contrast to this, palatal allophones of /ɣ/ merged with the already existing phoneme /j/, as may be seen by comparing E. *good, young, yield, yellow* with G. *gut, jung,* but *gelten, gelb*. A notable feature of this change is that it is shown as complete in the earliest OE orthographies; they all agree in equating [ÿ] and /j/, whether by the usual symbols *ge-, gi-* as in *geong, geolu, gieldan, geard* (cf. the Bewcastle runic spelling *gessus* 'Jesus') or by the rarer *i-* as in *iung, -ieard*. Yet at the time when the earliest OE orthographies were being established, the actual contrasts between /ɣ/ and those cases of /j/ that had arisen from [ÿ] must have been very few and limited to new cases of the sequence /ɣɛ/, as in *gegenga* 'companion'; it was only later, when the umlaut-vowels /ø/ and /y/ had become unrounded, that they were increased by the addition of forms like *gēs* 'geese', *gilden* 'golden', or, in some dialects, by forms with /g-/ from ON in the words for 'give', 'get'. Whereas, therefore, the phonemic integration of /tʃ/ was a gradual process, the status of /j/ from [ÿ] must have been established much earlier: phonemicisation of the split of [ɣ] and [ÿ] is barely relevant to the merger of [ÿ] and /j/.

3.7 Circular shift

It was suggested in 3.3 that the whole of circular shift (apart from continued differentiation within phonological space) might be regarded as non-systemic. But two of the other functional factors listed on p. 30 must now be considered.

(i) *Economy of distinctive features*

It has been observed of the Germanic consonant shift that, after the start of the initial change from voiceless plosives to fricatives (/p, t, k/ > /f, θ, x/), the remaining changes result automatically from the giving up of distinctive features rendered functionally unnecessary by the initial stage.[1] Thus, firstly,

[1] Cf. Fourquet (1948), and Lyons pp. 123–5.

in original /b, d, g/ the marked feature of voicing was no longer opposed to the lack of it in /p, t, k/ but to a different distinction altogether (fricativity), and it could therefore be dispensed with; and similarly, once original /b, d, g/ had been thus unvoiced to /p, t, k/, the feature of aspiration in the series /bh, dh, gh/ was no longer necessary to distinguish them from the new /p, t, k/, and this series also could therefore lose this distinctive feature and change to /β, ð, ɣ/ or [b, d, g] according to environment. Hence, although these processes could be regarded as special details of a drag-chain mechanism as it pertains to consonants, it is relevant to add that such a mechanism may be at least partly controlled by a principle of economy of distinctive features.

(ii) *Sonority*

From the fact that sounds of greater carrying power (e.g. the open vowels [ɛ, ɑ] compared with [i, u] when pronounced with the same degree of energy) are not obviously preferred in linguistic development, it has usually been assumed that sonority has no relevance for change. But, on the contrary, it provides an important link in processes of multiple shift.

In the case of consonants, sonority has relevance for the unexplained initial change of /p, t, k/ to /f, θ, x/ in the consonant shift. Whether the IE consonant-system was at that period in a 'transitional stage of instability' is not necessarily relevant here, though a case can be made that the predominance in it of plosives (whether voiced, aspirated or neither) made it inflexible and more prone to change. But, with or without such a case, the fact that fricatives are more sonorous than plosives can hardly be overlooked: mechanically, the change is one of the common 'irreversible' type (2.5), and in this case it was not inhibited by the presence of other fricatives in the system.

With regard to vowels, the assumption that sonority is of no relevance overlooks a curious paradox in the production of vowels – that greater stress and muscular energy have a close relation to, and often include, tensing, raising and fronting of vowels (2.5). Since, from an acoustic point of view, sonority is itself one of the elements contributing to stress, it follows that raising of the tongue in contexts calling for greater stress must defeat its own object, and that this will be remedied only by pronouncing the new raised vowels with more energy still. The ultimate result of such a process, if it took place unchecked, would be a concentration of vowels (or, by merger, of vocalic yields) in the high or high-front areas. The history of some languages (e.g. Greek, Scottish English) shows a high rate of change in this direction, but for functional reasons it can never be tolerated in full, and the usual assumption is that vowels already in the highest positions move to lower, more central or retracted positions by normal push-chain processes. What is overlooked is, firstly, that such lowered or retracted variants already exist, say, as unstressed forms or in relaxed style; and secondly, that variants that have arisen under conditions of *less* stress may in time be selected as more effective *stressed* forms than those nearer the original.[1] Such a process will supply an answer to the problem posed in 2.6: the functional reason for the switch in selection is not just the 'differentness' of the new forms, but their greater sonority which compensates for the loss of it in preceding changes involving raising. On this view, the Great Vowel Shift could be largely explained as (i) raising and/or fronting of the vowels in lower positions through selection of a preponderance of forceful-style variants, and then (ii) the lowering and/or centralisation of vowels in high positions through selection of original relaxed-style variants as new stressed forms.

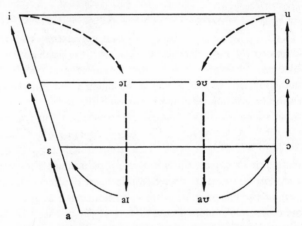

Fig. 2. Selection of variants in the Great Vowel Shift
———— selection of forceful-style variants
- - - - - selection of relaxed-style variants

Circular shifts of vowels are thus detailed examples of homeostatic regulation. The earliest changes are mechanical (though they may be triggered or accelerated by extralinguistic factors, cf. chapter 6); the later changes are functional, and are brought about by the favouring of those variants that will redress the imbalance caused by the mechanical changes. In this respect circular shift differs considerably from merger and split. Merger is redressed by split only in the most general and approximate fashion, since the original functional yields are not preserved; but in circular shift, the combination of functional and mechanical factors ensures that adequate distinctions are maintained. To that extent at least, the phonological system possesses some degree of autonomy.

[1] Cf. J. L. Fischer in Hymes (1964) 408: 'Obviously the threshold for a given variant does not *necessarily* remain the same, generation after generation.' For further discussion of the process see 7.1, p. 137.

As will be seen in chapters 4–5, such a regulatory process is paralleled in grammar and lexis; but, in addition, it fits the facts better than the view held by extreme adherents of the functional school – that *all* shifts arise from a previous asymmetry in pattern. A recent attempt at elaborating this latter view[1] multiplies the number of parameters by which a pattern is to be described, thus making it possible to show that all systems contain gaps in their patterns, and that the completion or elimination of one series always disrupts the symmetry of others, so that further changes are needed. According to this view, the parameters are 'the prime shapers and movers of the system' whereas disruptive changes are always to be regarded as temporary, transitional and – presumably on the assumption of a potent teleological drive that is active throughout – anticipatory of a stabilising solution. But there is no evidence that the better-known cases of disruptive change, especially split and merger, should be regarded thus. Certainly it is possible to envisage a set of chain-reactions – a series of changes each of which redresses the instabilities left by the last; but it is more probable that a majority of instabilities are due to a 'devaluation' of stressed forms that is purely mechanical in origin and which forms an exact parallel to the same phenomenon in grammar and lexis.

3.8 Alternatives to circular shift

Circular shifts are a typical manifestation of homeostatic regulation in vowel systems, but they are not the only possible one. There are other cases that show the same basic mechanical raisings and frontings but different solutions. The following are two examples.

(i) Certain dialects in S. Lancs. and S. Yorks. are exceptional in preserving extra distinctions between /ɛɪ/ in *meat, speak* (OE *mete, sprecan*) and /iə/ in *beat, deal* (OE *bēatan, dǣlan*), and between /oː/ or /ɒɪ/ in *coal, coat* (OE *col*, OFr. *cote*) and /ʊə/ in *oak, both* (OE *āc*, ON *báði*). These distinctions descend from a system of the following pattern:

i: *ride*		u: *house*	
e: *feet*		o: *good*	
ẹ: *beat*		ọ: *oak*	
ɛ: *meat*		ɔ: *coal*	
	ai *maid*	au *awe*	
	a: *made*		

In comparison with others, this is a 'crowded' system which might have been expected to show, under the fronting and raising pressures of the Great Vowel Shift, more mergers than elsewhere. But the distinctions were preserved by the selection of diphthongal variants for four mid-vowels as well as for the two high vowels. After the usual first stage in which /eː>iː, oː>uː, iː>əɪ,

---

[1] L. G. Heller and J. Macris, *Parametric Linguistics* (The Hague, 1967).

u:>əʊ/, the main pressures must have been in the areas of cardinal [e:] and [o:]. During the continual process of raising, two different sets of vowels raised to these areas were diphthongised by the two different processes referred to above in chapter 2: [e:, o:] in *beat, oak* became /iə, ʊə/, and a later [e:, o:] in *meat, coal* became /ɛɪ, o:/ or /ɛɪ, ɒɪ/. By these changes the space at [e:] was left for the normal shift upwards of the merged *made-* and *maid*-classes. Finally, since this system would by then have a large inventory of diphthongs (including the forms corresponding to *ride, beat, meat, house, oak* and often *coal*), it is not surprising to find that the earliest, in *ride* and *house*, have now been lowered and monophthongised to /ɑ:, a:/ and /a:, ɛ:/ respectively.

(ii) In the history of French, isolative changes are fewer than in English and do not constitute a circular or full shift; but it is notable that they all belong to the earlier period of the language, and consist of fronting and raising, viz. /u:/>/y/ (*murus*>*mur*), /o:/>/u/ (*tormentum*>*tourment*), /ɑ:, ɑ/>/e, ɛ/ (*gratum*>*gré, amare*>*aimer, carum*>*cher, talem*>*tel*). There have also been conditioned changes in the same direction, but the main feature of both isolative and conditioned changes since the early period has been a regulation of the imbalance by selection of lower and more retracted variants of different origins, resulting in /ɑ̃/ (*findere*>*fendre, tempus*>*temps*), /ɛ̃/ (*finem*>*fin, rem*>*rien*), /a/ (*femina*>*femme*), /o/ (*bellus*>*beaux*), /wa, wɑ/ (*me*>*moi*).

3.9 The vowels of unstressed syllables

It was suggested in 2.5 that vowels under conditions of less stress may show lowering or centralisation as a manifestation of normal mechanical change. If this is assumed for the vowels of unstressed syllables, it explains why syncretism under /ə/ is a common development: there is concentration in the central, not in the high or front areas as in the case of stressed vowels. Such syncretism may be remedied by new marked forms (5.5), but that is not the only possible development; there is often a process of systemic regulation which, as might be expected, takes place in the opposite direction to that for stressed vowels, by the selection of raised variants. But since systems of unstressed vowels are usually limited to fewer contrasts, this need not entail more than a slight raising within the central area from [ə] to [ɪ] or [ʊ], and by this means a proportion of less sonorous unstressed vowels is ensured. The raised variants for such systemic regulation are often provided by conditioning from neighbouring segments. In ME, where the vowels of the OE endings had been centralised to /ə/, we find widespread new raisings to /ɪ/, especially in inflexions ending in dental or alveolar consonants (*-is, -ith, -yn, -id, -ind(e)*). Since then, there has been constant distribution of the vowels of syllables newly unstressed to one or other member of the opposition /ɪ~ə/, depending partly on the inherited quality of the vowels and partly on that of the neighbouring segments: /ɪ/ is the commoner reflex of the vowels of ME *-es, -ed, -est, -edge, -less, -ness, de-, re-, em-, ex-,* whereas /ə/ represents the vowels of nearly all other unstressed syllables (the more important are *-ance, -and, -dom, -ence, -ent, -land, -man, -oun, -our, -ous, a-, con-, com-, cor-, sub-,* as well as syllabic /-l, -m, -n, -r/ and their reflexes wherever relevant). But there are exceptions to the expected distribution that are due to conditioning: the raising of /ə/ to /ɪ/ before /(d)ʒ, s/ as in *cottage, damage, orange, furnace,* and by vowel-harmony in *women* (also sometimes in *chicken, kitchen, linen*); and the same applies to other exceptions recorded in the past.[1]

Thus the pattern of development in EMnE was that new cases of /ə/ were continually arising from unstressed back vowels, but meanwhile certain cases of /ə/ with raised variants from conditioning were redistributed to /ɪ/. In present English, centralisation to /ə/ is again on the increase as dialects with higher proportions of /ə/ gain in prominence. Since this results in homonymy of pairs like *accept–except, allusion–illusion,* it may be regarded as a reactivation of the mechanical factor.

The evidence for such processes is often inadequate. The exact development of unstressed vowels in early Latin must remain hypothetical, since the pre-classical shift from initial word-stress is not fully documented. But it seems at least likely that contrasts of the type *ratus–irritus, facio–conficio, locus–ilico* are due to a similar process of reallocation of /ə/ to higher central vowels,[2] and that, here again, conditioning may have played some part (cf. distinctions like *incipio–occupo, regimentum–documentum*).

3.10 Phonaesthemes

Hitherto in this chapter it has been assumed that the smallest meaningful unit is the morpheme, and that phonemes cannot in themselves carry meaning, i.e. that the phonetic form of morphemes is arbitrary, not motivated. However, in most languages there is at least a proportion of morphemes (in some languages it is considerable) in which the relation of sound to meaning is not arbitrary. This is not to say that there is any direct connection between the sounds and their referents (in English, only a few words like *caw, miaow, hiccup* could be called imitative, and even they are only approximations); but

---

[1] For example, it is likely that /ɪ/ has at times been conditioned by a preceding affricate as well as a following one, as in *dungeon, truncheon* (Dobson (1957) § 336). But other cases of /ɪ/ recorded (e.g. in *waggon, obstacle*) are no more remarkable than the many cases of overlap or category-simplification found in dialects today, e.g. /ə/ in *possible, believe.*

[2] Such a view might explain why vowels that regained stress before a consonant group show *e,* not *i,* as in *facio–confectus, damno–condemno, aptus–ineptus.* It is reasonable to assume that in these syllables centralisation would not have proceeded so far (cf. the quality of vowels with intermediate stressing in MnE, e.g. in *aùthórity, hándfùl, préfèct, Nòvémber, yésterdày*).

there are, in each language, conventional and traditional associations between phonemes (or sequences of them) and meanings, for which J. R. Firth coined the term *phonaesthemes*.[1] For example, the phonaestheme /sl-/ may be assigned the values 'slippery' or 'falling' in *slide, slip, slime, slush, sludge, slough, slither, slink, sleek, slop(py), slaver, slobber, slur, slant, slope, sledge* and possibly *sling* and *sleet*; and it may also be assigned the closely related values 'inactive', 'degenerate' or 'morally worthless' in *slow, sloth, sleep(y), slumber, slack, slouch, sloppy, slug, sluggard, slut, slattern, slovenly, slump, slapdash, slang, slick* and to some extent in *sly, slander, slur, slate* (vb.), *slum*.

A frequent objection to the theory of sound-symbolism is that it never holds good for all cases, and that therefore the theory itself is invalid. In this example it might be claimed that /sl-/ in another group of words (*slit, slice, slay, slash, slot, sling, slap, slam, slog*) requires the value 'fast cutting or striking movement', which is distinct from those given above, or, at best, only marginally related to 'slippery' via 'motion'; and that there is still a residue for which no special value can be established – *slab, slag, slake, slate* (noun), *slave, sleeve, sloe, sloop,* and, in their modern meanings, *slight* and *slim*. The answer to such objections is that the validity of a phonaestheme is, in the first instance, contextual only: if it 'fits' the meaning of the word in which it occurs, it reinforces the meaning, and, conversely, the more words in which this occurs, the more its own meaning is strengthened; but if the phoneme or phonemes in question do not fit the meaning, then their occurrence in that context is of the common arbitrary type, and no question of correlation arises. Furthermore, just as a phonaestheme may or may not be significant, depending on its context, so it may have two or more separate values which are again contextually determined. It may often be possible to treat them as one, e.g. Firth classed all exponents of /sl-/ together as 'pejorative';[2] but, firstly, this entails a great loss of specificity, and secondly, it is clear from the historical evidence that we are dealing with two patterns that have in the main developed independently from separate roots containing the meanings 'strike' and 'sleep' in Germanic. It is therefore preferable to reckon in such cases with homonymous phonaesthemes; if connections subsequently develop that suggest their unity, this is no more than may happen with normal homonymy of free morphemes, as in the historically separate words *ear* (for hearing) and *ear* (of corn). As a further example, in earlier English there can have been little association of /gr/ in *greedy* and *grip*, that of *greedy* being associated rather with *grim*, as in the OE alliterative phrase *grim and grædig*; but, since the rise of *grab* and *grasp*, the link between *greedy* and *grip* has been strengthened sufficiently for all four to be included under /gr/ 'grasping'. This then becomes a subcategory of /gr/ 'unpleasant' (as in *grim, grisly, gruesome, gruelling, gruff, grunt, growl, grumble,*

---

[1] Firth (1964) 184.   [2] Firth (1964) 185.

grumpy, grouch, grouse, grudge, gross) as well as retaining its connection with /gr/ 'seize' (as in *grip, grope, grasp, grab, grapple*). Thus there are now links from the main group /gr/ 'unpleasant' not only via *grasping* to /gr/ 'seize', but also via *grating* to /gr/ 'abrasive', as in *grind, grate, gravel, graze, grit*.

The further problem, whether certain universal (cross-linguistic) patterns exist need not detain us here, since we are concerned only with those patterns that become established in given systems at given periods; if any universal patterns exist they will presumably be included automatically in any totals for a separate language that could be compiled, but no full description has yet been attempted. For English, some principal types have been established:

(*a*) initial consonants or consonant clusters, as /sl, gr/ exemplified above, and likewise /sn, fl, gl, b, kl, kr, skr, sw, tw, dʒ, br, tr/;[1]

(*b*) vowels+final consonants or consonant clusters, e.g. /-aʃ/ in *dash, gash, slash, bash*, /-ap/ in *clap, rap, slap, snap, tap*, and similarly /-ag, -ɪp, -ʌdʒ, -ʌmp/, often combining with those of (*a*) to form whole words, e.g. *trudge, clump, snip*;

(*c*) unstressed syllables, to express gradual process (*darken, harden, dampen*), iteration (*quiver, chatter, flutter, flicker*), useless or careless action (*fiddle, twiddle, fumble, quibble*);

(*d*) similarities in the total of distinctive features, e.g. plosive cluster+/ʌ/+ affricate+/ən/ in *truncheon, bludgeon*.[2]

(*e*) gradational variation, to be seen not only in formations like *singsong, riffraff*, but in the relation of nouns like *tip, drip* to *top, drop*.[3]

But all the lists of such features so far published are selective only; e.g. the fullest, by H. Marchand, instances under /kl/ 'words denoting sound' (*clatter, clang, clash, click, clamor*),[4] but omits the larger group in which /kl-/ suggests 'clinging' or 'coagulation': *cling, claw, clutch, cleave, clay, clog, cloy, clutter, clammy, climb, clamber, clasp, clamp, clench, cluster, clod, clot, clew, clump*.

The historical study of such groups shows how a phonaestheme may grow from minor, coincidental identifications between a few roots to much larger patterns. The type listed in (*c*) above appears to have originated in the re-interpretation of the /n, l, r/ that ended the roots of certain verbs in Germanic, e.g. *openian, nestlian, beterian*; the phonaesthemes /sl, gr, kl/ referred to above started from a nucleus of roots in Germanic or Old English and were strengthened by new formations (*slouch, slobber*) and loanwords (*grouch, grate*), but also by words which had earlier been unconnected in meaning but, through

---

[1] For examples see Bloomfield p. 245, Marchand ch. VII.
[2] D. L. Bolinger, 'Rime, Assonance, and Morpheme Analysis', *Word* 6 (1950) 117–36.
[3] The OED s.v. *tip sb.*[1] remarks: 'So far as is known, *tip* has no etymological connection with *top*; but the proximity of form and relative quality of sound in the two words have caused *tip* to be felt as denoting a thinner or more delicate *top*; cf. *drip, drop, chip, chop*.'
[4] Marchand p. 410.

motivation of their initial consonants, had entered the relevant semantic orbit (*clog, clasp*, cf. 4.2).

The growth of phonaesthetic patterns is of importance as a special type of linguistic change, but its implications for other types are often ignored. There are three possibilities that have to be borne in mind:

(*a*) a word changes in form because its existing meaning suggests the inclusion of a phonaestheme, or the substitution of a different one;

(*b*) a word changes in meaning because its existing form fits the new meaning better, i.e. its form thereby gains in motivation;

(*c*) a new word arises from a combination of both (*a*) and (*b*).

We shall return to (*b*) and (*c*) in chapter 4, but (*a*) is relevant here since it involves replacement of phonemes. Possible examples are to be found in the history of the phonaestheme /-ag/ 'slow, tired or tedious action', as in *drag, fag, flag, lag, nag, sag*: the only etymons that have been proposed for *flag, lag* and *sag* all end in /k/. Such a replacement of /k/ by /g/ differs entirely from the types of phonological change hitherto discussed. It is of neither mechanical nor functional origin within the phonological system; yet it is intrasystemic, and, so far as it is motivated, it is due to interference from patterns in the lexical, not the phonological, system. A similar process will explain the so-called 'expressive gemination': a pattern of consonant doubling which has arisen by normal mechanical change is extended, as suitable for reinforcing a meaning, to other contexts, e.g. to intensive and point-action verbs in Germanic (8.4).[1]

Lastly, there are individual cases which fall midway between this type of change and the blends mentioned above on p. 47.[2] In these, no real pattern is established, but a form is influenced by that of a semantically related word, e.g. late Latin *grevis* (cf. *grief, grieve*)<*gravis* under the influence of *levis*.

[1] This is not intended to imply that consonant lengthening cannot arise spontaneously under certain conditions of stress (cf. 2.5, p. 24); but 'expressive gemination' occurs in distributions that would be difficult to explain without semantic motivation, and it is therefore likely that extension of lengthening in phonaesthetic function also plays a part.

[2] Cf. further p. 61f below.

4 Grammar and lexis (1): variation

4.1 Introductory

The distinction between grammar and lexis is decided, for synchronic purposes, by various conflicting criteria, though it is usually possible to define some practical boundary. But no grammatical system is ever ideally 'complete', and therefore the boundary must be regarded as one that shifts in time. Meaning is carried by both grammar and lexis, and all meanings can be expressed primarily by one or the other, though often by devious circumlocution or expedient. Grammar is a selection of short-cutting devices for a certain number of the commonest functions, not for all. But since speakers are obliged by convention to use these devices even where the utterance, if spoken under ideal conditions, would not strictly need them (e.g. -s in *he goes*), grammar provides the language with a built-in level of redundancy that could not be achieved lexically, e.g. in the case just quoted it would serve to distinguish *he go* from *we go* if conditions for receiving the message were not ideal. But provided that that level is maintained, the actual choice of functions to be expressed grammatically may vary, not only from one language to another but also from one stage to another of the same language; at any given stage, the remaining functions are then expressed lexically, or left to be deduced from the context.

Thus in individual contexts it may appear that more is 'taken for granted' in one language than in another, e.g. Italian *ha* compared with British English *have you got*, American English *do you have*. But that is only one context where such brevity is permitted by the system of Italian. To say that it is compensated for by greater preservation of inflexional syllables elsewhere in Italian is probably an oversimplification; all we are really entitled to say is that the *overall* level of redundancy is maintained, but that the potential for grammatical redundancy in given contexts varies from system to system.

Of the universal grammatical categories capable of overt expression, some are essential (e.g. deixis, negation, syntagmatic relations), while others, like gender or verbal aspect, are optional. It is here that systems differ, for whereas the essential categories are always present, only certain proportions and combinations of the optional categories are included. The result is that some extreme variations are possible: some languages have a complicated verb-system but a simple noun-system, others the exact opposite. It has been suggested that there may be cultural reasons for such a distinction between 'event-dominated' and 'object-dominated' languages,[1] but the salient point is that there is always selection of sufficient categories to ensure maintenance of the level of redundancy.

This may be seen from comparing a single area (albeit one that is difficult to delimit) in the grammatical systems of Old and Middle English. Old English has a full formal system of grammatical gender, with agreement in case between modifiers and head-words. The communication value of grammatical gender may be questioned, but that is beside the point: the inherited system yielded a vast store of *expected* collocations, e.g. every time a speaker of Old English said *þære* rather than *þæs* he was automatically restricting the number of nouns that the hearer might expect, and *that* was its value to communication. In Middle English, this system (probably partly for mechanical reasons, cf. 8.2, pp. 155–7) broke down, and was replaced by a far more developed system of specifiers (determiners). This was a function very different from the previous: it was anaphoric and cataphoric only, i.e. it referred not to accompanying words, but to words elsewhere in the context. But, in communicative value, it served as an equivalent to its predecessor, i.e. *a(n)* and *the* served to limit the range of nouns that might be expected by the hearer.

The process of change between two such stages will be examined later (cf. 4.3–5, 5.5, 6.7, 8.2–4), but it may be summarised briefly thus: (i) the inherited spoken chain contains distributions, some accidental in origin, that are capable of being reinterpreted and given fresh systemic motivation; (ii) reinterpretation and/or realignment takes place when the overt expression of an old category is becoming indeterminate, and the change is to that extent a systemic regulation; but (iii) it is *ad hoc*, in that it embodies merely what can be most conveniently refashioned from the existing system, with the possibility of choice from hitherto covert categories.

The view outlined above conflicts with much that has been written in the past concerning a long-standing teleological drive towards perfection,[2] or concerning developments that are conditioned by 'growth in the complexity of human relations'.[3] The statement that English is an instrument that has continually progressed through the centuries could perhaps be regarded as partly true of the written language, but that is more or less coincidental. As a general thesis it can be questioned on a number of counts. Firstly, it often amounts to no more than that a grammatical means has been substituted for what was expressed with equal clarity before by lexical means, e.g. MnE *he had said* compared with OE *he sæde ær*. But the growth of grammar at the expense of lexis is of no advantage beyond a certain optimum point; too large

---

[1] Cf. A. Capell, *Studies in Sociolinguistics* (The Hague, 1966) 33.
[2] E.g. by Jespersen (1922 and 1941), Bradley pp. 38–49.
[3] Martinet (1964) 165.

a grammatical system will provide a higher level of redundancy than is needed, and is therefore uneconomical. In the above case, therefore, we may suspect that the development of a grammatically expounded pluperfect tense replaces other (possibly quite different) grammatical features that have been lost, but which contributed to the redundancy of the Old English system. Some hint of this appears from these particular words, for *sæde* varied for number and person in OE, whereas MnE *had said* does not; and although such a hint is insufficient for the precise measurement of loss and replacement of redundancy, it should at least warn us against thinking that the development of the pluperfect has necessarily enriched the language.

Secondly, grammatical distinctions are often lost without any replacement of the particular function that they performed. This happens more commonly where the main reasons are phonetic (cf. 4.3, 5.5), but not exclusively so. The sixteenth-century aspectual distinction between *he is come* and *he hath (has) come* can now be expressed only by lexical means such as *he is here* for the former and *he has made his way* for the latter. Since the phonetic syncretism in colloquial register of *he is* and *he has* to *he's* applies only to the third person singular, not to the other distinctions *am–have* and *are–have*, it can hardly be more than a contributory factor, and, as Fridén has shown,[1] the obsolescence of the auxiliary *be* in this construction is mainly due to the simple extension of *have*, which occurred regularly with more verbs and in a wider range of contexts (e.g. for repeated action and in negative, unfulfilled and concessive clauses).

Thirdly, comparison with other language systems can show that certain features of one language that are often regarded as highly developed and sophisticated are performed equally efficiently by more economic means in another. For example, English is praised for the number of 'levels' of synonyms in its lexical system that are available for the expression of register-distinctions. Yet at least part of this function is performed more economically by other means elsewhere, e.g. by the system of honorifics in Japanese, especially the complex obligatory distinctions in the verb between plain, polite and deferential (for address), or between humble, neutral and exalted (for reference).[2]

Hence in studying those processes of loss and replacement that constitute the history of grammar and lexis, it must be recognised that either system may be developed at the expense of the other, and that there need not be any obvious correlation of loss and replacement *within* each system. Nevertheless, it remains true that some functions in language (those which are more commonly regarded as corresponding to 'notions' in any given culture) are more conveniently expressed lexically, while other functions (those of placing the

---

[1] Fridén, especially 115–16.
[2] Cf. S. E. Martin, 'Speech Levels in Japan and Korea', in Hymes 407ff.

expounded notions in the desired relation to each other) are more likely to be expressed grammatically. It follows, therefore, that *some* correlations of loss and replacement should be detectable within each system, though, as pointed out above, the replacement may not fulfil precisely the same function. The most obvious case of this is in the lexical system, where verbal obsolescence and innovation by coining, word-formation or borrowing automatically keep pace with changes in culture; it is self-evident that there need be no correlation between the objects or concepts that are new and those that fall into disuse, and the same will apply to the words used to express them. But, as has already been partly shown above, it is extremely doubtful whether grammatical changes, or other lexical changes, can be attributed as directly as this to changes in culture. On the contrary, their more important conditioning factors appear to be intralinguistic; and although it would be difficult to prove that they are not indirectly related to cultural change, nevertheless their pressures are more constant and gradual, and less intermittent than those of cultural change. As in the case of phonological change, there are two basic factors, one of which is 'mechanical', though not in the same literal sense as for most phonetic change (cf. 7.2), and which is manifested in the two main *parole*-based sources of variation, *extension* and *intake*. The other factor is systemic, and will be discussed in chapter 5.

The term 'extension' will be used here broadly, for any process by which the use of a form is extended to a larger number of meanings or grammatical functions than it has hitherto possessed, its information-value being thereby reduced. For example, ME (*i*)*sely* until *c.* 1200 meant 'happy', 'blessed', but thereafter, by the simple addition to its denotations of those characteristics of its referents hitherto regarded as incidental, it could also mean 'innocent', 'harmless', 'helpless' or 'weak'.

4.2   Extension in lexis

Fluidity between forms and their referents (as exemplified above) has been recognised for centuries as a feature of human language, and needs no special explanation beyond the fact that, whereas common meanings (denotations) are accepted by all competent speakers of a language, individuals possess or develop new private links (connotations) between forms and their referents.[1] These links may be mistakenly identified by hearers as part of the established denotation; or they may be passed by special rapport from speaker to hearer, and reinforced by the context and/or situation common to them both. If

---

[1] The traditional terms denotation and connotation are retained here as convenient for dealing with semantic change; but 'denotation' requires qualifying to the extent that it includes, for each individual, elements which are private to him. These elements cannot properly be reckoned as connotations since they are part and parcel of the individual's view of the so-called 'agreed' meaning.

imitated in quantity, they may then enter the language and invade the semantic field of other forms.

Since the referents are themselves extralinguistic, the question again arises whether the process is cultural in origin: it could be suggested that the thirteenth-century extensions in the word *sely* mentioned above reflect a decline in the authority of the Church and in the respect hitherto accorded to religious people; and similarly its later extension from 'helpless' to 'foolish' could reflect the increased values placed on enterprise and initiative in the sixteenth century. It is often possible to make such identifications for particular words; but for our present purpose we need recognise only that such new connotations are *always* present as the material for extension, and that fresh extensions take place most commonly in two main directions, which to some extent parallel the variants arising in phonology from emphasis or the lack of it. In lexis, overstatement (exaggeration) could be regarded as corresponding to strong-stress phonological variation, and similarly understatement and euphemism would correspond to weak-stress phonological variation. The difference lies in the selection of discrete forms possessing 'stronger' or 'weaker' *semantic* (not phonetic) properties. The selection of a stronger or weaker form than the hearer believes the context to warrant will in time produce a devaluation: adverbs like *very, awfully, terribly, frightfully* or adjectives like *marvellous, glorious, stupendous* are typical examples of forms that have continually been used in contexts that did not require them in senses as strong as those they must originally have possessed. Such devaluation is by no means confined to adverbs and adjectives. Though a modern instance of the verb *die* as in *I'm dying to see you* may strike us as no more than an ephemeral exaggeration limited to certain colloquial registers, yet a parallel devaluation was permanent in the word *starve*, where the gradual weakening can be traced from its collocations: in ME it still meant 'to die', but especially of hunger or cold if these causes were specified (*sterue(n) of/for hunger*). Since 1600 it has usually had the weaker senses 'be on the point of dying' or 'suffer from extreme hunger', and the older sense, if required, must be expressed by *die of hunger* or *starve to death*. (For the specialisation of meaning in this word cf. 5.4 below.) Similar changes have been traced in the words *astonish, amaze, surprise*.[1]

Parallel to the devaluation of overstatements is that of metaphors. These, when first used, are expressive innovations, but later, when outworn, they supply little more than near-synonyms in a meaning already well supplied with forms, e.g. *ass* in the sense 'fool'.

The full scope of the opposite direction of extension, understatement of various kinds, is not always realised. It includes not only intentional euphemisms, but also understatements that may have been due to genuine miscalcu-

[1] Cf. Stern p. 399.

lations on the part of speakers. This may be deduced from the history of words meaning 'immediately', which normally show a blunting to the sense 'later on', as in *soon, anon, directly, presently*. Euphemism itself includes toning down what is feared (*inoperable* 'fatal', *emergency* 'war', *hardware* 'atomic weapons', *anti-personnel* 'killing') and deliberate manipulation or dissimulation for various purposes, e.g. political (*progressive* 'conservative', *recession* 'slump'), commercial (*medium* 'small', *reconditioned* 'second-hand'). The most predictable, and in some ways the most artificial, of such extensions arises from the avoidance of taboo: the speaker purposely chooses, as a euphemism, a related or more general term than that which he is avoiding (e.g. *lavatory* for *privy*), but, as soon as the euphemism is no longer recognised as such by other speakers, it has undergone extension to include that referent in its meaning; a new euphemism is then required (e.g. *toilet, bathroom*), and so the cycle is endlessly repeated.

The above two main directions of extension have been emphasised here since they are the obvious and continual sources of change arising from inaccuracy. They have long been recognised, as for example by Thomas Hobbes (*Art of Rhetoric*, 1681) in his requirement that a word be 'neither above nor below the thing signified'. But not all cases of inaccuracy or misapprehension fall under these heads. If all the semantic components in use were mapped in such a way that differences of degree were entered on a vertical axis, differences of quality or kind on a horizontal axis, it would be found that most everyday inaccuracies are on the former. But many extensions on the horizontal axis take place simply as reflections of natural – and to some extent predictable – overlappings in different people's attitudes to referents. For example, the history of the word *curious* shows that at some time in the past the same objects were regarded by some speakers as elaborate, by others as merely unusual; the change consists of substitution of essential defining characteristics of kind, not degree.

Conversely, the direction of extension may be influenced by purely intrasystemic coincidences – the phonetic or phonaesthetic similarity of forms that are historically distinct but semantically near enough to give opportunity for reinterpretation. Certain cases are well known since similarity of whole syllables is involved, e.g. *outrage* < *ultra* + -*agium* 'excessiveness', interpreted as *out* + *rage*, or *abominable* < *ab* + *ōmen* 'of ill omen', interpreted as from *ab homine* 'beastly'; and some possible cases where the same changes may at present be in process have been suggested, like *ebullient* from L. *bullire* 'boil' but influenced by the noun *bull*, and *scabrous* from L. *scaber* but influenced by the noun *scab*.[1] But such influences are often less obvious and appear only when the origins of a phonaestheme are examined: the histories of /kl-/ 'clinging, coagulation' (cf. examples listed in 3.10) and /br-/ 'vehemence' (cf.

[1] Cf. Read p. 307.

break, bruise, brute, brawl, brandish, brag) show the following sixteenth-century accessions:

	earlier meaning	*later meaning*
CLOG	fasten wood to (1398)	encumber by adhesion (1526)
CLASP	fasten (1386), enfold (1447)	grip by hand, clasp (1583)
BRAZEN	of brass (OE)	impudent (1573)
BRISTLE	stand up stiff (1480)	become indignant (1549)
BROIL	burn (1375)	get angry (1561)

A fuller example is provided by *prig*, which shows considerable changes in the space of two hundred years: 'tinker' (1567), 'thief' (1610), 'dandy, fop' (1676), 'precisian, esp. in religion' (1693), 'conceited, self-important and didactic person' (1753). It seems likely that its later meanings developed under continued influence of the phonaestheme /pr-/ 'conceited, fastidious' as in *proud, preen, prink, precise, prim*, though the meaning 'precisian in religion' may be partly due to influence from the seventeenth-century meaning of *Whig*.

4.3   Extension in grammar

Extension in grammatical systems does not differ radically from that in lexis, i.e. there must be a close connection (though this time of function rather than meaning) between the forms that spread and those they replace. But since one of the main differences between grammar and lexis is that the former comprises the commonest forms in the language, it is natural that the extension here should depend more on the purely quantitative distributions of forms in a system: that is to say, since grammatical extensions are usually of *learnt patterns* of wide distribution or frequency, they may be identified with what historical linguists have usually called 'analogy' – the copying of a proportional model and its application to a context in which it has not hitherto occurred.[1] It should be noted that lexical extensions could also be regarded as analogies (if often of only a situational or contextual type) and that the distinction between grammatical extension ('analogy') and lexical extension ('semantic change') remains a quantitative one;[2] but since the actual patterns of grammar are fewer and more highly structured than those of lexis, the types of extension that occur in it can be more easily distinguished, as in the following:

[1] This term is not to be understood mathematically. Proportional models in the linguistic sense are 'open-ended' in that (i) they may be applied to a single item only, or to any number of the items constituting a whole grammatical or lexical class, and (ii) multiple models may arise, depending on which of the possible points of comparison are selected, e.g. phonemes, distinctive features, morphemes, constructions. See further Leed (1970).

[2] The argument by King pp. 127–34 that grammatical analogy should be regarded as 'simplification by rule-loss' is a mere terminological quibble, and obscures the closer parallel between grammatical and lexical (semantic) extension.

C

(i) *Extension across paradigms (identity of function)*

Of two forms equivalent for the expression of a given function, the commoner may oust the rarer, e.g. the gradual replacement of the *-mi* ('athematic') by the *-o* ('thematic') conjugation, of verbs in Indo-European, or of the 'strong' gradational-type by the 'weak' verbs with dental suffix in Germanic. As we shall see later, other factors are often involved. The OE plural endings *-a*, *-e*, *-u*, zero, *-an*, as in *handa, cwene, scipu, word, bec, eagan*, were mostly replaced later by *-(e)s*, the reflex of OE *-as*, as in *hands, queens, ships, words, books, eyes*. This was a frequent ending, but except perhaps for plural-marking by mutation (which became productive in German), it was also phonetically the most distinctive. And even so, this change cannot be treated in isolation as a mere simplification of plural-marking, for it also contributed to the elimination of grammatical gender (8.2).

(ii) *Syncretism of paradigms with related functions*

The perfect and past tenses of Modern English will provide an example of how this might occur: although they are distinct in function, there are contexts where the difference of nuance, though present, could be regarded as irrelevant to the situation, e.g. *He didn't come?* and *He hasn't come?* This could lead to extension of one or other tense to other contexts, and some such change is to be presumed for early Germanic and Italic (where the aorist and perfect formally combined) as well as for the great growth of the perfect at the expense of the preterite in French and German (and to a lesser extent in English). In such cases the growth of one pattern at the expense of another may be supported by fortuitous inherited distributions, e.g. in the minor system of *is/has come* referred to above (p. 51), the original distribution of *is* had been determined by the semantic properties of intransitive verbs of motion, and was certain to be outnumbered by the use of *has* with transitive verbs.

(iii) *Syncretism within a single paradigm*

Levelling of two or more inflexional endings takes place in a number of ways, not all of which are strictly 'extensions', though the practical result is the same (cf. 4.5). Two endings may merge for phonetic reasons, e.g. the merger of early OE *-æ* and *-i* under *-e*. Such mergers may then act as proportional models for the loss of functional distinctions in paradigms with different endings. In late OE, the lack of distinction between the nominative and accusative in strong masculine and neuter nouns provided a model for the levelling of those cases in feminine nouns; and, conversely, the lack of distinction between the accusative and dative in feminine nouns supported a loss of that distinction elsewhere.

In the present tense of the OE verb, the *-aþ* in the first person plural is evidently an extension from the second and third persons. But, here again as in (i) above, analogical spread is not the only factor; functionally, the change could hardly occur before separate personal pronouns were in common use (cf. 5.5).

Where the forms of a paradigm are distinguished by more than one feature, levelling may eliminate one feature only, but leave others. In the French verb, forms with original radical stress have been generalised in the type *aime–aimons* (OFr. *aim–amons*) but the original alternation survives in the type *tiens–tenons*.

(iv) *Loss of distinction*

In the more marginally grammatical systems like intonation, a distinction may virtually disappear because the more commonly used member of the opposition ousts the other. In parts of the west of Scotland, the intonation-pattern typical of statements has become generalised to include questions (which must once, as in other Scots and English dialects, have had their own pattern). The result is that its information value is greatly lessened, as it now functions merely as a signal for the progress of the utterance.

(v) *Extension due to shift in function*

In grammar, just as in lexis, a form's incidental meaning may eventually assume special importance in certain contexts and become one of its essential functions. An example may be found in the MnE periphrastic future, as in *I shall be leaving*. The periphrasis originally increased in use as an expression of imperfective aspect, which remains its primary function overall. But the forms usually regarded as pure 'colourless' future (*I shall leave, I will leave, I'll leave, I'm going to leave*) all in fact carry some degree of modal nuance. The periphrasis *shall/will be leaving*, on the other hand, is well known for its 'actualising' or 'visualising' function: especially when it is used with non-durative verbs, it focusses more attention on the action of the lexical verb (*be*) *leaving* and less on the auxiliaries *shall/will*. It is therefore becoming more and more used as a colourless future without overtones of intention, wish, resignation or the like, and irrespective of whether the context demands a marked aspectual form. Such transfers of incidental and essential functions in grammatical forms provide one of the main positive ingredients for grammatical restructuring. The extensions exemplified in (i)–(iv) above are negative in that they produce syncretism without replacement. The third ingredient, the intake to provide replacement, will be discussed below (4.4 and later chapters).

The purpose of the present chapter is to show that variation due to extension is non-functional in origin, i.e. it is due mainly to factors of inertia or accident in the spoken chain. As mentioned in (i) and (iii) above, functional factors are always to be considered, especially since the cases of extension that survive from the past show by their very survival or recording in written texts that they belonged to *langue*, not merely to *parole*. The reasons for their acceptance into *langue* may still have been mainly non-functional (e.g. quantitative); the opposite situation, where for functional reasons a rarer variant ousts a commoner one, will be discussed in chapters 5–7. In the above examples the purely quantitative factor is perhaps least evident in (v), but the fact remains that even there the source of variation is an accident of collocation.

4.4 Grammaticisation

Innovations in grammar, in so far as they are not realignments of existing grammatical forms, consist of intake from lexis: extension of a lexical feature takes place to such a degree that it becomes 'grammaticised'. The process involves a loss, in information content, of those components of its meaning that restrict it to specialised contexts, and it is left with a function so general as to qualify it for near-universal, yet predictable, application. In its origins, the change does not differ from other semantic extensions, as may be seen from tracing the history of the MnE perfective passive quasi-auxiliary *get*, e.g. *got elected*, *got run over*. From its earlier meaning 'reach, attain', it had by Shakespeare's time developed a further sense 'succeed in becoming', e.g. 'How to get cleere of all the debts I owe' in *The Merchant of Venice*. Later (probably first in the seventeenth century[1]) this was extended to contexts where 'become' as well as 'succeed in becoming' would fit, e.g. *they got drunk* could be intended by a speaker to mean 'they succeeded in becoming drunk', but since to many hearers such a context required no connotation of success, the construction would be interpreted and used by them to mean 'they became drunk'. At the point when it is extended to adjectives or participles wholly incompatible with the notion of success (*get feeble/caught/punished*) it becomes sufficiently empty of lexical meaning to be grammaticised. Periphrastic tense-forms frequently derive from such 'weakened' lexical elements, especially (*a*) the future, as in English *will*, *shall*, *am going to*, German *werde*, Vulgar Latin *amare habeo* > Fr. *aimerai*, and (*b*) the perfect, which in both Germanic and Romance was an extension of forms expounding 'have' from a construction like 'I have the fish caught' to contexts where the notion of actual posses-

---

[1] The earliest example quoted in the OED (s.v. *get v.* v, 33) is *they were both gotten sufficiently Drunk* (1662). This at first sight seems ambiguous, but the wider context shows that it is active, not passive.

sion was not uppermost. But 'weakening' need not be the only change in grammaticisation; it may also include a shift of function like that referred to in example (v) of 4.3 above. As J. Kurylowicz has well said regarding both types:

'Such shifts as *iterative > durative, static present > perfect, desiderative > future, adverb > "concrete" case > grammatical case, collective > plural* . . . recur constantly and independently in all languages. They represent diachronic universals and must be somehow enrooted, directly or indirectly, in the elementary speech situation.'[1]

Other grammatical innovations may result from a change in the class and rank, rather than the meaning, of lexical items. This applies especially to the origin of prepositions, whether simple or complex. Most simple prepositions derive from adverbs, and, since there are fewer limitations on the position of adverbs than on other word-classes, would arise at a stage of the language when they functioned at clause-level, e.g. as an adverb, *to* could occur either in the position *he cwæþ þæm monnum to* or in the position *he cwæþ to þæm monnum*. But by a different analysis on the part of hearers, it was associated with a following dative, and thus came to function at group level, i.e. its use was extended to the position before oblique cases that had hitherto expressed the same function independently. Many later additions to the inventory of English prepositions resulted from a similar process of historical rankshift, e.g. *concerning, regarding, according to, owing to*, and (more recently) *due to*. In the case of this last, purists still insist that it may be used only as qualifier or complement, as in *My lateness was due to an accident*, and not as a preposition introducing an adverbial group as in *I came late due to an accident*; and in the same way *considering* and *bearing in mind* are criticised as 'dangling participles' if they do not refer to the subject of the clause. Such critics ignore the fact that *owing to, regarding*, etc., are all the result of the same processes in the past: reallocation of functions within the same linear sequence. In *he is suffering from illness due to neglect, due to neglect* is transferred from the function of qualifying *illness* to the status of adjunct to the clause, and is therefore extended to contexts like *he is ill due to neglect*.

The reason for regarding the intake to grammar as lexical in origin is clear in the above examples, but it applies equally to those parts of grammar where the lexical origin is less evident, e.g. the case-endings in the earlier Indo-European languages (cf. 5.5). Nevertheless, some grammaticisations are merely transitional, not lasting. The OE *ge*-prefix was grammaticised as a marker of the past participle (much as in Modern German) in the southern dialects of ME, appearing even with polysyllabic verbs of French origin (e.g. *yconfermyd, yordeynyd, ydelyueryd*), and it survives as such in the form /ə-/

1 Kurylowicz, Preface.

in south-western dialects today. But in the late Old Northumbrian of the
Lindisfarne glosses it shows signs of grammaticisation as a reinforcer of
verbality at clause-level, occurring most frequently in the very syntactical
contexts where it had, in earlier systems, expounded lexical *Aktionsart*, i.e.
not only in the past participle but in past tenses, the infinitive after auxiliary
verbs, and the subjunctive. That this distribution is independent of glossing
habits or the Latin original is proved by the same distribution of the particles
of and *um* in early Old Norse.[1] As its functions were so wide, it must have
continued to lose information-content; and this factor, coupled with that of
phonetic weakening, is sufficient to account for its disappearance in the earliest
Northern Middle English texts. But, furthermore, there were in Old Norse
special rhythmic reasons for its elimination (cf. 5.6), and its disappearance
from North-Midland as well as Northern ME may well have been furthered
by Norse influence.

4.5 Extension and change of form

It may be deduced from the examples in 4.3 and 4.4 that in both grammar and
lexis the 'raw material' of change is produced in a manner parallel to that of
phonetic change, but at a different and probably higher level of the brain-
process. Instead of inaccurate or ineffective *articulation* by the speaker who
initiates a change, it is in this case aberrant *selection*. However, there is the
important corollary that in the case of grammar and lexis the effects of
changes lower in the hierarchy, at the phonetic and phonemic levels, must be
added to those that have just been described.

Grammar and lexis are often left unaffected by phonological change, but,
when they are affected, it is usually found that the result is in the same direction as that taken by extension proper. Thus in lexis, homonymy brought
about by phonemic change has the same practical result as semantic extension – that the same form henceforth serves for more meanings. There is
naturally the difference that, since the relation between form and meaning is
more often arbitrary, the connection between meanings for the same form
may be close in polysemy but random in homonymy; but this does not lessen
the fact that coalescence of form has the same result as extension – the
lowering of information-content.

In grammar, as already mentioned in 4.3, syncretism of form through
phonetic merger of inflexional endings is often found working in combination

---

[1] At the time of their grammaticisation in both Old Northumbrian and Old Norse,
the particles were greatly weakened as markers and expressed *neither aspect nor
Aktionsart*, a point not sufficiently emphasised by J. W. Lindemann in his critique
of previous work in *JEGPh* 64 (1965) 65–83. That the same prefix may be purely
lexical in some contexts but grammatical in others is amply demonstrated by *ge-* in
Modern German. See further Samuels (1949 and 1950–1), Dal and Kuhn.

with extension or 'analogical levelling'. That this should occur more often in grammar than in lexis follows from the much smaller range of forms used. Nevertheless, since grammatical syncretism has the same effect irrespective of whether it is due to phonetic merger or extension, the two factors are often difficult to distinguish (cf. 5.5).

4.6 Innovation and intake in lexis

In contradistinction to the intakes of the closed systems of phonology and grammar, intake to the open system of lexis is (although often complex in its details) basically a simple process when viewed as change. Reference was made above (p. 17) to its more obvious manifestation (the naming of new concrete objects), and it may be presumed that when forms like *transistor* or *Hoover* are selected, they do not coincide in form with any already in common use. But these, in any case, belong to the least structured part of lexis.

The exact sources of new lexical intake vary from language to language. In English, an important source is extrasystemic (loanwords: cf. 6.4), and the main intrasystemic sources are:

(i) compounding of various kinds, as in *blackbird, airport, breakfast, carefree, curly-haired*;

(ii) phrases constituting single lexical items, e.g. *give up* 'surrender', *win over* 'persuade', *fall of leaf* 'autumn';

(iii) terms invented from a combination of roots found in Greek and Latin which are not always free forms in English, e.g. *photograph, thermonuclear, hydro-electric, psychedelic*;

(iv) coinages from initial letters, e.g. radar, NAAFI, UNESCO;

(v) blends, e.g. *smog* from *smoke+fog, mingy* from *mean+stingy, slithy* from *slimy+lithe*;[1]

(vi) formations from established phonaesthemes, e.g. *twirl, trudge, splutter, flurry*;

(vii) derivation by means of prefixes or suffixes, whether of native or foreign origin, e.g. *un-, be-, re-, extra-, super-, semi-, -hood, -ion, -ize.*

All these types belong, with all the variants discussed hitherto in chapters 2 and 4, in the sources of variation leading to innovation, but they differ from them in that they produce new forms which cannot strictly be termed 'variants', however close to their antecedent models they may be. As complete innovations from the start, they demand (*a*) more motivation on the part of the first user, and (*b*) more effort in understanding them on the part of hearers. But although there is this broad line of division between lexical intake and

---

[1] This type of blend should be distinguished from purely formal blends that result from contact of two systems, for which see 6.5 below.

variants resulting from phonetic change or semantic extension, there are, within the lexical intake, very great differences of degree in both motivation and ease of reception. Some of the above-listed types are clearly artificial (iii, iv and v), and require special contextual cues to their meaning when first used; and certain examples of the other types may be conscious artistic inventions, e.g. compounds in the poetry of G. M. Hopkins. But the rest all occupy positions somewhere between this extreme and the variants resulting from extension discussed in chapter 4, 2–3. Compounding, phonaesthetic coinage and derivation all agree with the latter in being essentially extensions of existing patterns, but with the former in their lesser degree of predictability. In the case of compounding, the problem may amount to no more than assessing the familiarity of the compound as a collocation, e.g. *dare-gale* compared with *curly-haired*; but the problem is more difficult in the case of phonaesthetic coinage and derivation.

Phonaesthetic formations like *flurry* are best regarded as consisting of base (e.g. *-urry* as in *hurry*)+phonaestheme /fl/, which replaces the /h/ of the model. (Formation from two phonaesthemes would in theory be possible, and in some cases the base is indeed a phonaestheme in its own right.) They are distinct from the more artificial type of blends in that the latter result from straightforward telescoping of words that need not contain any phonaesthetic properties at all, e.g. *smog, brunch*. But to distinguish the two historically, we must have evidence of the existence of the relevant phonaestheme(s) at the time of the formation. For example, the base *-udge* first appears in *grudge* (1450, from earlier *grutch*) and *drudge* (1494, probably from a native root meaning 'labourer') though the verb *drudge* 'toil' is not evidenced till 1548 in the OED. *Trudge* (1547) is said by the OED to be of obscure origin, but its meaning, 'tread laboriously' is precisely that which would result from *-udge* in *drudge*+phonaestheme /tr/ 'walk, travel' as in *tread, travel, tramp, track, trail, trip, trot*. Although such formations *can* result from forethought, they are more likely to arise as spontaneous *ad hoc* coinages in speech, easily apprehended since the alteration in meaning is precisely that supplied by the phonaestheme(s).

Derivation demands least effort of all from either speaker or hearer, since it consists of an established base and a prefix or suffix that is habitually added. It is this facility of production that has given rise to the long-standing argument whether derivation belongs to grammar rather than lexis. The main objection to this is that the choice of one or other affix is not predictable. Not only are many of the slots filled by affixes now no longer productive (e.g. *longness* cannot replace *length*), but, even among those that are productive, functions overlap, so that, for each individual base, one affix is more acceptable than others, and the use of the others causes at least a momentary bar to communication. This preference for one affix is often the result of a long period of competition. For example, *-ness*, *-(i)ty* and *-itude* all denote mainly 'condition' or 'quality', while *-ion* denotes rather 'condition' or 'action'. Because of this overlap, *propension* (1530), *propenseness* (1568), *propensity* (1570), and *propensitude* (1607) were all used in the seventeenth century for the general senses 'inclination', 'disposition', 'tendency', and only later did *propensity* become the preferred form. Furthermore, competing forms often develop nuances (e.g. *inedible* 'not for eating', *uneatable* 'spoilt in cooking'), and even the criterion of easy intelligibility is not conclusive, for it is open to observation that new forms like *insightful* are not immediately intelligible when first introduced. Although derivation is the most 'grammar-like' part of lexis and consequently demands least effort as a process, it cannot be ignored as part of the lexical intake.

The fact that the lexical intake is more motivated in origin than the majority of phonetic variants and semantic extensions does not alter its initial status as 'raw material' of change. Each new form is individual in origin, and many are abortive and never become part of *langue* proper. Some of the factors affecting such selection will be discussed in subsequent chapters.

5 Grammar and·lexis (*II*): systemic regulation

5.1 Introductory

It is evident that if the multiplication of new meanings for a single form, or of new forms for a single meaning (i.e. initially 'pure synonyms') were to continue on the lines set out in the preceding chapter, without any counterbalancing or regulating mechanism, the language would break down as a system of communication. But that would occur only if there were an abnormal preponderance of 'form-directed' utterance (cf. 3.1) in which speakers were taking only the immediate context into account. The counterbalance is 'function-directed' utterance, in which the speaker consciously or subconsciously considers more than immediate context, i.e. the overall system or those parts of it that are relevant to the utterance. Every individual, whether his utterance be commonplace or unusual, careless or creative, must, if he wishes to avoid ambiguity and remain intelligible, allow for the system to which his utterance belongs; and to that extent his utterance can be regarded as collective as well as individual in significance.

Avoidance of ambiguity means that of all the alternative forms available to a speaker, whether in grammatical paradigm or lexical set, he selects only those that are clearest and least likely to give rise to ambiguity, i.e. in each of the many acts of selection necessary for the utterance, he must prefer some forms and reject others. Now, just as all the extensions discussed above are spread by imitation, so the avoidance of features may also be spread; not everyone exercises the same degree of care in selection, or avoids the same features, but the collective effect is a regulating mechanism which takes the form of processes that will counteract extension: limitation, and differentiation. Earlier writers on semantic change listed various 'laws' for these processes without recognising that they are the most obvious manifestation of *ad hoc* regulation, by the system, at pressure points created by extension and other changes of the mechanical type. In Bréal's pioneering work on semantics (1897), the chapter on *Restriction* precedes that on *Expansion*, and that on *Specialisation* precedes that on *Irradiation*. Yet the simple principles on which these processes of limitation and differentiation depend show that they are regulators:

1. *Ambiguity and limitation.* If a form has two meanings – whether as the result of polysemy or homonymy – so incompatible that they cause ambiguity, one of the meanings dies out, or, more rarely, the form itself becomes obsolete.

2. *Synonymity and differentiation.* Language possesses no *pure* synonyms, and this fact is not likely to be accidental. As Bréal remarked in the same work, 'the memory does not willingly burden itself with two mechanisms working concurrently towards one and the same end'.[1] If, for extralinguistic reasons such as cultural borrowing or foreign conquest, two exact synonyms exist for a time in the spoken chain, *either* one of them will become less and less selected and eventually discarded, *or* a difference of meaning, connotation, nuance or register will arise to distinguish them. Only in rare cases can genuine free variation be said to exist, and, in those with which we are today acquainted it seems probable that one or other of the two processes just mentioned is already at work, though the result, for want of controlled observation, escapes us.

Whether a synonym is discarded or differentiated, the process is complex; it is not sufficient to say that, since at the level of idiolect the individual brain observes the principle of economy referred to above, a collective preference for one or other form is thereby automatically established. But the beginnings of a choice will appear as soon as conversation takes place, since rapport cannot be set up without a common terminology; and the speed with which the choice then spreads will depend on how closely knit the speech-community is (6.7, p. 118f). Similarly, the survival by differentiation of two forms originally synonymous may depend on many factors: the privilege of occurrence of each may be narrowed, or one of the forms may be increasingly selected in a meaning hitherto marginal; slight differences in contextual meaning may be gradually magnified, or the process of extension in the direction of connotations hitherto dormant may be hastened by the presence of the other (newer) form (cf. 6.7, p. 116f).

3. *Functional pull* ('*filling of an empty slot*').[2] Conversely, if one of the meanings of a word is discarded because of ambiguity as in (1) above, and there is no new form that is encroaching on the area of the lost meaning, a new slot-filler may arise from borrowing or creation, or the 'pull' of the empty slot may hasten a new process of extension in another existing word. Such slot-fillers are often ready to hand as 'affective' near-synonyms; their extension need consist of no more than the disappearance of such special connotations

---

[1] Bréal p. 62.
[2] 'Empty slots' never exist literally, since circumlocutions in lexis and marked forms in grammar are always available. But the degree to which circumlocutions are tolerated is limited, so that the ultimate effect is the same as if empty slots actually existed.

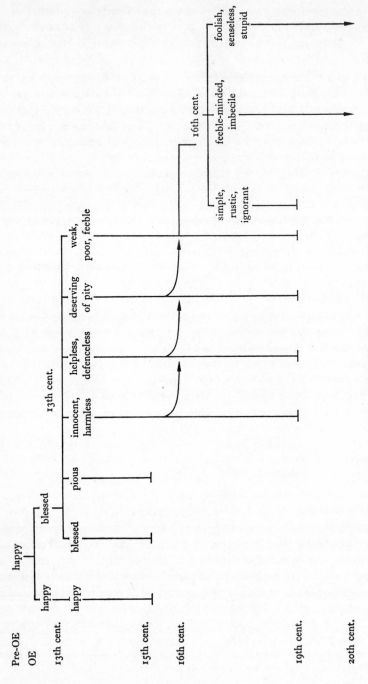

Fig. 3. Dating of semantic changes of the word *silly*, OE *(ge)sælig*

(e.g. jocular) as have hitherto differentiated them from the recessive form or meaning.[1]

As an illustration of the regulation, by these processes, of mechanically induced extension, any of the well-known examples of 'concatenation' will serve. Fig. 3 shows a schematisation of the OED evidence for the dating of semantic changes in the word *silly*, OE *(ge)sælig*. All the meanings other than the original must initially have resulted from extension, but it is much harder to establish the relative importance of the regulating processes – limitation, differentiation and functional pull. It seems reasonable to suppose that meanings as unlike as 'happy' and 'pitiful', if their occurrences overlapped, would give rise to ambiguity, and that that is the main reason for the obsolescence of the meaning 'happy' in the fourteenth and fifteenth centuries, and of the meaning 'harmless' in the eighteenth and nineteenth centuries. But the problem is not, as might at first sight appear from the diagram, merely one of extension and limitation. That would be true only if we had proof that new words like *blissful* (1240), *joyful* (1290) or *happy* (1375) had been formed or borrowed specially to fill the slot left empty by the extension of *sely/silly* after its older and newer meanings had become incompatible; but such words may enter the system for other reasons, and it would therefore be equally possible to regard the great extension in the meanings of *silly* as due to differentiation from these words, which could have been exact synonyms to the earlier meanings of *silly* when they entered the system.

Here, then, lies a central problem in the history of both lexis and grammar: is it the *availability* (for mechanical, extralinguistic or extrasystemic reasons) of new forms that causes the shift, by differentiation from them, of older forms? Or is it the prior shift of the old form to a new meaning (by extension and limitation) which creates the *need* for a new form?

Since this problem is the grammatico-lexical counterpart to that of push- or drag-chain mechanisms in phonology, the relative importance of the factors involved must be discussed further.

5.2 Homonymy

It has recently been questioned whether homonymy should be regarded as any more than a minor, incidental factor.[2] The few well-proven and documented examples of homonymic clash are accepted, but for the rest it is claimed that context provides the safeguard, and that the danger of ambiguity is small. Admittedly, it is fair to assume that homonyms of different word-classes are not normally confused, e.g. the verb *(to) bear* and the quadruped *bear*. Again, even if they belong to the same word-class, but to specialised fields within it,

[1] Cf. von Wartburg p. 146.
[2] Weinreich (1968) 101 n.; cf. Wang p. 10, where homonym prevention (together with other factors) is regarded as 'unsatisfyingly ancillary and particularistic'.

there is little chance that their ranges of collocation will overlap: no one confuses *calf* 'young cow' with *calf* 'part of the leg', and although *mould* 'rust, fungus' has virtually displaced the older *mould* 'earth', there is apparently no confusion with *mould* 'shape'. Furthermore, even in a language with no distinctions of grammatical gender, other distinctions prove adequate: *peace* as an abstract noun is only rarely preceded by a determiner and never occurs in the plural, whereas *piece* is usually either preceded by a determiner or used in the plural; or, with a different distinction, *son* is usually either modified by *my/his/her*, etc. or qualified by an *of*-group, whereas *sun* is normally preceded by the definite article.

However, the mere fact of the survival today of homonyms that are not obviously safeguarded in one of these ways does not prove that they are no disadvantage. For example, the verbs *lie* 'recline' and 'tell lies' are both intransitive, and *lie* 'recline' need not necessarily be followed by an adverb of place. Here, the fact that *he lies/is lying* is often replaced by *he tells lies/is telling a lie* (or by *he's a liar*) shows that interference exists.

The difficulty is that proof of homonymic clash is usually only accepted when it is supported by impressive evidence from linguistic geography, and that is available only when the sound-change causing the homonymy is restricted to certain dialect areas of the language. If the boundary for the replacement-form(s) is then found to coincide with that of the sound-change, the case is complete. The best-known and most often quoted example is from South-West France, where *faisan* and *vicaire* replaced the older word for 'cock' in the precise area where the reflexes of Latin *gallus* 'cock' and *cattus* 'cat' had fallen together under the form *gat*. Similarly, in English dialects the obsolescence of the word *quean* 'harlot' can be shown to belong to those areas where it coincided in form with *queen*, whereas it survives in areas where the ME phonemes /ɛ:/ and /e:/ remain separate. Such evidence is also available when a loanword that is adopted only in part of the country causes homonymy: in Northern English and Scottish dialects the variants *yate*, *yett* 'gate' were selected in preference to *gate* because, in almost the same area, that form existed in its Scandinavian meaning 'way, road'. A further variation occurs when a replacement is needed in one area because only that area uses another form that causes the clash: *lug*, probably a semi-jocular metaphor, partly replaced *ear* in Northern English and Scottish dialects, where *an ear* could be confused with *a neer* 'a kidney', whereas in Southern dialects where *kidney* was used, *ear* continued as the only form.

But such cases are in a minority; more often, the two words have existed, so far as our evidence goes, in the whole language-area, and the part played by homonymy is then judged according to whether the date for the start of obsolescence followed fairly closely on the sound-change or borrowing that gave rise to the homonymy. Well-known examples are ME *brede* 'bread' (OE *brēad*) and 'roast meat' (OE *brǣde*); ME *hele(n)* 'heal' (OE *hǣlan*) and 'cover, hide' (OE *helan*); other possibilities are ME *here(n)* 'hear' (OE *hēran*) and 'praise' (OE *herian*), *dare* 'dare' (OE *durran, dearr*) and 'cower, fear' (OE *darian*), ME *bidde* 'ask' (OE *biddan*) and 'pray' (OE *gebiddan*). The verb *not* 'to clip the hair' became obsolete in the seventeenth century following on the rise in the sixteenth century of the verb *knot* (there is evidence that the change /kn-/ to /n-/ had begun before 1600, though it was probably not accepted into formal London English till later). However, the dating is not always clear-cut, as may be seen from examining the evidence for such an obvious clash as *let* 'allow' and *let* 'hinder'. First, the replacement of the ME verbs *lette* and *werne* 'hinder' (the latter itself probably ousted by a clash with *warn*) was a very gradual process for which a number of verbs have to be considered, e.g. *restrain* (1340), *withstand* (1385), *hinder* (1400), *accloy* (1430), *stop* (1440), *prohibit* (1523), *bar, debar* (*c.* 1550), *damp* (*c.* 1550), *check* (1581), *impede* (1605), *obstruct* (1647), *prevent* (probably not before 1650 in this sense). Secondly, the date at which the two words *let* became homonymous cannot be narrowly delimited, since the replacement of /ɛ:/ by /ɛ/ in *let* 'allow' took place over a long period in which both variants existed side by side; all we know is that it was probably complete in the standard language by the mid-sixteenth century, for spellings with *ee* or *ea* then become rare, and the early orthoepists, Smith and Bullokar, attest a short vowel.[1] Thirdly, the process of obsolescence of *let* 'hinder' appears to have been correspondingly gradual: the OED quotations suggest (though they hardly prove) that it has been becoming more obsolescent and archaic since 1600, except in the construction *to let* (*a person*) *from* (*doing*), which is less ambiguous and therefore survived till later. A sceptic could hardly be blamed, therefore, if he maintained in this case that the main reason for thinking that the obsolescence of *let* 'hinder' is due to a clash with *let* 'allow' is that their meanings are exact opposites (the same would apply to the gradual obsolescence of *cleave* 'part asunder' and *cleave* 'adhere' and their replacement by *split* and *stick* respectively).[2] But, having admitted the existence of homonymic clash for the few cases where the homonyms are antonyms, the sceptic can then reject it for all others that are not fully documented, on the grounds that native words were in any case often replaced by French words when no homonymy was present, and that the same can apply to, say, the replacement of ME *hele(n)* by *cover* and of ME *here(n)* by *praise*.

This scepticism may be natural in studying the etymology of individual words; but, for the general theory of linguistic change, there is no justification for elevating it to the status of a dogma. On the contrary, instead of insisting that every one of a certain list of conditions must be satisfied before the possibility of homonymic clash can be considered, the pressure of homonymy

---

[1] Jacobsson p. 70.
[2] Cf. further on p. 161 below.

Map 1

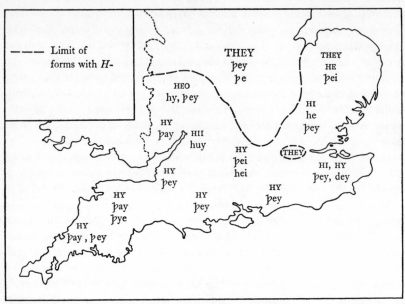

Principal forms in later Middle English (southern area) for 'they' (Map 1 above) and 'though' (Map 2 below)

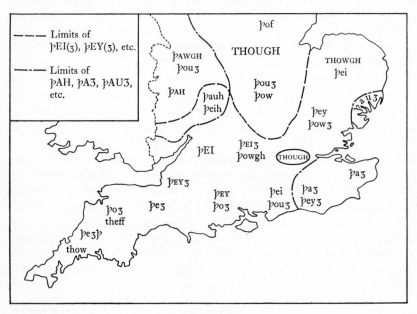

Map 2

should be regarded as potential in some area of most semantic fields, always present to combine with other factors to cause redistributions within that field, and irrespective of whether it eventually causes obsolescence or not. This view can be supported on a number of grounds.

Firstly, the established canon for judging homonymy is by no means sacrosanct. For example, the restriction to members of the same word-class can be outweighed by considerations of distribution and frequency, as may be shown from a study of the forms for 'they' and 'though' in the Middle English dialects. These two words are in some respects the most important of those words of Scandinavian origin that greatly exceed the Danelaw area, spreading over the whole country and ousting the corresponding words of Old English origin. It would in any case seem likely, even without the evidence we have for the rest of the country, that the Scandinavian form for 'they' was adopted in the Danelaw area as providing a more effective distinction from the singular *he* than the inherited English plural forms *hi*, *heo* and *he*, but the proof for such a theory comes from the fourteenth- and fifteenth-century evidence of dialects south of the Danelaw. This allows us to examine the repercussions of the adoption and spread of *they* (*þei*, etc.) in some detail. It was adopted gradually and at first in stressed positions only, so that in the fourteenth century it was still a minority variant compared with the native *h*-forms. Meanwhile the forms *þeiȝ*, *þeih* 'though', which had developed normally in most of the southern area from OE *þeah* (late OE *þeh*), were in process of losing their final fricative. The form *they* (*þei*, etc.) was thus being adopted into an area that already possessed the same form in the meaning 'though', and, according to the usual formula restricting homonymy to members of the same word-class, this should have caused no difficulty. In fact the evidence shows that there was always a clash, which was remedied shortly after by the further adoption of the form *though* (*þo(u)ȝ*, *þo(u)gh*, etc.). A schematisation of the early fifteenth-century position (see maps 1 and 2)[1] shows that, in the area where there was no complication from the forms *þa(u)h*, *þa(u)ȝ*, the boundaries between the forms of the two different systems coincide almost exactly: the system spreading southwards from the Danelaw combines *they* and *though*, while the southern system that is yielding to it combines *hy*, *he*, etc., 'they' and *þei(ȝ)*, *þey(h)*, etc., 'though'. Furthermore, there is convincing evidence that the adoption of *though* always followed (never preceded) the adoption of *they*: in some hundreds of texts written in dialects of the southern area, the combination of *hy* 'they' with *though* as the main forms never occurs;[2] but there is just a small fraction of

[1] For the evidence on which this and the subsequent maps are based see McIntosh (1963).
[2] This statement does not apply to early texts from *within* Norse-settled areas (e.g. the *Peterborough Chronicle*) where the conditions under which these two words were adopted were different.

texts that use *þey* for both 'they' and 'though'. The existence of these few texts shows that there was an interval between the adoption of *they* and *though*, and their paucity suggests that that interval was always short. These indications are corroborated by the scribes of these few manuscripts themselves, who, in their perhaps unconscious attempts to remedy the awkwardness of the sequence 'though they', provide us with evidence which is, in its way, just as revealing and convincing as that of a modern dialect informant. The scribe of MS Caius College 386 (*Prick of Conscience*) normally writes *þ*^{i} for both words, but in this sequence *þ*^{i} *he* (ff. 4^b and 6^a), using an archaic form for 'they'; and in MS Rawlinson Poet. 138 of the same work, *yei* is usual for both words (with rare *yow* 'though') but for this sequence the scribe wrote *y*^{ei} *yat hee* on f. 101^a, and then *yow yei* shortly after on f. 102^a, as if dissatisfied with his first attempt. The scribe of Rawlinson C. 35 of the *Prick of Conscience* was confused by the sequence *þey þey*, and at first wrote only one *þey*, inserting the second afterwards (e.g. on f. 36^b), while the scribe of C.C.C. Oxford 201 of *Piers Plowman* made use of his less usual and archaic spelling for 'though' (*þeyh3 þey*, f. 10^b). But the sequence *þai þai*, written by the third scribe of the Auchinleck MS without apparent qualm, is a decidedly rare phenomenon.[1]

It should now be clear why the development described above does not fit the normally accepted canon: both 'they' and 'though' are functionally important words that can co-occur; but, judged by frequency, the importance of 'they' outweighs that of 'though'. The evidence shows, firstly, that if pressure for the adoption of a new form in the commoner (here pronominal) function is overriding, that form will be adopted *in spite of* the fact that it clashes with the form already in use in the less frequent (here concessive) function; and secondly, that after such an adoption, the *proportionately minor* (though not in itself small) problem of homonymic clash is automatically remedied by a process of *ad hoc* regulation.

Besides the question of frequency, there is another factor that must be balanced against the usual contextual criteria for judging homonymy: the associations of a given form that exist irrespective of context. Ambiguities of this kind are continually present, especially in the written language. For example, President Nixon was reported in the national press on 30 April 1969, as having said: 'when we find situations where students, in the name of dissent and change, terrorise other students and *rifle files*' (italics added). Even the reader who at once construes *rifle* as a verb may well add to it extra connotations of violence derived from the referential meaning of the noun *rifle*. Speakers and writers are often prepared to run the risk of such ambiguities, and indeed may even cultivate them for literary purposes. But, whether consciously or not, they often avoid them, especially if the associations of one

---

1 It is pointed out by F. C. De Vries on p. 48 of his edition of *Floris and Blauncheflur* (Groningen, 1966).

word of the pair are unpleasant, or if it is a taboo-word. The verb *flee* is obsolescent, and has as yet no replacement in formal register; we are here in a position to judge while the event is still in progress, and there seems no reason to question Jespersen's and Orr's views that it is due to the associations of the noun *flea*.[1] Similarly, for all we know, the loss of the verb *queth(e)* 'say' in earlier English may have been connected with the associations of the adjective and noun *qued(e)/queth(e)* 'bad, wicked person, Devil'. The possibility is not restricted to forms with unpleasant associations; it may depend on the fact that the form is phonaesthetically more suited to the meaning of one word of the pair than the other: the adjective *neat* was introduced from French in the sixteenth century, and the obsolescence of the noun *neat* 'ox, cattle' seems to have set in shortly after (for the phonaestheme /-iːt/ cf. 7.3).

It would thus appear that the application of a strict canon to decide whether homonymy should be accepted or rejected as a factor in any given case is unjustified; rather, homonymy should be graded according to the evidence on a scale of 'more or less', and not simply of 'absent or present'. Attention has been too often focussed on actual obsolescence, while there has been neglect of the study of potential homonymy, of its effects on the frequency and semantic area of a given word, and of the relation of those effects to other words in the same semantic field. For example, if one were to suggest that homonymy of *heart* and *hart* had ever been an operative factor, the suggestion would be dismissed on the grounds that both words survive, and that their main meanings are much the same as those of OE *heorte* and *heorot* respectively. But to anyone seeking to explain the restriction and specialisation of *deer*, the possibility must be explored. The restriction of *deer* from 'animal' to its present meaning is described by the OED as 'a specific application of the word, which occurs in OE only contextually, but became distinct in the ME period, and by its close remained as the usual sense'. In its older sense it was in process of being replaced during the ME period by *beast* (from French) from about 1200 onwards, and that evidence only might suggest that *deer* was specialised simply as a process of differentiation from *beast*, i.e. a push-chain mechanism depending purely on the availability of a French loanword. But, for much of the ME period there are signs that the MnE meaning 'deer' was coming to be expressed by the masculine *hert(e)* 'hart'; this word, besides being used occasionally instead of the female *hind*, was used more often than *deer* in compounds where no restriction to masculine can have been intended – *hart-skin, -hide, -leather, hart's tallow, -marrow* and perhaps also *hart-hunting* and *-hunter*. After the fifteenth century this extension ended, and *hert(e)/hart* was even more restricted to its masculine meaning than it had been in the OE period, being replaced by *deer* wherever the generic meaning was required. A possible reason is that the increased frequency and semantic sphere of *hert(e)*

[1] Jespersen (1941) 76; Orr pp. 1–8.

'hart/deer' had involved it in a clash with *hert(e)* 'heart', so that in general, unspecialised contexts and registers, *deer* would be used increasingly to avoid ambiguity; but, if restricted to specialised contexts and registers (e.g. hunting treatises), *hert(e)* 'hart' could survive without ambiguity as a precise term in opposition to the other specialised members of its subsystem, *hind, buck, doe, roe*, as well as to more peripheral members like *stag*. Hence, although this homonymy caused no actual obsolescence of form, it could well have caused a restriction in the meaning and frequency of *hart*, and with it a functional pull towards specialisation of *deer*. Two other minor factors may point in the same direction. Firstly, there would be in Middle English some homonymic pressure, mainly of an associative type, between *deer* and *dear* adj. (OE *dēore*, ME /de:r(e)/, later ME variants /de:r/ and dɛ:r/). This is certainly tolerable today when *deer* has its restricted meaning, but might be less so when its meaning included wild and savage animals. Secondly, the connotations of brutal, non-human attributes in *beast* came to the fore early in its history, and that may account for the further introduction of *animal*, c. 1600; but it also suggests that there would have been ample room for both *beast* and *deer* in the general field 'animal', and therefore no great push-chain pressure for *deer* to become specialised as it did. As we have seen, consideration of potential homonymies suggests that drag-chain pressures (the need to fill partially vacated slots) were the more important.

It is a commonly held view that English stands apart from other Germanic languages because of the great influence of French on its lexis, and this view presupposes a push-chain pressure of extrasystemic origin. But in the case just discussed, it is noticeable that the other Germanic languages show far fewer parallel homonymies: *Herz* and *Hirsch*, *Tier* and *teuer* are distinguished in German, *hart* and *hert*, *dier* and *duur* in Dutch, *hjerte* and *hjort* (Swedish *hjärta* and *hjort*) in the Scandinavian languages, with *dyr* alone as a homonym in the latter. Such comparisons confirm that the drag-chain pressures resulting from a higher rate of intrasystemic change in English have hitherto been underrated, and that they should often be accorded more weight than the mere availability of French loanwords.

Finally, although homonymy is the most obvious repercussion of phonetic change on lexis, there is another possible result to be considered here: ambiguity of form which is due to reduction of phonetic substance. This applies more to the Romance languages than to Germanic with its greater consonantism. Some well-known examples are: Latin *dies* replaced by *diurnum* (Fr. *jour*, It. *giorno*), *avis* replaced by *avicellum* (Fr. *oiseau*, It. *uccello*), *apis* replaced by *apicula* (Fr. *abeille*, It. *pecchia*, Sp. *abeja*), *sol* replaced by *soliculum* (Fr. *soleil*), *flare* replaced by *flatare* (It. *fiatare*) or by *subflare* (Fr. *souffler*, It. *soffiare*, Sp. *soplar*), *edere* replaced by *comedere* (Sp. *comer*) or by *manducare* (Fr. *manger*, It. *mangiare*). Naturally it is difficult to assess margins of tolerance for phonetic distinctiveness, and the problem is not eased by the fact that replacement often occurs in some Romance languages but not in others. It is possible that actual homonymy, not merely the ambiguity associated with 'near-homonymy', is always involved even in such cases; certainly an adoption like 'little sun' seems to lack semantic motivation, and is reminiscent of the expedients used for homonymy. But the fact remains that it is always the longer forms that replace the shorter, and this suggests that phonetic attrition should be regarded as a separate factor which works in the same direction, and requires the same remedies, as actual homonymy.[1]

5.3 Polysemy

As pointed out in 4.5, the effect of polysemy is in principle the same as that of homonymy – the representation of two or more meanings by a single form. And here again, the safeguards normally provided by context are adequate: no ambiguity arises from differences between the meanings of *soon* in 'as soon as' and *soon* 'presently, later on', or between those of *curious* 'inquisitive' and *curious* 'strange, odd'.

Nevertheless, there is some difference in the types of change that result. For whereas homonymy is, as it were, forced on the system in such a way that it is pure chance whether the collocational ranges of the two words will overlap or not (with a consequent clash in some cases), the process of polysemy is more gradual: the collocational ranges of new meanings resulting from extension can evolve without overlapping, and if, eventually, a meaning develops that is incompatible with older meanings, the overlap of collocational ranges will be smaller, its onset less sudden, and the required regulation will be less spectacular, than in the more obvious cases of homonymic clash. Total obsolescence of the word is therefore rare, the usual consequence being the loss of one or more meanings. Some of the best-known examples are of changes spread over many centuries, in which, however, the period when two incompatible meanings coexisted was comparatively short. The extensions in the meanings of OE *uncuþ* 'unknown' may be schematised from the OED evidence as follows:

```
1 Unknown........OE————————————————1650
2 Unfamiliar, strange OE ——————————————————— obsolescent
3 Strange and unpleasant ........ 1380————————————————→
4 Uncomely, awkward, clumsy ...........1513————————————→
5 Rugged, rough  .....................1542————————————→
6 Uncultured  ...........................1694————————————→
```

From this it may be seen that the original meaning (1) survived the slight

---

[1] Possible examples in English are to be seen in the loss and replacement of the OE forms *ā* 'ever', *ǣ* 'law', *ǣg* 'egg', *ēa* 'water, river', *eoh* 'horse', and the suppletion of *īeg*, *ēg* to *island*.

degree of pejoration seen in (3) for two hundred and seventy years, but the greater degrees of it seen in (4) and (5) for much shorter periods.

This, and the cases examined by Menner[1] and Rudskoger,[2] are fairly straightforward examples of the part played by incompatible meanings in the process of limitation (cf. 4.2, 5.1). Others are more complex, and perhaps also more revealing. The word *quaint* had a varied range of meanings in ME and EMnE, mostly inherited from French:

1 Wise, knowing, skilled, clever: 1250–1728.
2 Cunning, crafty, given to scheming: 1225–1680.
3 Cunningly or skilfully made (of things), elaborate: 1290–1631.
4 Beautiful, pretty, dainty, handsome, fashionable, elegant: 1300–1784.
5 (Rarer meanings) proud, haughty: 1225–1430.
  fastidious, prim: 1483–1678.
6 Ingeniously elaborated, refined, smart, full of conceits, affected: 14th cent.–1783.
7 Strange, unusual, odd, curious: 14th cent.–1808.
8 Unusual but attractive in an old-fashioned way: 1795–

Senses (1), (2), (3) and (5) were all obsolete or obsolescent by the seventeenth century. (2) had been ousted by the developments of (3), which, when transferred from things to persons, resulted in (4), (6) and (7). (4) and (7) then combined in (8), and then, *as soon as this had happened*, (4), (6) and (7) vanished. This is shown by the evidence of the dates: 1784, 1783 and 1808 are the last dates for (4), (6) and (7) respectively, with (8) beginning in 1795. Until the late eighteenth century, wide polysemy had been tolerated in this word, but as soon as it was extended to a complex meaning with an individual twist, all the other meanings had to come to an end. The development is pejorative only by comparison with meaning (4), and the reasons for the peculiar twist in sense for this word are probably extralinguistic, e.g. the younger generation might hear the word applied in meaning (4) by their elders to objects, qualities or persons still admired by the older, but not by the younger generation, who would thus come to interpret it in meaning (8).

But the most frequent and obvious reasons for the obsolescence of older meanings are that the new meanings are (a) pejorative, as seen in the history of *crafty* and *cunning*, or (b) have associations of taboo, e.g. *lewd*, *undertaker* and more recently *intercourse*, or (c) have lost greatly in information content, e.g. *very*, *awfully*. In all such cases, once a word has come into use in its new meaning, it is likely to be useless and avoided in its older meanings, the functional slots for which have then to be filled by other words. (The special and somewhat artificial way in which the slots for certain taboos have to be continually refilled was mentioned in 4.5.) The indications of a drag-chain process to regulate these types of polysemy are thus clearer than in many

---

[1] Menner (1945).
[2] A. Rudskoger, *Fair, Foul, Nice, Proper: A Contribution to the study of Polysemy* (*Gothenburg Studies in English I*, Stockholm, 1952).

cases of homonymy. An outstanding case where a grammatical item was replaced because of a peripheral lexical extension has been suggested for Middle High German, where the preposition *after* developed the meaning 'posteriors' and was replaced by *nach* for its main functions.[1]

But in cases where there is no such 'devaluation', the regulation of polysemy may take place in a different way, which is nevertheless equally indicative of the same direction of functional pull: by the differentiation of two existing free variants, or by the adoption of a variant form of the same word which may be ultimately either from another dialect, or from the same original paradigm. Examples are *person* and *parson*, *cloths* and *clothes*, *shade* and *shadow*, *morn(ing)* and *(to)morrow*, *belly* and *bellows*. A parallel solution that applies only to the written form is the adoption of different spellings, as in *metal* and *mettle*, *discreet* and *discrete*; but this may in turn affect the pronunciation, as in *human* and *humane*, and, in some pronunciations, *flour* and *flower*.

5.4 Other factors

It appears from 5.2–3 that in many cases of shift, whether through obsolescence and replacement or specialisation and replacement, both homonymy and polysemy are relevant for assessing the degree of drag-chain (i.e. functional) pressure. But, since it is often difficult to account for the preference of one form or meaning rather than another, yet further factors must be taken into account.

Firstly, one lexical root may be less capable of integration than another. The OE verb for 'to plough' was *erian*, ME *ere*, EMnE *ear*, obsolescent after the seventeenth century except in northern and south-western dialects; and the verb *plough* itself arose in the fifteenth century, formed on the noun *plough* from a root rare in OE but becoming commoner in ME. The obsolescence of *ear* vb. could be due to interference from two other words in the same semantic field, *ear* (of corn) and its derivative verb *ear* 'to ripen', and, at least in certain periods and dialects, also from the verb *hear*, in a context like 'he (h)ears but poorly'. But the survival of *ear* 'to plough' in dialect, as well as the survival of the noun *sullow* 'plough' (<OE *sulh*) partly in the same dialects, suggests that the homonymic factor is not decisive in this case. A more likely reason for the preference for *plough* in Standard English is that both noun and verb *plough* could reinforce each other, whereas the verb *ere* could not be integrated in the same way, since the formation of a new noun **ear* 'plough' would have increased existing homonymic pressures beyond the margin of tolerance.

Secondly, phonaesthetic factors may influence the choice of meaning for forms involved in a shift (cf. 4.2). This can be seen from the development of

[1] Jespersen (1941) 75–6, with reference there quoted to Öhmann.

the OE words for 'to die', *sweltan* and *steorfan*, which in OE were supplemented by the periphrasis *wesan dēad*. It seems probable that *sweltan* and *steorfan* were euphemisms for *dēgan, and that they had originally in Germanic meant 'burn slowly' and 'grow stiff' respectively. Whether the unrecorded *dēgan survived or not is unknown, but in ME the root was either revived or reintroduced under influence of ON *deyja*, supported by the existing noun and adjective (OE *dēaþ, dēad*). From then on, *swelte(n)* and *sterue(n)* were specialised in the direction of their original meanings – *swelte(n)* 'swoon or faint with heat', *sterue(n)* 'die of hunger or cold', 'starve or freeze to death' (for the later meaning of *starve* cf. 4.2). The very fact of their specialisation in these directions would appear to rule out the possibility of taboo as a cause of the shift; and, since there is no trace of these special meanings in OE, it is most probably to be attributed to two factors: availability of ME *deye* (push-chain factor), and by differentiation from it, specialisation of *swelte(n)* and *sterue(n)* to meanings that derive from the relevant phonaesthemes in ME. For *swelte(n)* cf. OED s. vv. *sweal* 'burn, be scorched', *swalm* 'faintness' (1300–1609), *swoon, swow, sway* 'swoon' (fourteenth and fifteenth centuries), *swime* 'a swoon' (OE – 1460); the growth of the phonaestheme /sw-/ is shown especially by *sweam* ('affliction', 1250–, but 'fainting fit, swoon', 1400–) and by the later extension of *sweal* to 'melt, waste away', 1653–; and *melt, swink* and *sweat* may also have contributed. For *sterue(n)* cf. *stark, stiff, derf, stern, steeve* 'rigid', *stith* 'unyielding, severe', *steep* 'glaring', *stour* 'severe, grievous', *strain* 'afflict, distress', and 'toil', *strait* 'pressing, severe', *stress* 'affliction', *stretch, strive, stubborn* and perhaps ON *starfa* 'toil'; and more marginally *stare, stand, stone*. On this view, the change involves a return to the meanings of phonaesthemes that had to some extent existed earlier in Germanic. The different development in Old Norse, where *svelta* took on the meaning 'starve', does not constitute an objection, since different phonaesthemes had developed there meanwhile.[1]

But thirdly, and conversely, where a number of forms are in competition for the filling of a slot, phonaesthetic factors may account for the preference for a given form for that meaning, and not, as in the previous case, for a given meaning for a form that is vacating the slot. The earlier history of the main words for 'throw' in English shows various primarily mechanical changes: introduction of Scandinavian *cast*, the extension and specialisation of ME *werpe(n)* to 'weave' and then 'warp', and of *þraw/þrowe(n)* from 'twist' to 'throw'. But the later history is one of a curious competition between *cast* and *throw*: *cast* was more firmly established in EMnE, but has been largely ousted by *throw*. *Cast* survives in a range of peripheral collocations where the con-

---

[1] The original connection of *svelta* with 'heat' had been weakened in Norse, which possessed similar forms in the opposite meaning – *svalr* 'cool', *svala* 'to chill', *svell* 'ice', while *svæla* had been specialised to 'smoke'; and a new connection with 'starve' would be supported by *svangr* 'hungry', *svengd* 'hunger'.

notation of violent physical action is not required (*cast a vote/shadow/skin/ metal*; *cast-off clothes, downcast, overcast*), whereas *throw* is the normal word where there is emphasis on physical action. A possible reason is that *cast* contains no suitable phonaestheme, whereas /θr/ in *throw* is matched by that in *thrust, thrash, thring* (= 'throw', 1400 onwards); the same applies to the forms of *hurl* and *fling*. Such preference for forms of greater phonetic suitability can be paralleled. It has been shown in detail[1] that, during the period when *nime(n)* and *take(n)* 'take' were in competition, *take(n)* was used for the 'full' senses like 'seize', 'accept', while *nime(n)* more often occurred in quasi-auxiliary use as in *take care/leave/vengeance*. That *take(n)* might be selected for greater 'expressiveness' than *nim* can be shown by examining groups of words of similar form (*take* can be paralleled by *make, shake, quake*, but *nim* has no such parallels: cf. 7.3).

Such phonaesthetic factors work only gradually and more slowly than the other factors hitherto mentioned. They may be regarded as mechanical (since based on analogies with other groups of words containing a relationship of sound to meaning), yet also functional, inasmuch as they enable greater use to be made of the system – however partial it may be – of phonaesthemes. In this respect they probably occupy a midway place in the scale of push- and drag-chain pressures.

5.5 Assessment of systemic shift

To return now to the main question posed above: how far can the degree of push- and drag-chain pressure be assessed in given cases of shift? Most shifts can be divided, according to the evidence available, into (*a*) those taking place in a semantic field containing few items, the more significant of which are known to us, e.g. *animal, beast, deer, hart* in the example given on p. 73f; and (*b*) those in a semantic field containing numerous items, where replacement may be by whole groups of words, as presumably in the cases of *silly* (4.2, 5.1), *uncouth*, and *quaint* (5.3). In (*b*), not all the obsolete words or meanings that are relevant are known to us, since they are recorded only alphabetically in the OED, and no historical thesaurus exists to present them classified by fields.[2] In the present state of our knowledge, therefore, shifts of type (*b*) cannot be assessed; but it is reasonable to suppose that, if we had the evidence, such shifts would differ only in complexity, not in principle, from those of type (*a*).

Push-chain pressure can often be recognised without difficulty, e.g. the introduction of French legal terms like *judgement* was extralinguistic in

[1] A. Rynell, *The Rivalry of Scandinavian and Native Synonyms in Middle English, especially* Taken *and* Nimen (*Lund Studies in English* 13, 1948).
[2] Work is in progress at the University of Glasgow to remedy this need (cf. ch. 9 below).

origin, and accounts amply for the specialisation of *doom*. The extent of drag-chain pressure is assessed partly by dating and partly by the nature of the replacement, i.e. whether it was readily available or of obscure and makeshift origin. The following are two typical but contrasting examples:

(i) The noun *harbour* (ME *hereberʒe*) originally meant 'protection' and was extended to a wide range of meanings: 'shelter', 'lodgings', 'entertainment', 'haven for ships'. In the sixteenth century there was confusion with (*h*)*arbour* (ME (*h*)*erber*) 'a green plot' or 'bower'. Since then, all the more general meanings of *harbour* like 'shelter' or 'lodgings' have become obsolete; only the most specialised sense, 'haven for ships', where there was no danger of ambiguity, has survived. The noun *shelter* is first recorded from 1585 and is of obscure origin, and this suggests that it was called into use to remedy the ambiguity.

(ii) *Cod*, meaning 'bag', 'husk' or 'pod' occurs from OE times till the eighteenth century. It would be liable to confusion with *cod*, the fish, recorded from 1357, and it is probably no coincidence that the compound *peas*(*e*)*cod* 'pea pod' is first recorded just after that, in 1362. This compound was an adequate, if unwieldy, remedy for the ambiguity, and the modern form *pod* did not arise till the late seventeenth century, when 'peasecod gatherers' were given a presumably slang contracted title *podders*. The first solution, *peas*(*e*)-*cod*, was evidently functional in origin; as regards the rise of *pod*, although both mechanical and functional factors were present, they seem from the evidence of the chronology to have operated in such a weak and fortuitous manner that the question of push- or drag-chain pressures hardly arises: a chance mechanical development was eventually found convenient, and it was accepted.

It would thus appear that pressures towards shift may be both strong and weak, and they may be either push-chain or drag-chain. In some cases we may surmise that both types operated (e.g. if both homonymy was present and a replacement was readily available, as when ME *here*(*n*) was replaced by *praise*) but in the sphere of lexis the evidence for single words is usually not full enough for certainty on this point. In the sphere of grammar, however, the coverage is much greater and there is no lack of evidence; and it is probably for that reason that the problem of mechanical and functional change in grammar has been the object of more controversy in the past. In particular, attention has been focussed on the apparently cyclic swing between synthesis and analysis as the means of grammatical expression, e.g. (1) OE *þæm cnihte*> late ME *to þe knight*, L. *canto*>Fr. *je chante*, L. *cantabo* replaced by *cantare habeo*>Fr. *chanterai*; (2) the descent of the original Indo-European case-endings from adverbs grammaticised as bound morphemes; (3) signs that the periphrases of modern French may be giving place to new bound forms.[1]

The older view, which antedates the neogrammarians but had them as its

---

[1] Pulgram (1967) 1642–7.

main supporters, is essentially that the syncretism or loss of inflections through 'phonetic law' creates the need for new periphrases, i.e. a drag-chain process. This view was not without critics in the nineteenth century, but the main criticism has come from the so-called 'functional' school of W. Horn and his successors Lehnert and Berndt,[1] who maintain that the new forms arise from a 'Streben nach grösserer Deutlichkeit' and that the loss of both function and form in inflections is merely a result of this (i.e. a push-chain process). The main arguments advanced are:

(1) that the introduction of periphrases always antedates the loss of inflections by a long period, and this (it is claimed) proves that they were introduced before any actual need arose; and

(2) that the loss of endings must be due only to lack of function, and not to a sound-change, since the same endings often survive if they perform a useful function, e.g. English *-en*, preserved in the past part. *written*, or German *-n*, preserved in plurals not distinguished by the definite article (fem. *die Nadeln* pl., *die Nadel* sg.) but otherwise lost (masc. *die Schlüssel* pl., *der Schlüssel* sg.).

These arguments can be answered, but the answers (to be given partly here and partly in the next chapter) themselves entail modifications of the neogrammarian hypothesis, the result being a more complex hypothesis. The main weakness of argument (1) is that it takes no account, firstly, of redundancy as a permanent and necessary feature of grammatical systems, and secondly, of the concept of marked and unmarked forms functioning in a minor system.

Since one of the functions of grammar is to ensure redundancy, it is not surprising that there should be a refinement in its mechanism that dispenses with the use of heavily redundant forms when they are not required: a minor system of marked and unmarked forms (e.g. *he does go* ~ *he goes*) is used according to the degree of stress required by the context. It is a minor system of this type that appears during the long period of overlap between the adoption of new means (e.g. prepositions, pronouns) and the discarding of the old (i.e. inflections): in many contexts the inflections alone still suffice, and where periphrases with pronouns or prepositions occur as marked forms, they at first include the inflections as part of the maintenance of a normal level of redundancy. The overlap is thus to be expected, and argument (1) above proves nothing either way. But even if it were valid, it would fail to show why, if the inflections that have functioned adequately for centuries are still doing so, new periphrases enter the grammatical system at all. The 'urge towards greater clarity' that is supposed to explain this necessarily entails the notion of 'progress', of bringing the language to greater perfection. But this, as was shown earlier (4.1), is untenable: the extent of such an urge (except in nonce-

---

[1] Horn (1921), Horn and Lehnert (1954); R. Berndt, *Form und Funktion des Verbums im nördlichen Spätaltenglischen* (Halle, 1956).

instances of *parole*) must be assumed to be constant for all periods of all languages, and an increase in it (comparatively speaking) can occur only if the existing inflections are not functioning adequately. Since one of the premises of the argument is that *no* general need for the new periphrases exists when they are introduced, it would appear that the argument fails as an explanation. If, on the other hand, the possibility of a need is admitted, the problem once again becomes tractable. The fact that inflections continue in Latin, Old English or Old French texts side by side with prepositions or pronouns (and are written in their full form) does not mean that they could not have lost part of their effectiveness, in both function and form, when compared with their antecedents in a fully synthetic language system. Such a loss of effectiveness could be due to (*a*) phonetic weakening (but not loss), especially where, as in Germanic, inflections did not receive the main stress, (*b*) extended functions and consequent lowering of information-content, and (*c*) syncretism resulting from both (*a*) and (*b*), and leading to still further loss of information-content. It must be emphasised that only a slight weakening of phonetic distinctiveness, as in (*a*), need occur to cause imbalance; then, especially under conditions of contact between speakers of different languages, dialects or registers (chapter 6), a greater range of emphatic devices is called into use, whether by an increased use of existing marked forms or from lexical sources.

We are thus led to argument (2), which criticises the neogrammarian concept of inflections weakened or lost through 'sound-law'. It is true that this concept needs reformulating (see 6.7) but there can be no grounds for denying it altogether. Some preliminary points may be mentioned here. Firstly, there is clear historical proof that such a change exists, and that its results may occasionally remain unremedied: forms like the plurals *sheep* and *deer* are inconvenient, and the absence of plural marking in these words could not be functional in origin; it must go back to a purely mechanical loss of inflections that was remedied in the majority of the other words in question. Secondly, no one denies that merger causes homophony of root-syllables, and consequent lexical ambiguities, and it is therefore extremely unlikely that a parallel change of form should not affect inflectional syllables; the only difference is that in grammar, the replacements, new marked forms, are likely to exist already as frequent lexical collocations, whereas remedies for lexical homonymy are often obscure or makeshift. Thirdly, and likewise, no one denies the existence of lexical polysemy, and it is therefore reasonable to expect a parallel extension of the functions of inflections, with resultant loss of information value.

On the basis of the above discussion, the following stages for the change from synthetic to analytic structure may now be suggested:

Stage 1. Inflections are the normal forms. Pronouns and adverbs are available, but are used for emphasis only as part of normal lexical collocation. There is no question, at this stage, of their availability acting as a push-chain influence towards the weakening of the forms or functions of inflections.

Stage 2. As a result of any or all of the factors (*a*), (*b*) or (*c*) mentioned above, inflections are slightly weakened. Pronouns and adverbs become grammaticised as part of new marked forms which continue to include inflections (drag-chain process). Unmarked forms consisting of inflections only are still used more commonly than the new marked forms. Certain adverbs are reinterpreted as prepositions, with rection of a case-ending.

Stage 3. Over a long succession of *états de langue*, the unmarked forms increasingly give rise to ambiguity in their rarer functions, and the marked forms become more common (drag-chain process continued). But at this stage the reduced functional value of the inflections appears: in certain early Middle English texts like the *Peterborough Chronicle*, a reduced form of inflection (*-e*) may be selected for use after a preposition, compared with fuller forms (*-ne*, *-en*) when no preposition is used (start of push-chain process).

Stage 4. Grammatical relations are now shown mainly by a fixed word-order at clause level, and by periphrases at group level. As a result of conservatism and inertia, reduced inflections are preserved, with a surviving but gradually decreasing contribution to redundancy (push-chain process continued). At this stage there may be systemic selection of different inflections (or of zero) to form new subsystems, e.g. in late Old Northumbrian, *-en* is found more commonly in the preterite indicative, *-e* in the preterite subjunctive. The process of selection will be discussed in chapter 6; suffice it to say here that it cannot be used as evidence that the earlier stages result from push- and not drag-chain pressures, or that mechanical pressures towards loss of inflections are irrelevant. These latter are present throughout, though of more importance in the earlier than the later stages of a cycle which may last for anything between one and two millennia.[1]

The view outlined above, though more complex than earlier views, accords better with the facts. As we might expect from a problem that concerns a

---

[1] It has been claimed that in Old French the earliest uses of personal pronouns are mainly rhythmical in origin (e.g. as propwords after weakly-stressed conjunctions), and that their rise is therefore not connected with the weakening of endings (cf. von Wartburg pp. 63–75). But the position in Old French is by no means abnormal. The contexts in which the pronouns are found are all such as might be expected for new marked forms in stage 2, irrespective of whether rhythm or emphasis are the conditioning factors; and the later generalisation of the pronouns, after the loss of endings, follows the usual pattern.

major structural feature of grammar, the various factors – extralinguistic, mechanical and systemic – that were found to apply in uneven proportions in lexis, combine here more evenly, constantly and gradually. New forms for intake into grammar are always available in lexis, but, in the early stages, drag-chain pressures (which may or may not be extralinguistically induced) are uppermost; in the later stages, when the new forms have been grammaticised, push-chain pressures become more prominent, though the original drag-chain pressures continue to operate in combination with them.

The process just described is seen at its most obvious in the replacement of inflections, but it applies equally to the replacement of free grammatical forms that lose in phonetic substance or distinctiveness and are replaced by heavier forms. Here again, the loss of phonetic substance is not 'caused' by the availability of heavier forms in lexis (or, as the Horn–Lehnert school have it, by 'loss of function'), but, initially, by frequent use in contexts demanding little stress; there then ensues a period in which the later (heavier) and earlier (lighter) forms combine as marked and unmarked members of a system. Examples are especially common in the pronominal and deictic systems: in Latin, *ille, iste, idem, ipse* were all originally marked forms in opposition to *is*, but, in so far as they survived without suppletion in Romance, they were largely 'down-graded' to supply personal pronouns and the definite article (Fr. *le, la, il, elle*; It. *il, la, lui, lei, esso, essa*); in their demonstrative functions they were replaced by forms which must, from the evidence of their etymology, have originally been marked, but have in turn been reduced: *ecce iste* > Fr. *ce(t)*, *eccu(m) istum* > It. *questo*, *eccu(m) illum* > It. *quello*, **metipsimum* > Fr. *même, istu(m) ipsum* > It. *stesso*. The process continues with reinforcement to new marked forms in Fr. *ceci, cela*; for Gmc., cf. **aiwa galīkaz* > *each*; IE pronominal **te + se* 'see' > OE *þes* 'this', Mn dial. *this here*, Swed. *den här*, ME *þe ilke* 'the same' > South-West E. dial. *thick(y)* 'that'.

5.6 Evidence of correspondences

The cases discussed above have been mainly limited to single semantic fields or grammatical functions, but the same essential problem may sometimes be solved by the detection of correspondences in fields or functions that are not immediately related, or by comparison of developments in geographically adjacent systems. The possible types of evidence vary greatly, as may be seen from the following:

(i) In Old Norse, unstressed prefixes (mainly preverbal) were lost much earlier than in other Germanic languages, so that e.g. *nema* occurs in the meaning not only of the original simplex but also of the compounds **and-, *bi-, *fra-, *ga-* and **undneman*. This change has been the subject of a controversy parallel to that concerning the loss of inflections (5.5), and here again the claim that prefixes were lost because they had become functionally superfluous[1] seems unlikely in view of the fact that more ambiguities were left to be resolved by context only, or were remedied by the addition of post-verbal adverbs like *upp, fram, saman, (i) sundr*. But there are also other, functionally unrelated, developments in Old Norse which tell against such a view: (1) the proclitic negative *ne* was replaced by the suffixed (i.e. enclitic) *-a(t)*; (2) a suffixed definite article *-inn* was developed, in contradistinction to the prepositive article of other Germanic languages; (3) enclitic pronouns *-k, -þu, -er, -it* were used more extensively than elsewhere in Germanic, and the suffixing of the reflexives *mik* and *sik* led to a further peculiarity of Norse, the medio-passive verb-category in *-mk, -sk*. Here again, as in the case of inflections, it is not practicable to state that proclitic syllables were lost in early Norse 'by sound-law' (cf. 6.7). But the fact that they were either avoided or replaced by enclitics in categories as functionally diverse as those listed above suggests that the basis for this change lies primarily in the spoken chain, not the system.

(ii) The extreme functional view regarding loss and replacement of inflections (5.5) would postulate that the OE present indicative endings *-eþ* (sg.) and *-aþ* (pl.) must have merged in *-eþ* in early ME as a result of the clearer distinctions rendered by the increased use of personal pronouns. But further light may be cast on this problem by comparison of systems. In fact, during the period of the syncretism, the distinction rendered by pronouns of the third person was either static or decreasing, according to dialect. In Northern and Southern dialects it continued to be made by *he* (sg.) and *hi* (pl.), in the North in combination with verbal *-es*, not *-eþ*. But in the Midlands, especially the East and Central Midlands, the OE form for both 'they' and 'she', *heo*, was becoming unrounded to *he*, which now had to supply all three functions, 'he', 'she' and 'they'. This problem of the ambiguity of the *h*-pronoun was eventually solved overall by the introduction of *she* (6.7) and *they* (5.2); but, long before that happened, the plural *-eþ* had been replaced by *-en* in the Midlands, and early ME texts from East Anglia show this feature as their only distinction of number, e.g. in *he comeþ* sg. ∼ *he comen* pl. It is usually explained as an analogy, for which there were models in the auxiliary (preterite-present) verbs, in the preterite indicative, and in the present and preterite subjunctive. It would also be supported, in the Midlands and North, by the proportional model: ON infinitive *-a*: 3rd pers. pl. *-a*:: ME infinitive *-en*: 3rd pers. pl. *-en*. But this does not explain its adoption and currency in precisely those areas that show *he* 'they', whereas in the North *-es* continued (with *-e* or zero used only directly after personal pronouns), and *-eþ* in the South. The explanation for that must be that it was required for regulation of the imbalance caused by homonymy of pronouns which affected the Midlands more than elsewhere. In

[1] Modéer pp. 70ff.

the North, *hy* (presumably) survived until it was replaced by *they* (*þai, thai,* etc.), while in the South, where *hy* survived longest, the contracted singular remained as an extra distinction in many verbs, e.g. sg. *sekþ, fint* compared with pl. *secheþ, findeþ.*

(iii) In early ME, the relative *þat* was extended from its limited use in OE to all contexts after neuter antecedents, and, in some dialects, a special system was evolved whereby the distinction animate–inanimate was expressed by the forms *þe* and *þat* (8.2). Yet this system was soon disrupted by the generalisation of *þat* as relative pronoun, in spite of the fact that it was already heavily overloaded with other functions. The model for this extension would no doubt exist in the stressed demonstrative *þat*, which was generalised from neuter to all genders. But the most probable reason for it is systemic – that the definite article had meanwhile developed to an invariable form *þe*, so that (*a*) it was confusing to have the same invariable form serving for all genders in the definite article but differentiated from *þat* and serving for animates only in the relative pronoun, and (*b*) the alternative solution whereby *þe* was revived as an invariable relative pronoun as well as a definite article would have been unbalanced (cf., on the one hand, German, where a diverse paradigm survives as both definite article and relative, making full contribution to the level of redundancy, and, on the other, Scandinavian with its invariable relative form *som*, distinct from the suffixed article and the demonstratives *den* and *det*). In other words, the generalisation of *þe* as invariable definite article was remedied by the generalisation of *þat* (in preference to *þe*) as relative pronoun.

A recent writer on this problem, K. Kivimaa, thinks that 'the article *þe* probably had little influence on the disappearance of the relative *þe*',[1] and adduces cases like *þa boc þa* and *þe boc þe* (Laȝamon A) to show that the combination of both was possible. But such cases are mere survivals of the 'diverse' position that still obtains in German; they do not prove that *þe*, when fully generalised in both functions, would not eventually prove inconvenient.[2] His second argument seems at first sight more cogent: in a single Early Middle Kentish text, MS Digby 4 of *Poema Morale*, the definite article forms *se* and *si* survive, yet the replacement of the relative *þe* by *þet* is almost complete, i.e. it *precedes* the generalisation of *þe* as article. But this evidence should not be accepted without further scrutiny. The problem, if posed in the simple form 'why was the form *þe* avoided in one type of Kentish of *c*. 1200?' finds an answer in a special innovation of Kentish – the merger of late OE /y/ and /e/. It is quite possible that the less stressed forms of the instrumental (OE *þy̆*) would have coincided with *þe*, and that explains both

---

[1] Kivimaa pp. 137–8.
[2] The MnE sequence *that man that* provides no parallel, since the two types of *that* differ in stress, whereas both the article and the relative *þe* must have been unstressed in early ME.

the later survival of *se* and *si* and the earlier extension of *þet*. What seems at first sight a puzzling exception turns out, on further comparison of dialects, to confirm rather than weaken the original hypothesis.

It may be seen from these further examples that a sequence of mechanical change followed by systemic regulation is normal and to be expected in the historical study of grammatical systems. The basic processes of change in grammar and lexis are closely parallel: homonymy and polysemy in lexis, syncretism and extension of functions in grammar, loss of phonetic substance and systemic regulation in both. The processes of differentiation and special-isation so common in lexis have parallels in grammar too, and these will be taken up in chapters 6 and 8.

6 Diversity and contact

1. Introductory

The purpose of chapters 2–5 has been to examine the types of possible intrasystemic change; and if such change is regarded as a whole, without specifying any given type or direction for it, then some degree of it can be regarded as predictable for all systems in normal use.[1] But some obvious further questions have been deferred until now, namely, why is there more of such change in some systems than in others, and why sooner in some than in others? To answer these, other perspectives must be used: the extralinguistic and extrasystemic factors – hitherto treated only incidentally from the viewpoint of a single system – must now be discussed in more detail.

As was pointed out in 1.4 (p. 7) the exact delineation of the spheres of these two terms can at times be difficult, but there are certain unambiguous uses of 'extralinguistic' that can be disposed of at the outset. Cultures and communities differ; their needs, their customs and their ways of looking at things differ. This point should not be pressed too far, since there is more to unite the total human experience than to divide it; but it is sufficient to account for many superficial differences, not only in the names for the actual objects or concepts in use, but also in the type of distinction chosen for marking. An obvious example is the way that the colour-spectrum is differently divided in different languages, but more abstract systemic differences could also be considered in this connection, e.g. the division of the deictic function into *this/that* in Standard English but into *this/that/yon* in N.E. Scots, *este/esse/aquele* in Portuguese.

The reasons for such differences may be accepted here as purely fortuitous, or as outside the scope of the discussion. But there are borderline cases that cannot be marked off as either purely fortuitous or purely extralinguistic; for example, the choice between internal word-formation, calque or loanword in lexical intake. Superficially it might appear that the difference of choice between English *telephone* and German *Fernsprecher* (or Icelandic *talsími*) is wholly extralinguistic – a matter of national outlook. Yet word-forming habits depend partly on the structure of the language that has been inherited. In German, the original habit of initial stress has been preserved because foreign

[1] The whole subject of 'possible linguistic change' has recently been referred to as 'constraints', but this seems too limiting a title for so wide a field. Cf. Weinreich (1968) 101–2, 183–4.

words with different stress-patterns were not – as in English – imposed on the language by invasion; no pattern was established for the acceptance of such words, and native word-formation is therefore preferred.[1] The preference is thus the result of a combination of factors: extralinguistic (absence of invasion) but also intralinguistic (absence of pattern). Again, superficially it might appear that the gradual ousting of *wireless* by *radio* in British English is fortuitous. But the existence of both is due to the very fact of *diversity* of systems (American and British), and the spread of one at the expense of the other is due to *contact* of systems. Both these subjects, diversity and contact, have intralinguistic (but more often extrasystemic) relevance.

6.2 Diversity

Diversity, ultimately, depends on the concept of the idiolect – that no two persons speak exactly alike because there are always at least some minor differences in their respective upbringings, environments and physical make-up. These differences are important for the origins of change (cf. 2.1, 6.7), but, when viewed as belonging to single individuals in isolation, they have no relevance for systemic change. The minimum unit relevant for change leading to systemic diversity is a speaker and his interlocutor, or rather (since there are often no practical reasons for preferring one interlocutor to another) the group forming his habitual interlocutors. Such groups have been termed 'closed networks',[2] and are to be distinguished from 'open networks' resulting from overlapping between groups (cf. 6.7, p. 118).

If the vast range of variants discussed in chapters 2 and 4 is now reconsidered, it will readily be seen that, given two closed networks, there is a much greater probability that different variants will be selected in each than that both will coincide precisely in their selections. This is not a matter of pure chance: in the first place, each group contains a different set of idiolects, and its 'common core' is therefore already slightly different from those of all other groups; then, if a choice is available, it is only partly a matter of chance whether a different choice is made in each group, for it may also depend on the precise and unique combination of extralinguistic factors operating within each group whether (for example) a higher proportion of relaxed variants is used, or whether certain features of voice quality, rhythm or intonation become more prominent than in other groups; similarly, the choice of one particular

---

[1] In Modern Icelandic, the intralinguistic reasons for avoidance of foreign formations are even stronger than in German, Dutch, or the continental Scandinavian languages. Its morphological system is extremely conservative, and would be disrupted if the number of new words that do not conform to the inherited pattern rose above a certain level. Cf. R. J. McClean, *Growth of Vocabulary in Modern Icelandic* (Inaugural Lecture, Birkbeck College, London, 1950).

[2] Gumperz pp. 34f.

semantic extension rather than another can be accounted for by the peculiar combination of group-conditions and the individual past experiences of the members of the group. And just as with mechanical change, so systemic regulation may vary from group to group: different ambiguities and pressure-points arise, and are remedied in different ways.

It is thus the mere fact of *isolation* or separation of groups that accounts for all simpler kinds of diversity. Complete separation, whether through migration or geographical or other barriers, may result in dialects being no longer mutually intelligible; and thus, if there is no standard language to act as a link between them, new languages come into being. Lesser degrees of isolation result in what is known as a dialect continuum – a series of systems in which those nearest and most in contact show only slight differences, whereas the whole continuum, when considered from end to end, may show a large degree of total variation. Dialect continua are normally 'horizontal' in dimension, i.e. they occupy a region in which fresh differences, which would be represented on a map as a network of isoglosses, continually appear as one proceeds from one village to the next; but in large towns they may also be 'vertical', i.e. the different groups belong to different strata in the social scale.[1]

Although a horizontal dialect continuum might in theory be expected to show gradual changes, this applies only to areas where the population is distributed evenly. In addition to natural geographical barriers, there are always more sparsely populated belts over which there is less communication, and these coincide with a greater concentration, or 'bundle' of isoglosses than elsewhere. Furthermore, larger cities are often centres for standardisation (cf. pp. 93 and 103 below); different types of regional standard radiate outwards from each centre, and, at the points where the different types meet each other, secondary 'bundles' of isoglosses may be expected.[2]

Country and class dialects often do not embrace such a range of lexis as the standard language, and, especially when used by not fully 'competent' speakers, have been referred to as 'restricted codes'; but with some possible exceptions to be mentioned below (p. 109), they are normally autonomous systems of communication sufficient for the needs of the groups they serve. But a type of incompleteness that is more relevant to diversity is represented by 'subcodes' of existing systems. Other terms used for these vary from the more general 'register' to the more particular 'field of discourse' or 'domain' (specialised language, e.g. of occupations and professions) and 'style' or 'tenor' (language used in particular situations, e.g. submissive, commanding, sympathetic, sarcastic). In what follows, the terms *register* and *style* are preferred.

If a grid is constructed to accommodate all dialect, occupational and stylistic variants, the number of slots is vast. Naturally, not all the slots in such a grid

---

[1] Cf. Halliday p. 86.
[2] For a full demonstration of this process, see Malkiel (1964).

would be filled by a different variant, e.g. some occupations tend to coincide with certain classes; the same forms may recur in both dialects and registers that must on other criteria be regarded as separate. Nevertheless, register remains an important, if as yet not fully explored, source of variation. For our present purpose, we are less concerned with the specialised lexis of technical registers (though even they may provide items like 'safety-valve' that enter other registers as metaphors) than with the phonological variants, especially those of stress and intonation, which typify so many situational registers (styles), and which have already been mentioned above and in 2.2 in connection with distinctions like *forceful–relaxed, formal–colloquial, careful–slurred.*

Register is not invariably classified as intralinguistic or intrasystemic; some linguists have preferred to regard register-variants as extralinguistically conditioned, in much the same way as degrees of loudness or softness could be said to be conditioned by the distance a spoken message has to cover, or by the amount of other noise it has to overcome. But the variants (e.g. assimilated forms typical of fast colloquial style) are capable of exact description; each speaker has more than one register at his disposal, and, in 'switching style', he will be largely changing from one set of discrete forms to another. Although his selection of them is conditioned by his relationship with his interlocutor, they are not created anew by these conditions each time, but have been previously learnt by imitation. A dialect system could thus be said to consist of a whole range of register variants; it is only through them that it can be expounded, and it is therefore preferable to regard them as intrasystemic. It follows that change in register-variants may be regarded from two aspects: as exponents of system, they may diverge from each other within the limits feasible in that system; but they may also diverge, *qua* exponents of dialect, from their counterparts in other dialects. Apart from these possibilities, however, the concept of register-variants *within* a system may cast further light on the process of dialect divergence already referred to. The exact combination and proportion of different registers used by each group depends not only on the occupations but on the habits, tastes, and temperaments of the members of the group. For example, even if we assume that two groups have 'the same' regional or class dialect and occupation and habitually discuss the same topics, one group may do so in a light-hearted, bantering way, the other in a more serious, committed, or 'intense' way. The former group may then be expected to use a higher proportion of relaxed and slurred variants, the latter a higher proportion of forceful variants, and this increases the chances that the groups will diverge. In this way, registers appear as the intralinguistic and intrasystemic counterparts to the external conditioning of each group.

Linguistic diversity is thus of great relevance to linguistic change, and this will be shown further in certain examples to be given in chapters 7 and 8. Indeed, it is the very existence of diversity that prompts the basic questions asked earlier in this chapter; and since its existence can be explained, that explanation answers, at least in part, the first question: why more in some languages than in others? To carry the answers further, we are concerned less with the fact of divergence itself than with *contact* between either different languages or any of the divergent types of a single language enumerated above.

6.3   Contact

The study of contact between different types of language is of importance because it can provide reasons – often the most simple and straightforward ones of all – why a type of language changes: it is influenced by another type as a result of contact between its own speakers and those using the other type. Such influence is variously named, e.g. 'borrowing', 'loans' or 'loanwords' are often used of the receiving system, while more neutral terms are 'mixture' or 'convergence' (of varieties) and 'spread' or 'transference' (of features).

The spread of features takes place in no predictable order, and is evidently determined by the special social conditions that apply in each individual case of contact (see further on pp. 103–10). In general, lexical spread is the more frequent and noticeable between languages that are *not* mutually intelligible, whereas between closely related dialects of the same language (which already have a lexis that is largely common to both) it is the spread of phonological and phonetic features that is of greater interest. But we must distinguish carefully between the spread of individual features and the spread *en bloc* of so many features as to constitute a virtual spread of system. If we take the normal dialect continuum as an example, the possibilities are as follows (though, in theory at least, they apply to other situations too).

Firstly, the isogloss for a given feature may or may not shift. If it does shift, there may be complete levelling resulting in the elimination of the recessive form, or a new compromise form may arise. Secondly, the receiving systems (or their subgroups) may be variously affected by these three possibilities as they apply to all features of the system, so that *either* (*a*) further, 'secondary' divergent systems are created, which must be added to the divergences already discussed in 6.2, *or* (*b*) there is a shift of so many features that the receiving system itself becomes *less* divergent from its neighbour than before, retaining only relic forms from its antecedent.

The outcome will depend on the precise conditions of contact, to which we return below; but it is useful to distinguish two main types of contact:

Type A: stable and continuous contact between neighbouring systems that are adjacent on either the horizontal (regional) or the vertical (social) axis;

Type B: sudden contact, resulting from invasion, migration or other population-shift, of systems not normally in contact hitherto.

The distinction applies both to systems that are mutually intelligible and to those that are not. The specific results of both types, *A* and *B*, could theoretically be the same, but, in contact of type *B*, speakers must inevitably make adaptations at a higher rate: a larger proportion of stressed and marked forms will be used, so that, quite apart from the specific reciprocal influences of each system, the normal internal processes of change in phonology, grammar and lexis (chapters 2–5) will be intensified and accelerated.

It is thus probable that contact of type *B* provides part of the answer to the problem of varying rates of change (cf. pp. 108, 133f). But it is not always possible to make an absolute distinction between types *A* and *B*; some cases of contact fall somewhere between the two extremes. For example, in centres of commerce, especially capital cities, there are continual contacts between speakers of non-adjacent dialects and therefore a permanent 'weak' type *B* situation. This may result in a faster rate of change in a capital city than in the rest of the country. The assumption cannot be made automatically, since capital cities are usually cultural centres with a high degree of literacy, which may act as a conservative influence; but large cities usually show a higher rate of innovation than surrounding areas (to which the innovations then radiate), and hence the classic situation in linguistic geography of an 'innovating central area' flanked by 'conservative peripheral areas'.

6.4   Contact of languages

For the study of contact between different languages, a further distinction is necessary: whether the contact takes place via competent bilinguals or not. If not, we have what is in effect an extreme case of type B contact, where neither speaker has more than a few words of the other's language at his disposal. The result is a *pidgin* language, or, if it becomes established as the first language of a community, a *creolised* language. These are not simply mixtures of the two languages in contact; their structures include much that is new, based on the earlier speakers' misunderstandings of their inter-locutors' intentions. Since pidgins start from the need of two speakers of mutually unintelligible languages to find a mode of communication, their formation is wholly unpredictable, and not typical of language contact as a whole.

More usually, the contact takes place via bilinguals who have some degree of competence in the second language. For contacts of type *A*, the numbers of these vary according to which geographical frontier is in question, but, however small the frontier trade, there are always some bilinguals. These, when speaking their second language, include (through the psychological process known as 'interference') features belonging to their first language, and such features may then be adopted and spread further by the monolingual interlocutors, thus crossing the language boundary. For lexical features, admittedly, contact via genuine bilinguals is not essential: names of objects can be transmitted by speakers whose knowledge of the second language is negligible; or their spread may take place through the written language or mass communication media, though here it is likely that the author, or other person first responsible for their introduction, will have more than a rudimentary knowledge of the second language.

In contacts of type *B*, the bilinguals are usually those who learn the second language for reasons of prestige or livelihood – the subjects in a conquered country, or foreign immigrants in an expanding country.

As already mentioned (6.3), the most obvious transfers between different languages are in the sphere of lexis. Words are borrowed mainly for one or both of two reasons:

(i) the donor language is of greater prestige in the field of the borrowed words, e.g. French terms for government and organisation, cookery and many other fields, in Norman England;

(ii) there is a vacant slot for the word in the receiving language, not yet filled from within the system (cf. 5.1, p. 65).

The usual result is that the language that is of less prestige receives a greater number of loanwords, e.g. Middle English in Norman times, or the German and Scandinavian of immigrant communities in the United States. The lack of prestige of the language may be due simply to the low status of its speakers; but in educated communities the language that has the greater literary status has a clear advantage, e.g. in Switzerland, Romansh, for lack of a literary standard, shows both a great dialectal diversity and also a large intake of words from literary Swiss German. Such gaps in prestige between the two languages may have a long historical standing, but the prestige factor in borrowing remains the same: Latin was the language of learning in the Middle English period, and when it was gradually replaced by English in this function in the fifteenth and sixteenth centuries, the influx of Latinate words into English reached its highest level. It can be no coincidence that writers throughout this period characterised English as 'rude' and lacking in eloquence.[1]

The above indications of the direction of transfer from the 'upper' to the 'lower' of two languages in contact bears little relation to the ultimate survival or obsolescence of the languages themselves, which usually depends more on the sheer numbers of the speakers of each. Thus the languages of immigrant communities in the United States tend to lose their hold after a few generations (and this is only partly due to their large lexical intake from American English), while French, the 'upper' language in medieval England, eventually

---

[1] For a review of such statements see R. F. Jones, *The Triumph of the English Language* (London, 1953) ch. 1.

gave place to English. Furthermore, there have been special cases of contact in the past where none of these general indications apply. The Viking invasions resulted in a strong concentration of Scandinavian speakers in the Danelaw area, and in the following centuries many Scandinavian words of a commonplace, not specialised, nature (e.g. *hit, take, egg, husband*) and even grammatical forms like *they* and *though* (cf. 5.2) displaced their English counterparts. The probable reason for this exception is that the two languages were cognate, and may have retained some degree of mutual intelligibility, not only at the time of the first contacts but increasingly as hostility between the two communities died down.

A factor that is difficult to assess is purist reaction and resistance to loanwords. Superficially it appears to exert strong pressure, but, as we have seen in the case of German (6.1), even if it succeeds, it may be an outward manifestation of less obvious systemic factors. The sixteenth-century purist movement against foreign loanwords in English achieved little, for, although many of the much-criticised inkhorn terms did not survive, there were still fewer survivals of the purists' native coinages like Lever's *naysay* 'negation'. In this case, the outcome might be held to suggest that the movement was based simply on national sentiment or rationalism, but it provides no more than a vague indication. As we shall see later (p. 107) there are other areas where the functional and extralinguistic factors merge and are difficult to distinguish.

If interlanguage contacts were restricted to lexis, this part of the subject would – apart from problems of the type just raised – be a comparatively simple aspect of linguistic change. But grammatical, phonological and phonetic features may also cross language boundaries, as is shown by the spread of uvular [R] to replace the original trilled [r] in much of Western Europe, or by the spread of retroflex consonants from Dravidian to the Indo-European languages of India. The best-known example of grammatical spread in a limited area is from the Balkans, where Romanian, Bulgarian and Albanian (unrelated except ultimately as members of different branches of Indo-European) share a number of features, e.g. the postpositive definite article. English, because of its geographical separation from the Continent, provides fewer and less obvious examples. The best known, which resulted from a type *B* contact, is the split of OE /f/ to /f, v/ and of OE /s/ to /s, z/, as a result of the French loanwords that required this distinction in initial position. But there are some features of South-Eastern ME dialects that may have resulted from trade contacts with the Continent. One example is the replacement of ME /ð/ by /d/ in words like *de* 'the', *dis* 'this', *dykke* 'thick' which became common in the fifteenth-century dialects of Kent, east Sussex and east Surrey, and still survives in Kent and east Sussex in demonstrative words. In the continental Germanic languages, this replacement took place over a long period of geographical spread, which started in South German in the eighth century and reached Middle German in the ninth and tenth centuries, Low Franconian in the eleventh, Low German in the twelfth, Danish in the fourteenth and Swedish in the fifteenth. If we assume that it spread from Flemish to Kentish in the fifteenth century, the date parallels that of the spread from Danish to Swedish; and the assumption is borne out by the fact that the only other English dialect from which it is reported is Pembroke-shire,[1] where it resulted from a contact of type *B* – an enforced settlement of Flemings in the early twelfth century.

In addition to the above types resulting from direct contacts, there is another, less direct, channel of influence from foreign languages, via learning and education, and this may sometimes interfere with what might otherwise have been regarded as the normal processes of internal change. A sound change that is, from the point of view of Modern English, notably 'incomplete' is that of ME *-er-* to $/\alpha(r)/$ as in *carve, heart*. It is known from spellings during the period 1500–1800 that variants with $/a/$ existed for most of the words in question, yet $/\varepsilon r/$ or its reflexes ($/ɜ(r)/$) were preferred in the bulk of words that had counterparts in French or Latin, e.g. *certain, clergy, concern, confirm, deter, desert, deserve, divert, fervent, infer, mercy, prefer, sermon, serve* (and derivatives), *universal, verdict, virtue*. It seems probable that this preference was due to awareness of continental pronunciations.

There remains the problem of transference from a substratum. This applies primarily to phonological features, for, if lexical or grammatical features are deduced to have been transmitted from an obsolete and displaced language like Etruscan to dialects of Italic, the transmission is regarded as due to normal contact, and there is no special assumption of substratum influences. But as regards phonology, the claim has often been made that features typical of a displaced language may recur in the newly adopted language, and an extreme view claims that this is due to genetically transmitted differences in the organs of speech. This latter view, though it has not lacked supporters even in recent years, is so obviously contradicted by, say, the broad Glaswegian of the children of Indian or African immigrants that it is not likely to make much headway. But there can be no objection to the view that suprasegmental features of stress or intonation are *environmentally* transmitted through generations of speakers of the displaced language, and that these features may – even long after the displaced language has disappeared – produce changes in the segmental phonemes of the adopted language. Such a view need presuppose no more than an instance of bilingualism in the past, irrespective of whether the language that supplied the traits has left a survivor (Welsh, Gaelic, Basque) or not (Gaulish, Pictish). The difficulty lies in the evidence, which

---

[1] Wright (1905) §311. The same phenomenon in Shetland and Orkney is due to continued contacts with Norse.

is often too scanty for proof. For example, the theory that the change of Latin /u:/ to /y:/ in French is due to the Gaulish substratum is attractive, though the simple fact of contact would be sufficient to explain this change (cf. pp. 23 and 133); but if one is further tempted to regard the great differences between the northern and southern dialects of French as due to different degrees and types of contact between Gaulish and Latin, one finds that these differences are as well, or better, explained by later events such as sterner control by the Franks in the North compared with the survival of Roman civilisation in the South under the milder rule of the Goths.

But although the evidence for substrata in the past is usually deficient, there is enough evidence from present-day dialects of English like those of Wales or the Scottish Highlands to show that periods of bilingualism provide some foundation for the theory. Whether Welsh or Gaelic will themselves survive depends on the success of revivalist movements directed against English mass-communication media; but if present trends are not reversed, it is possible to envisage a situation where the English dialects of Wales and north-west Scotland will have outlived Welsh and Gaelic, yet will still retain special phonetic features derived from the period of bilingualism. The theory of biological inheritance is rightly castigated, but we tend to forget that, in eras when the standardising influences of the mass media did not exist, the intonation- and stress-patterns surviving from Welsh or Gaelic 'substrata' might well have led to further phonetic changes in the English of those areas.[1]

6.5 Contact of dialects

In theory, the processes of spread could be regarded as the same, irrespective of whether the contact is between dialects of the same language or between different languages. This is because the dispositions and attitudes of those who have something to communicate are parallel in both situations; in both, there is a common tendency for speakers to adjust their speech to bring it nearer to that of their interlocutors. That this tendency is universal has been questioned,[2] and it evidently does not apply to all speakers; there are many exceptions that are due to environment, upbringing and social grouping.[3] However, it is a common way of seeking rapport or sympathy, a natural method of enhancing the process of communication, and the parallel therefore remains. The obvious difference is that, in the situations just discussed in 6.4, the speaker must go so far as to use a second language for the purpose; whereas, if his interlocutor speaks an adjoining regional dialect, he may do

---

[1] Quite apart from the above considerations, the operation of substratal influences has been amply proved from pidgin and creole languages. Cf. Hall (1952) 143–4.
[2] Weinreich (1968) 113.
[3] Bernstein 1964*a*, 1964*b* and references there quoted.

no more than select those variants in his own system that he knows to coincide or to be nearest to those of the neighbouring system in question. Within this wide range, there are intermediate cases, e.g. one speaker may switch to a different class dialect, or, if they both speak widely separated dialects of the same language, both may switch to their own nearest approximation to the standard language.

In practice, since there is more scope for natural and uninhibited 'give and take' between speakers of mutually intelligible systems, it is the study of dialect- rather than language-contact that can tell us more about linguistic change, especially in its more structured aspects of grammar and phonology.[1] The alterations and adjustments common in contact situations may be divided into two main groups – adaptations (compromises) and switches (shifts).

(i) *Adaptations*

Adaptations occur frequently in the neighbourhood of a regional isogloss, and demonstrate well the gradual nature of variations in the dialect continuum. They are likely to occur especially at points where isolation was once greater (through older settlement or cultural divisions) but, since normal contacts over the area have been resumed, some compromise is necessary. They are a frequent feature of dialect maps, e.g. in the Northern counties of England, the word 'ask' is predominantly /ask/ in the East, /ɛks/ or /aks/ in the West, but between these two areas there lies a narrow corridor running through northern Cumberland, northern Westmorland and north-west Yorkshire where the form is /as/.[2] In Middle English, the form *noiþer* is found between *noþer* and *neiþer*, and *hei* between *hy* and *þei*.

The choice of a compromise vowel appears sometimes to be socially conditioned. In northern Switzerland, in an area where speakers are conscious of a local dialect division between /ɑː/ and /oː/, some speakers select /ɔː/ to avoid committing themselves one way or the other;[3] and in Bengali speakers often use a vowel midway between [ɔ] and [o], avoiding [ɔ] as too affected, [o] as too colloquial or 'uneducated'.[4]

Whether such variants are to be accorded phonemic status depends on their frequency and exact distribution, but, for the horizontal axis, it has been established that a small border community sometimes shows a larger inventory of phonemes than either of its more numerous neighbours.[5] An example that is partly horizontal and partly vertical in direction is provided by Standard

---

1 This general statement is not intended to cover the special field of creole and contact-languages. Cf. p. 92 above, and Hall (1952).
2 Kolb p. 41.
3 Moulton (1960) 179.
4 C. A. Ferguson and M. Chowdhury, *Language* 36 (1960) 39.
5 A. Haudricourt, *L'Homme* 1 (1961) 175–208.

Southern Scottish, which possesses an extra phoneme to bridge a difference of distribution between Standard English and the Scottish dialects. In Scottish dialects, *ever, never* have the same phoneme as *sit*, realised as low and central [ɪ]. In Standard Scots, the /ɪ/ of *sit* is higher than in Scots dialect and nearer that of English, but in *ever, never* the original /ɪ/ is retained, so that it has the same quality as in Scottish dialect but is nevertheless nearer in quality to English /ɛ/ in *never* than it would have been if it had the same phoneme as Standard Scottish *sit*. There are thus three phonemes in Standard Scots corresponding to two in both Scottish dialect and English.[1]

	Scottish dialect	Standard Scottish	English RP
sit	ɪ {	ɪ	ɪ
never		ɪ	} ɛ
sever	ɛ	ɛ	

The origin of such compromise forms and systems is usually transparent: they result from the two *different* and *older* forms or systems adjacent to them on each side. But this is not always the case. The ME form *euch(e)* 'each' is comparatively rare, occupying a belt running south of Hereford and Worcester, between *vch(e)* to the north and *ech(e)* to the south (see map 3), and it might appear at first sight to be no more than a phonetic compromise between the two latter. Yet *euch(e)* has the OE etymon *eghwilc (æghwilc)* to which it is convincingly connected by the attested middle stage *ewilc(h)*; and *eghwilc* is, for the OE period, a by no means obvious compromise to occur between *ylc* and *ælc*, the respective etyma of *vch(e)* and *ech(e)*. We can only assume that *eghwilc (æghwilc)* was more widespread in OE and occurred in free or conditioned variation with other forms, but that it became obsolete everywhere except in the precise area where its ME reflex was suitable as a compromise; but also conversely, that its precise phonetic development (which was only one of a number possible) was due to the forms adjacent to the area to which it had become restricted. In other words, *euch(e)* is partly the product of its own history within its own system, and partly that of its geographical environment. Simpler, purely phonological, parallels to this situation are common in dialect maps, e.g. /əʊ/ occurring between /uː/ and /aʊ/ in Northern England in words like *house, about, cloud*.[2] It can hardly be a coincidence that such compromises between undiphthongised and diphthongised forms are precisely those that a phonetician would postulate as the

[1] Cf. K. J. Kohler in *Linguistics* 23 (1966) 49ff.
[2] Kolb pp. 257–63.

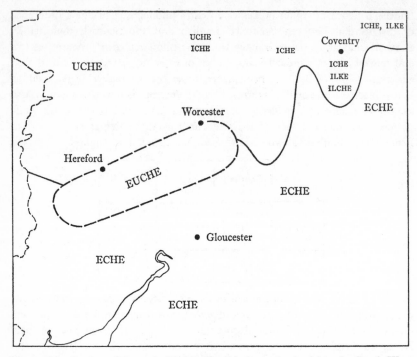

Map 3. Distribution of the main Middle English forms for 'each' in the South-West Midlands

chronologically intermediate forms in the process of diphthongisation. Viewed historically within its own system, each form has undergone a normal development, ceasing at just that point that fits it to act as an intermediary between the progressive and the conservative forms to each side of it. (For the dynamic counterpart to this static view, see below, p. 114.)

In general, the distinction just drawn corresponds to that between dialect continua of long and undisturbed existence (contact of type *A*), and contacts resulting either from population shifts (type *B*) or, secondarily, from the meeting of regional standards that radiate outwards from different centres. In the former, *every* form is, in a sense, a gradual compromise, but this is a secondary aspect of its history; in the latter, more forms come into being as simple blends, i.e. compromise is a primary aspect of their history.

(ii) *Switch and spread (shift of isogloss)*

The other common result of contact between dialects is that the speakers in one dialect or its subgroups 'switch' or give up a feature of their own dialect in favour of the corresponding feature in a neighbouring dialect (i.e. one feature recedes, the other spreads, and the isogloss shifts; cf. p. 92 above). The intrasystemic factors in this process in the receiving system have already been discussed (ch. 2–5); from an extrasystemic viewpoint, we must again distinguish three main factors.

(*a*) *Mechanical.* If the variants that lead ultimately to sound-change (ch. 2) are already in use in system *A* or in any of its subgroups, and the sound-change has been accepted in a neighbouring system *B*, then normal contact will hasten its acceptance into system *A*. An example of this process is the loss of initial *h-* in the word 'it' (*hit, it*) in the ME dialects. It will be seen from map 4 that isoglosses in this type of spread are likely to be discontinuous:

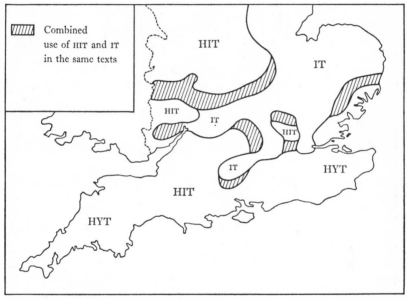

Map 4. Distribution of the forms for 'it' in later Middle English (southern area)

the change may arise more or less independently in a number of centres and radiate outwards from each, but the innovating areas do not always link up immediately, and there may be small conservative enclaves where unshifted forms survive till long after (in this particular case, *h*-forms still survive in certain positions in the modern dialects of Scotland and Ireland).

(*b*) *Functional.* The situation here is quite different: there exists, in each system in the language, or in the systems of certain regions of it, a functional slot left empty for one of the reasons outlined in chapter 5. A remedy can be found from resources within each individual system, but the commoner

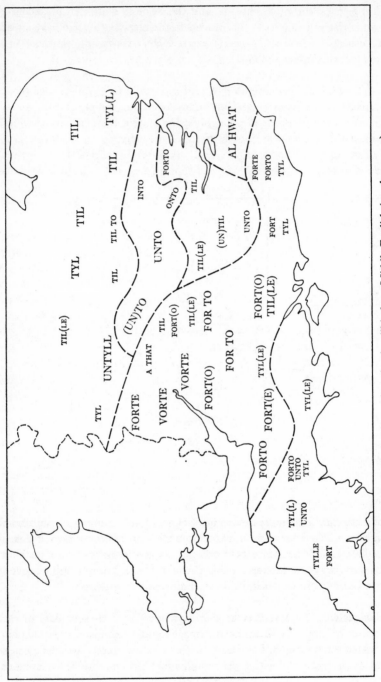

Map 5. Main forms for the conjunction 'until' in later Middle English (southern area)

solution is for the most suitable slot-filler to spread from the one or more systems where it has initially arisen to all other systems that require it. Two related examples of this type were given in chapter 5: the spread of *þei, þai,* etc. 'they' southward beyond the Danelaw boundary to replace the original *h*-forms, and of *þouȝ, thogh,* etc. to replace original *þei(ȝ)* 'though'. The isogloss in such cases spreads more quickly and cohesively than in (*a*) above; there are fewer conservative enclaves and, on the contrary, progressive enclaves are formed in *advance* of the main isogloss because the shift reaches important centres as a result of commerce or immigration (cf. the enclaves of both *they* and *though* in the London area on maps 1 and 2).

Map 5 gives an example of the more complex situation where a number of different slot-fillers arose in different regions of the South as a result of internal solution, but were ultimately replaced by a more suitable remedy from the North. The OE for 'until' (*oð þe* or *oð þæt*) occurs rarely in early ME in the reduced forms *þat* and *a þe(t)*, but these forms were apparently ambiguous and lacked phonetic substance. They were replaced by the native expedients *fort(o)*, *vort(e)*, etc. in the South and South-West, *al hwat, -huet* in the South-East, by (*un)to* (*þat*) in the South Midlands, and further north by (*un)tyl* (*þat*), the latter two from OE *til* and *to* but strongly supported by ON **und* and *til*. Of these forms, all except (*un)tyl* were to some extent ambiguous, and their displacement by the one unambiguous form (from systems further north) is therefore significant. The spread of (*un)tyl* was a fairly quick one in the fifteenth century, and, as in the case of *they* and *though*, can be shown to have taken place before the newly evolving written London standard had had any effect on the rest of the southern area.

(*c*) *Extralinguistic.* Here again, as for language contact in general, the most important factor is the greater prestige of the users of the forms that spread; but its effects on the dialect continua of both region and class are more complex, especially on the latter. Probably the largest and most widespread effect is the imitation, for the purpose of social or economic advancement, of the speech of urban centres by speakers of country dialect, and, in cities, of the speech of the social class a speaker wishes to enter. Where a standard language exists, this too may provide a model to speakers of lower-class dialects, especially through the medium of broadcasting. But the dialect of national broadcasters may not necessarily coincide with the regional prestige dialect of a particular city; both are likely to influence other dialects in the same general direction, but they cannot be entirely equated.

A remarkable feature of the imitation of prestige dialects is that it is largely a conscious process. Certain traits of the dialects that lack prestige are stigmatised, while the corresponding forms in the favoured dialect are regarded as prestige-markers; and it has been shown that the stigmatised traits are avoided more in careful than in casual style. Little research has so far been carried out on the precise details in British English, but W. Labov has made a detailed study of the dialects of the Lower East Side of New York City,[1] and established an exact correlation between social class and avoidance of such features as the following:

(1) use of initial [t] or [tθ], not [θ], as in *thing, think*;

(2) absence of preconsonantal or final /r/, as in *dark, never*;

(3) use of diphthongs [ɪə] or [ɛə] as exponents of /æ:/ in *bad*, and of [ʊə] or [ɔə] as exponents of /ɔ:/ in *caught*.

The movement of speakers towards prestige dialects is not a straightforward matter. Firstly, there are always some speakers with limited social goals who make no attempt in this direction, but remain content as speakers of 'broad' country dialect or of lower-class urban dialect. Secondly, there are inhibiting factors that may in special situations be equally powerful. Linguistic geographers have long recognised that standardisation can be countered by the 'esprit de clocher' – parochialism and a pride in local speech or in the class or occupational dialects of particular groups; and this in turn may lead to actual hostility towards prestige dialects, and to the feeling that they are snobbish or affected, while local forms flourish because, like the passwords to a secret society, they foster a spirit of 'togetherness' in minor groups. Normally, since the groups are fragmentary and divided, their influence is no more than a minor obstacle to the spread of a well-established standard. But if there are historical reasons for stronger and more widespread separatist or even quasi-national sentiments, the two forces may be more evenly balanced. An illustration may be found in present-day Southern Scotland where, for most purposes, 'Standard Southern Scottish' and English Received Pronunciation are equally acceptable as prestige dialects, though in certain situations either may have the advantage. In many types of polite Southern Scottish, the original trilled [r] or flapped [ɾ] has for long been replaced by [ɹ] (with varying degrees of constriction), presumably under English influence; a strongly trilled [r] or [ɾ] before consonants carries some degree of social stigma, and tends to be avoided in the upper middle class, except by professing nationalists. But its distribution in the word remains that of the Scottish dialects, i.e. it is retained in preconsonantal and final position; the pronunciation of *burn*, [bəɹn], coincides neither with RP [bɜːn] nor with Scottish dialect [bʌɾn]: both [ə] and [ɹ] are approximations to existing RP phones, but [ɹ] is used in a position normal in Scots only. The reason is that /r/ in these positions is little less than a national shibboleth, and a Scot who does not use it is in danger of being regarded as ashamed of his heritage. Its survival is supported by normal English orthography, and it is taught in most schools. In general, a pronunciation like /bɜːn/ is regarded as affected and excessively

[1] Labov (1966*a* and 1966*b*).

Anglicised, and is liable to arouse various subjective value-judgments in Scottish hearers, e.g. that English speakers are slack or lazy for their omission of /r/. Such feelings are aggravated by the existence of the English linking-*r* (the so-called 'intrusive *r*' as in [lɔːr ənd ɔːdə] 'law and order'): many educated Scots whenever they hear this phenomenon assure themselves that they speak their language 'better' than the English. Some indication of the strength of these opinions is provided even by those Scots who normally speak RP and pronounce *burn* as [bɜːn], for, when they have occasion to name a national figure like Burns, they have been observed to switch to pronunciations like [bəˈnz] or even [bʌˈnz].

6.6 Dialect contact: further complications

In addition to the two main factors (unifying and divisive) discussed above, there are a number of further complications that arise from contact of dialects. These may (as in the case of the last example given in 6.5 above) in the first instance affect idiolects only, but they are assumed here to have potential systemic relevance, in the same way as for all the variants discussed in chapter 2.

The ensuing sections (i)–(iv) deal with some further consequences of social cleavage, section (v) with the process of standardisation, and (vi) with the effects of the written language.

(i) *Incomplete imitation*

A learner of a new dialect may direct all his attention to certain features of which he is aware, but ignore others. The result is a hybrid system that is not recognised as either his original dialect or that which he is imitating. In time, however, if a number of speakers follow the same course and are imitated by others, such a dialect may achieve some status. This is likely to happen if the imitated dialect contains more phonemic distinctions than the learner's own. For example, many Scots speakers who aim at acquiring RP concentrate on, and even exaggerate, the difference between Scots [eː, oː] and RP [eɪ, əʊ], but fail to distinguish between RP /ʊ/ and /uː/ (as contrasted in *pull* and *pool*) or between RP /ɒ/ and /ɔː/ (as contrasted in *cot* and *caught*). Still further divergence arises where the distribution of phonemes differs. An example is provided by the Scots and RP distributions in words of the types listed overleaf. A Scottish speaker who automatically identifies the vowel of *glory* with that of *coat* will 'translate' it to [gləʊɹɪ], a hyperform not easily recognised or understood by RP-speakers.

	Scots	RP
coat	} o {	əʊ
glory		} ɔː
caught	} ɔ {	
cot		ɒ

(ii) *Hypercorrection*

The example just given shows that contact can lead to innovation as well as spread, and this type of innovation must be distinguished from the adaptations already discussed on pp. 98–100 above. When it occurs as a result of an avoidance (usually conscious) of a feature of the speaker's native dialect, it is known as *hypercorrection*. As in the last example, this is due to a difference between the two systems, or in the distribution of their categories, but the use of the term 'correction' implies that, to the speaker at least, the replacing feature seems 'better' than his own. A well-known occurrence is when Midland or Northern English speakers apply a formula 'Northern /ʊ/ = RP /ʌ/ in all cases', resulting in forms like /pʌt/ 'put', /bʌtʃə/ 'butcher' and /ʃʌgə/ 'sugar'. The fact that some of such forms exist historically in dialect (and that the two developments may combine) does not mean that they cannot be distinguished in individual cases. Another example is to be found in those Scottish speakers who substitute /ər/ for Scots /ʌr, ɛr/ not only when the /r/ is preconsonantal (as in *burn, pearl*) but also in other cases like *thorough, currant, herald*, the resulting pronunciations being /'θərə, 'kərənt, 'hərəld/.

(iii) *Polarisation of social origin*

Polarisation of the difference between two phonetic variants can take place when a speaker who is aiming at a prestige pronunciation is so intent on avoiding the features of the stigmatised variant that he exaggerates the difference and produces an 'affected' form. Such exaggeration is especially common among those whose native dialect was not of prestige value,[1] but it may also be produced or imitated (with further exaggeration) by any with the same social goals. Thus a speaker avoiding the retracted Cockney [ɑɪ] or [ɒɪ] (as in *time*) may prefer a variant more fronted than RP [aɪ], i.e. nearer [æɪ]. Conversely the Cockney, in reaction against this affectation, may prefer the more retracted variant [ɒɪ]. There are corresponding polarisations in the

[1] Weinreich (1953) 78–9.

neighbouring diphthongs of *tame* and *boy*, so that wide systemic differences result.

	'tame'	'time'	'boy'
RP	eɪ, ɛɪ	aɪ, ɑɪ	ɔɪ
'genteel'	ẹɪ	æɪ	ɔɪ
Cockney	æɪ, aɪ, ʌɪ	ɑɪ, ɒɪ, ɑː	oɪ

Such polarisations follow the directions normal in mechanical change (cf. ch. 2), but the social factor is important, since only a certain selection of sounds in the system are stigmatised or favoured, and these may then change at a faster rate than the rest. Within minor class dialects, they entail further systemic adjustment. It may be suspected, for example, that the diphthong /oɪ/ in Cockney *boy* is not typical of the main mechanical changes in that dialect (retraction and lowering), but is a result of push-chain reaction to them.

Exaggerated forms are frequently criticised, but it does not follow that they conflict with the system or will be rejected, and there are historically attested cases where they have eventually been accepted into the standard language (cf. p. 132f below). However, if a pronunciation that is criticised as affected is also functionally less efficient, it is likely to be replaced by a wholly different variant. A possible example from present English is the near-merger, in some types of RP, of /ə:ʊ/ with /ɜ:/ as in *goal* and *girl*, *own* and *earn*, or of the more affected /ɛ:ʊ/ with /ɛə/, as in *don't* and *daren't*. The gradual replacement of 'RP' variants /ə:ʊ/ and /ɛ:ʊ/ by non-RP variants like /ʌʊ/, /æʊ/ may then be due to a reaction against forms regarded as both affected and unintelligible; i.e. it is due to a social factor – reaction of the younger generation against what they regard as the 'mincing tones' of the Establishment, and a favouring of the accents of their own popular entertainers, but also to the fact that they find the latter more intelligible. At this point, the social and functional factors merge and cannot be distinguished: to many members of the younger generation, 'he talks like a square' and 'I can't understand him' would be merely two sides of the same coin.

In past cases of class differences, the extralinguistic factor may appear as paramount: the best-known example is the replacement of upper class /wɛ/ in French *roi* by lower class /wa/.[1] Since this occurred at the time of the French Revolution, it appears to result simply from the sudden move upwards of a whole social class. But even in this case it is not certain that functional factors are to be entirely discounted (cf. the resumption of this discussion below, p. 133).

[1] Cf. Hall (1964) 286, with reference there quoted to K. Nyrop, *Grammaire historique de la langue française* I § 158.

(iv) *Stigmatised forms and the grammatical system*

Social influences on grammatical forms may lead to situations similar to those arising from taboo in lexis, but fall for discussion here rather than in chapters 4–5 because the forms are rejected only in the standard language, and less in dialects. Since the standard language is thus automatically cut off from its normal sources of replenishment, its grammatical system may be left incomplete. The best-known example is the pronoun of the second person: the familiar and less polite form *thou* was replaced by the originally plural *you*, and the grammatical system has, ever since, lacked the means of distinguishing singular and plural in the second person. The reason for this is not the lack of slot-fillers, since new forms like *youse, youse 'uns, you all, y'all* have arisen to complete the system in dialect. But these forms are rejected as vulgar, and in polite English the lack has therefore to be remedied by various lexical means according to context and register, e.g. *you people, my friends, you chaps, those present*. Somewhat similarly, polite modern colloquial English has no contracted form for *I am not going* that will correspond to *he isn't/we aren't going* because the original contractions *an't, ain't* have been rejected as vulgar. The gap has to be filled from a different paradigm (*I'm not*), though in the interrogative *am I not* is rarer than *aren't I*, a curious analogy from the plural that probably masks the originally stigmatised *an't*, and persists in spite of the new formation *amn't* (*ammen't*) that has arisen from time to time in dialect.

(v) *Functional utility*

Especially when shifts of population have taken place, the process of standardisation is likely to depend as much on the overall 'functional utility' of forms as on their prestige value. The term functional utility is used here not in the intrasystemic sense of a form's suitability within its system, but in the quantitative sense that it is the form that is most readily intelligible to the largest number of speakers, irrespective of what system they use. An example is provided by some of the more standardised features of fourteenth- and fifteenth-century Anglo-Irish texts. The language of these texts shows that the English settlers must have been predominantly from the West Midlands and South-West of England. But it tallies with the dialect of no single restricted area of England; it consists mainly of an amalgam of selected features from the different dialects of a number of areas: Herefordshire, Gloucestershire, Somerset, Devon, Shropshire, and to a lesser extent Cheshire, Lancashire, and possibly Wales. Most of the standardised forms are those that were current in large parts of this total area, but they are not from the same parts in each case, e.g. *streynth* 'strength' and *proȝ* 'through' are common West Midland forms, whereas *hyre* 'hear' and *ham* 'them' are more typical of the South-West. One form stands out as of especial interest – *euch* 'each'. This form was rare in England (it is restricted to S. Herefs. and S. Worcs.), and, as suggested above (p. 99), it probably survived there at least partly because it was a convenient compromise between *uch* to the north and *ech* to the south; but it is the form selected as standard in the Anglo-Irish texts, where *uch* and *ech* are rarer. The possibility that a majority of the settlers were from Herefordshire has already been precluded by the rest of the evidence; rather, we must assume that a majority of the early settlers used *uch(e)* or *ech(e)*, and only a minority *euch(e)*. The spread of *euch* to the position of majority form can therefore be explained only in one way: that there was a *continued* preference for it as a compromise form in the many newly founded communities in which users of one or other of all three forms had combined. Such a situation thus demonstrates the principles of overall functional utility in two ways: firstly, the numerically superior forms were selected irrespective of their original areas of provenance, and secondly, an initially rarer variant spread at the expense of the commoner variants because of its suitability as a compromise between them.

(vi) *The written language*

Once a standard has come into being, from whatever diverse spoken origins, the most potent force in its acceptance, propagation and preservation is the written language. Written Standard English has not changed radically since it first emerged as the vehicle of official business and administration around 1430 (for its development prior to that see 8.5). In its pronunciation, change and dialectal variation continued on a large scale till 1750, and on a smaller scale to the present day. But the basis of the standard throughout has been its written form, which provides a codification for what otherwise would be far more fluid. The full extent to which this is true can be shown only by comparison with those languages that possess no written form of their own. An extreme example is provided by creole languages that exist in an unstable relationship to a model language; in these, it can be extremely difficult to ascertain the spoken norm, or the nature of the systems underlying the behaviour of the speakers, without reference to the written form of the model language (Jamaican Creole appears to be such a case).[1] In the more usual situation where systems are complete, a comparison of three Dravidian languages in southern and western India (Kannada, Tamil, and Tulu) has shown that in the first two, which exist in written form, simplificatory changes of phonology and grammar take place more slowly in formal spoken register than in colloquial register, whereas in Tulu, where literacy exists only through the medium of Sanskrit, Kannada, or English, there is no such differentiation. On the

[1] Le Page p. 205.

other hand, lexical innovation (especially by borrowing) is not inhibited by the written form in these languages, and is actually commoner among literate speakers.[1]

The relation of the spoken to the written language that appears from these comparisons is amply confirmed by details from the history of English. Whereas a large proportion of lexical innovations has entered through literate channels (cf. 6.4), the conservative influences of the written language on phonology and grammar are often shown by the further complications to which they can give rise. Not only do older pronunciations of words like *forehead*, *often*, *waistcoat* or the present participle *-ing* show that the present pronunciation is due to the spelling, but mere vagaries of spelling like the *th* in *author* or *throne* have led to 'unetymological' innovations in pronunciation. In the field of grammar, the influences of literacy are still further complicated by the existence of *prescriptivity*. This consists largely of the teaching of prestige forms, but is at its most obvious when one form (e.g. *It is I*) is preferred and prescribed at the expense of another (*It's me*). The phenomenon would in theory be avoidable if a majority of speakers were trained in linguistic objectivity, but such majorities never exist. The result is the curious mixture of further extralinguistic influences that stem from the prescriptive grammarian – the decision in favour of one variant or another according to personal opinion, whether bolstered by logic, or the analogy of foreign languages, or mere prejudice. Such decisions may run counter to functional factors in the spoken language, and a state of conflict or vacillation then ensues, which in turn is a fruitful source of hypercorrection. This situation is amply attested in Fowler's *Modern English Usage*, where sequences like *a candidate likely generally to be accepted* receive the following characteristic comment: 'The above writers are bogy-haunted creatures who for fear of splitting an infinitive abstain from doing something quite different, i.e. dividing *be* from its complement by an adverb.'[2]

One type of change that is apparently uninfluenced by the written language is isolative circular shift. The values of the symbols simply change with those of the phones without any awareness on the part of most speakers (would-be spelling-reformers in all ages are the main exceptions). The extent to which this is true of the Great Vowel Shift is shown by the fact that it was only *exceptions* to the shift that were adjusted in spelling. Thus the spellings *ou, ow* for ME/u:/ remained but were changed in value to represent the diphthongisation (e.g. in *house, town*) and similarly the spelling *oo* (ME/o:/) later represented the raising to /u:/ as in *food, foot*. But, where ME/u:/ occurred before a labial, unshifted variants were preferred, as in *room* (ME *rowme*, OE *rūm*; cf.

[1] Bright (1964).
[2] H. W. Fowler, *A Dictionary of Modern English Usage*, 2nd edn, revised by Sir Ernest Gowers (Oxford, 1965) 580.

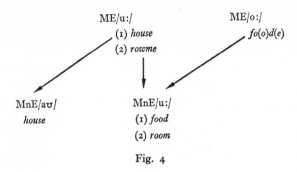

Fig. 4

fig. 4). Other cases are *droop* (ME *droupe(n)*, *drowpe*), *coop* (ME *coupe*), *stoop* (ME *stoupe*, *stowpe*). Here it is significant that adjustment in spelling from *ou/ow* to *oo* was automatically made only in those few contexts where the phone remained unshifted, and not in the great majority affected by shift. Evidently the shift took place irrespective of the spelling, which has, for correlations between original long and short vowels, remained 'irrational' ever since; only in minor exceptions (where it would in fact have been 'rational') was it regulated to conform to the majority.

Whether literacy in a more general sense can be said to have relevance for isolative shift is open to doubt. There may be some connections between direction of shift and social class (cf. pp. 131–3 below), but, if so, they are more likely to depend on the repercussions of social cleavage (p. 105ff) than on literacy itself.

6.7   Contact and linguistic change

The extrasystemic dimension, briefly outlined above, can cast further light on the nature of linguistic change, and is an essential complement to the intrasystemic dimension which predominated in chapters 2–5. It will now be considered in relation to five problems hitherto left outstanding: (i) the process of change in general (ch. 2); (ii) the distribution of sound-changes (ch. 3); (iii) the process of isolative vowel-change (ch. 2–3); (iv) regrouping and restructuring in grammatical systems (ch. 5); and (v) the relation of spreading features to systems (cf. 6.3).

(i) *The process of change*

Examinations of this problem from an intrasystemic point of view have produced few signs of agreement so far. The conventional view is that changes are always manifested by differences in speech between the older and younger generations, whatever the precise source of such differences. Such a view is implicit in the answers to dialect questionnaires that a form is 'rare' or 'used only by older people'. The reason may then be either that the form has changed gradually by minute and constant alterations in transmission, or that there has been gradual replacement of one discrete form by another, with continuous alteration in the proportion of the two forms in use. Any gap between the generations is presumably bridged partly by (*a*) the cognition of new features by the older generations so that they understand them without themselves using them, or (*b*) by accommodation or 'switch' by the younger generation to older variants, whether of dialect or register, when addressing their elders, or (*c*) by an increase in the use of redundant forms on both sides; but, in any case, the greater the difference in age, the less likelihood that the gap is ever adequately bridged at all. There is discontinuity of transmission from one generation to the next which provides much of the inaccuracy of transmission already assumed above in chapter 2 (p. 17), and there can be little doubt that at least the foundations of this discontinuity are laid during the language-learning process in youth. The Chomsky–Halle hypothesis[1] goes so far as to claim that every language-learning process in childhood embodies a restructuring of the parents' system that would be impossible in later life; that changes may take place in the systems of adults if they consist of addition of rules, but not if they consist of their elimination or simplification, which are delayed until restructuring takes place in the next generation.

In itself, this process is no doubt a possible one; the main objection to it is that its authors regard creation and spread of rule as the only explanation necessary for linguistic change in general. But there are other considerations to be taken into account.

(*a*) Even if it were admitted that all restructuring takes place in the younger generation only, the fact remains that it could not take place at all if the necessary variants did not already exist in the speech of older generations (ch. 2 and 4). In his continual experiments and efforts to conform during the learning process, the child produces many variants, but it is only those that are known and familiar to others that are likely to receive reinforcement. His significant innovations are those of distribution, such as transference of collo-quial variants to formal register.

(*b*) The hypothesis that it is simply the parents' system that is restructured rests on the assumption of a homogeneity that is exceptional. Normally, children are affected as much by the model of other children's speech as by that of their parents. Whereas the influences of their parents' model are mainly normative, their contact with persons from outside their family could be regarded as a type *B* situation in microcosm: the processes of adaptation are similar to those of standardisation (though the systemic relevance is much less), and it is here that most of the innovations originate.

[1] Halle (1962 and 1964).

(c) We have no proof that restructurings are confined to single generations. The evidence of change in the past suggests that the stages necessary for a change of rule were spread over a number of generations,[1] and it was only as a result of this continual process that a restructuring eventually took place. As regards the present, it is unlikely that further research on language-learning processes could cast light on this problem, since it is so difficult to maintain the stable controls necessary for continuous research over a number of consecutive generations.

The Chomsky–Halle hypothesis overweights the factor of discontinuity of transmission during childhood, while omitting one that is equally important: exposure to great variety of variants and systems from speakers outside the child's immediate family.

More light can be cast on the problem by starting from an area much wider than a single community or its subgroups and studying, with the aid of such details as dialect-geography yields, the process of a change viewed extra-systemically, as it moves over an area from one system to another. Evidence is available from the few languages that possess a quantity of records surviving from a period before standardisation and therefore written in local dialect orthographies. Middle English texts of the thirteenth, fourteenth and fifteenth centuries yield more information on the dialect continuum than might have been expected, since they are only partly influenced by regional centres. By use of this evidence, comparison of the earlier with the later texts shows that major changes, once initiated in one or more centres (ch. 2) consist essentially of a process of *spread*. The isoglosses in the maps for 'they' and 'though' (maps 1 and 2 above) are based mainly on early fifteenth-century evidence, and it is clear from fourteenth-century and late fifteenth-century texts that these iso-glosses moved southwards over a major part of Southern England during a century and a half. Phonological changes are understandably less reliably indicated in spelling, but local dialect orthographies of that period, though traditional, were less impervious to change than the standardised and more monolithic orthographies of later periods. Most of what has been written regarding the inability or unwillingness of scribes to mark subphonemic change is valid enough, but it is reasonable to suppose that, after spread of a phonemic change, altered spellings would ultimately spread in its wake. For example, in early ME, the reflex of OE/ɑ:/ is written *o* in texts south and east of the Severn but *a* west and north of it, whereas in later texts the *o*-spelling has moved up to the Ribble boundary. The exact relationship of phonemes and their orthographic representation is rarely capable of absolute proof, but it seems perverse to deny that such a spread in *o*-spellings reflects a corresponding spread of phonemic change.

[1] Cf. von Wartburg pp. 32–3 and references there made to the works of L. Gauchat and E. Hermann.

Furthermore, provided we bear in mind that some changes are limited in scope and may never shift far from the place where they started, we may utilise further the general principle that the diachronic axis of change can be 'translated' and equated with the diatopic axis of spread: if there are sufficient details of the stages of the spread, they should correspond to the stages of change on the diachronic axis, albeit the evidence comes from the mouths (or quills) of different informants. Fig. 5 shows a hypothetical change that took a hundred and fifty years to complete: on the vertical (diachronic) axis X–X, *a*, *b*, *c* denote three texts from the same place, *a* showing the initial stage 1, *b* the transitional stage 2 and *c* the final stage 3; on the horizontal (diatopic) axis, Y–Y denotes a cross-section of the earlier dialect map, in which A, B, C represent the depth of an isogloss and its environs, area A

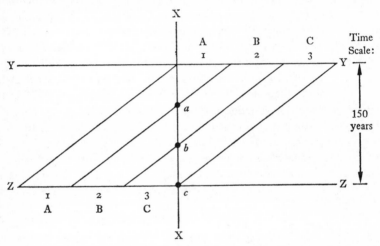

Fig. 5. Correlation of the diachronic axis of change to the diatopic axis of spread

showing the old form, C the new form and the border area B the transitional form; similarly Z–Z denotes a cross-section of the later dialect map in which the isogloss has shifted stage by stage to the other side of the place in question.

A demonstration of the above process is provided by the development of new forms for 'she' in Middle English. The ME reflex of OE *heo* was *he*, so that large areas of the country were left without a formal distinction between 'he' and 'she', while even in the remaining areas the other surviving forms (*hy*, *heo*) were not ideal for the purpose. This systemic gap, which can be shown from the ambiguities in many surviving texts,[1] was filled by a typical

[1] For example, in certain MSS (Cambridge Univ. Lib. Gg. 4.27.2, BM Harley 2376 and Add. 19677) the curious variants *hei*, *hey* are used for 'he', and in one (BM Add. 19677) *hei* 'he' occurs more often when in close proximity to *he* 'she'.

drag-chain process – the selection of originally rare variants, the stress-shifted forms /hjo/ and /hje/. These then changed, via the intermediate stage /ço, çe/ to /ʃo, ʃe/, perhaps first in the heavily Norse-influenced Cumberland–Yorkshire belt which provides numerous parallels for the change.[1] But the change is demonstrated diatopically as well as diachronically by Middle English dialect texts: firstly, the intermediate stage with /ç/ is shown in forms like *ȝhe(o), ȝho, ghe,* but these never survived for long in any

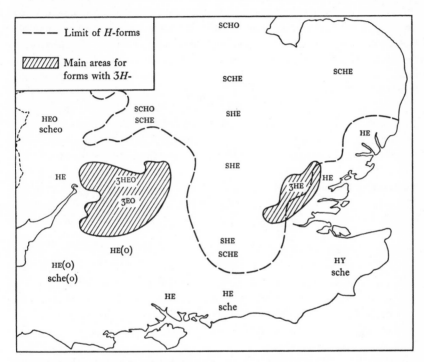

Map 6. Schematisation of forms for 'she' in later Middle English (southern area)

given area, presumably because /ç/ as a marginal phoneme gave place to the equally distinctive but better integrated /ʃ/ ;[2] secondly, /ç/ is always found in border areas dividing the newer *s(c)he/s(c)ho* from the older *h*-forms; and thirdly, these border-areas with /ç/ can be shown to have moved southwards across the country in advance of /ʃ/, until, at the end of the spread, /ç/ is found only in the southern fringe-areas of Devon, Dorset, and Kent. This last deduction follows from the startling contrast between the later Middle

[1] Cf. A. H. Smith, *RES* I (1925) 437–40; E. Dieth, *ES* 36 (1955) 209–17.
[2] Cf. Vachek (1954) and (1964) 21–9.

English evidence (schematised in map 6) and that of early Middle English texts, which show that in that period *ʒho, ghe, yo*[1] were used in the North and East Midlands at points which later have *sch-* forms, while *h-* forms were still used in areas later showing *ʒhe* and *s(c)he*.[2]

It is not certain whether, in the later stages of this spread, the original phonetic process was always exactly repeated; but the fact that the same order of change persisted is sufficient to show how the process must at first have operated in full. A further qualification is that, in examining geographical spread, one is sometimes confronted with evidence that suggests a reversal of the order that might be expected from the principles discussed in chapters 2–5. Such reversals are presumably extralinguistic in origin, for, where the required non-linguistic evidence is available, it shows that they are due to factors like immigration or increased prestige of speakers using conservative forms (cf. 6.8 and 8.5 below).

The spread of *s(c)he* is exceptional in that the intermediate stage seen in the *ʒh-*forms was itself a substantial development; normally the stages of a phonetic change take place at subphonemic level and are not expected in written records. However, the evidence for transitional stages that shift with an isogloss is by no means restricted to such rare cases. They are commoner when the change consists of the replacement of one discrete form by another; in such cases, the map often shows both forms combined in a single minor system. For example, the texts from a border-area in the fourteenth century (area *aa* in fig. 6) show *it* as the normal form but *hit* in initial or more stressed positions; but the isogloss A was moving westward, so that in the fifteenth century texts from area *aa* show *it* only, and there is a new border area, with a subsystem combining *hit* and *it*, in the region of isogloss B further west.[3]

Even in texts where two forms appear at first to be in free variation, we may detect scribal preferences which, though they can hardly be said to show systemic patterning, may cast light on the reasons for the spread. Thus for

---

[1] In Orm, *Bestiary, Genesis and Exodus* and *De Clerico et Puella* (BM Add. MS 23986).

[2] Cf. *hie* and *he* in *Vices and Virtues*, *hie* and *heo* in the *Trinity Homilies*.

[3] Examples of such subsystems are to be found in MSS BM Royal 18 A.x, Harley 211 and 2403, Sloane 2027 and Add. 36791; Bodl. Rawlinson B.171, Bodley 416 and Laud Misc. 108; Trinity College, Dublin MSS C.v.6 and F.v.8; and MS Lambeth 551.

The exact functions of *hit* and *it* vary according to text, and, in border areas at least, depend on the relative frequencies of the two forms in the spoken chain (cf. p. 128 below). In MS Univ. Coll. Oxford 97, *hit* is rare, but is apparently used as a stressed form in: *Let the world wexe vil to þee, eer þou be vil to hit* (C. Horstmann, *Yorkshire Writers* II 439). In MS Bodl. Rawl. B.173 (ff. 186 to end), *it* is rare, but is in contrast with *hit*, as in: *They answered and seide, yff it like you to yeue him any goode, hit were well do* (fol. 195ᵃ). See further N. Davis 'The Epistolary Usages of William Worcester', in *Medieval Literature and Civilization: Studies in Memory of G. N Garmonsway*, ed. D. A. Pearsall and R. A. Waldron (London, 1969) 273.

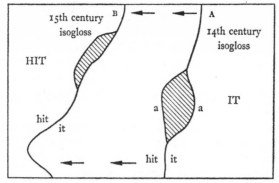

Fig. 6. The process of recession of the form *hit* 'it' in later Middle English

the past tense of the verb 'see', certain scribes[1] use the progressive *saw(h)* more often in the first person, but the recessive *say(h)*, *sey(h)*, *sei(h)* more often in the third person. In the first person, *I(ch) sey* 'I saw' was not sufficiently distinct from *I(ch) sey(e)* 'I say', whereas in the third person, *he say/sey* 'he saw' was sufficiently distinct from *he sayþ/seyþ* 'he says'. This suggests not only that the reasons for the spread of *saw* at the expense of *sey/say* were functional (cf. 5.2, pp. 69–72) but also that the change took place via a stage in which both forms were in conditioned variation.

That the two forms, the new and the old, can occasionally exist in wholly free variation is a possibility that has not yet been disproved, but, as Bloomfield rightly remarked: 'where a speaker knows two rival forms, they differ in connotation, since he has heard them from different persons and under different circumstances'.[2] Differentiation is therefore likely to be the norm: a common core of agreement on the status of the two variants is gradually established in each group, and they henceforth carry various distinctions, e.g. of function, meaning, stress, register. Later, depending on systemic or extra-linguistic factors (cf. 6.5, pp. 100ff), the distribution of the two forms in the system may gradually change so that one form is eventually ousted, but this is not necessarily the outcome: the minor systems mentioned above need not be mere transitions, but may survive. One example has already been mentioned above (6.5, p. 101); similarly the minor system for *they* and *hi* found in ME texts[3] was reported by J. Wright for the counties of Lincolnshire, Warwickshire, and Shropshire in the forms /ðei/ or /ðeə/ ~ /ə/.[4] The

---

[1] E.g. MSS BM Cotton Caligula A.ii and Add. 39574, Bodl. Digby 171 and Douce 78. The scribe of MS Univ. Coll. Oxford 45 wrote *I seye* at first, but then deleted *seye* and wrote *saw* after it.

[2] Bloomfield p. 394.

[3] The functional distinction may be conveniently demonstrated by a sentence from the unpublished British Museum MS Burney 356: *þey mow now3t be asoyled fort hy haue ymaked satysfaccyon* (fol. 54ᵃ).

[4] Wright (1905) § 410.

distinction between stressed *them* and unstressed *hem*, which appears in Caxton's earlier (i.e. more dialectal) prints, might, from the point of view of written English, be regarded as 'transitional', since in his later prints he adopted the practice of his London contemporaries in using only *them*; but the unstressed /əm/ is still widespread in dialect, and it is only the spelling *'em* that prevents its recognition as more than a colloquial variant in Standard English (see further p. 128f below).

Since the differences between regional and class dialects are those of degree and complexity, not of principle, we may proceed further and assume that the spread of a feature through the various groups and strata of urban communities takes place in the same way. Just as, for the purpose of convenient abstraction, we may speak of 'the system of English' and yet simultaneously admit that it consists of a multitude of smaller heterogeneous systems between which there is a constant interchange and spread of new features, so we may speak of a system of Birmingham English and yet assume interchange and spread between the heterogeneous systems used by the groups that go to make up its community, e.g. those of the family, school class and playground, and of social, religious, commercial and professional groupings. Here, to a greater extent than for the language as a whole, it is an oversimplification to say that a feature spreads from one small group to another; each individual belongs to a number of overlapping groups (cf. 'open networks' p. 89) and usually there are also the influences of the mass-media which are more or less simultaneous on all or a large proportion of groups. But in so far as it is permissible to speak of spread *within* an urban group (rather than, more generally, of spread 'among peers'), it is a matter of common observation that the spread is faster than that encountered in regional dialect geography, at least as regards grammatical and lexical features. But apart from such differences in the speed of the spread, the innovation takes its place in the recipient's idiolect in the same way, i.e. unless it is one of those ephemeral or vogue-words that suddenly oust their antecedents, it will normally form or augment a minor system as a functional or register variant. The table below shows the effect of the spread of the forms *yeah* and *yup* on the system of affirmatives used by the present writer and certain of his associates over a period of about five years.

But the direction of this change is known: *yeah* and *yup* were once not used at all in these idiolects, and they are now becoming still commoner and invading polite register. The system shown in the table is therefore merely a transitional one. Once a new form has entered an idiolect in this way, its distribution in the system may then increase merely as a result of contact with other speakers in whose systems it occupies a larger place; in this particular case, the ultimate source might be traced to those radio or television programmes in which *yeah* is the preponderant form. But, since such exceptional extrasystemic pressure is not always present (and existed less in the past),

	Register	
Context	Polite	Colloquial
Normal	*Yes*	*Yeah*
Hurried interjection	$\left\{ \begin{array}{l} \textit{Yes, quite} \\ \textit{Agreed} \end{array} \right\}$	*Yup*
Unemphatic	(Nod)	/mˡhm/
Indication of awareness	(slight nod or smile)	/m/

other reasons must be sought for any increases that take place. It is sometimes suggested that they are to be accounted for by the phenomena known as (*a*) 'style-switching', i.e. intrasystemic changes to different sets of register variants according to situation, and (*b*) 'code-switching', in which the speaker actually changes from one system to another, usually because his regional or class dialect corresponds to his familiar or informal register, while for formal purposes he uses his own or the local approximation to the standard language. But there are a number of unresolved problems here; some speakers possess wide ranges of register variants and distinguish them carefully, while others have a smaller repertoire or are less conscious of any need to switch style. In code-switching, it has been observed that a speaker using his formal code may, under conditions of stress or emotion, 'relapse' into his colloquial code,[1] which suggests that, for some speakers at least, their colloquial code is their native 'first language', whereas their formal code is a learned one that requires more effort and concentration. In any further research on these mechanisms of change, account will have to be taken of such cross-currents. For the present, two of the simpler possible mechanisms may be assumed here: (*a*) inaccurate recognition, by speakers of one class or regional dialect, of the register distinctions used by speakers of another, and (*b*) simplification and redistribution by younger generations of the systems of register variants used by their elders. The latter is itself subject to extralinguistic factors such as the ebb and flow in fashions of formality and informality, but, to take a simple example, the following differences between two sets of favourable responses to a proposal suggest that some such simplification does take place:

	Mother	Daughter (15)
Polite	*That'll be very nice*	$\left. \begin{array}{l} \\ \end{array} \right\}$ *That's fine*
Informal	*Right-o*	
Colloquial	*Right you are*	$\left. \begin{array}{l} \\ \end{array} \right\}$ *All right*
Familiar	*O.K.*	

[1] W. Labov in Bright (1966) 111. For parallels in bilingual situations, cf. S. R. Herman 'Explorations in the Social Psychology of Language Choice' in Fishman pp. 501–2.

E

This particular case may have depended on differences in temperament, but, if it is linguistically significant, it should not be too readily identified with the phonological simplifications postulated by Halle and Chomsky (p. 112 above); rather, it suggests that ability to use a greater variety of register-variants grows with experience and competence in the adult.

A question that remains here is: how far can code- and style-switching be assumed for past periods of the language? Code-switching between class-dialects has presumably become commoner since the growth of industrial communities, but is likely to have existed, if only on a limited scale, in any period when there was a distinctive language spoken in court or government circles. In an extreme form, it is seen in the widespread bilingualism in French and English during the earlier part of the Middle English period; but the orthographies of Middle English texts also suggest that there may have been a choice between parochial dialect and the regional standard of the nearest cultural centre, and it is likely that there was some spread of spoken regional standards in the fifteenth century, though this is hardly proof of code-switching as a common practice. On the other hand, style-switching has probably always existed in varying degrees according to temperament and status of the speaker. The evidence of early rhetoricians, as well as of much early literature itself, is sufficient to show that differences between 'formal' and 'less formal' must antedate writing (e.g. in oratory and oral recitation). No doubt the complexity of modern life has meant an increase in the diversity of spoken registers, but there seems no reason to question that they have always existed to a degree sufficient for the present argument.

(ii) *The distribution of sound-change*

The traditional (neogrammarian) view is that a sound-change, once stated in a way that provides for special phonetic conditioning, admits of no exceptions, and that any apparent exceptions are borrowings of unshifted forms from another dialect. This view was accepted by Bloomfield, and admittedly it was a reasonable assumption that, if a phoneme changes in a closely knit community, it must change in every instance if it is to remain intelligible (the same assumption is implicit in current statements by 'rule' for changes in distinctive features). But its validity depends on the degree of homogeneity that can be assumed for communities or groups; in practice, *every* dialect contains exceptions for one or other of its features, and it is this fact that has led other linguists to accept the possibility of 'weak' or 'sporadic' change. The older formula is a theory only, which could apply only to a dialect that was completely homogeneous, immune from all contact with other dialects, from the written language and learned channels of transmission, from variation in sub-codes and registers, and from any of the functional and phonaesthetic pressures discussed in chapter 5. Since no such dialect exists, the formula can be accepted as a theoretical basis only; it must then be fully qualified to fit what is actually found in utterance and text.

In the first place, it appears that, even from a purely intrasystemic viewpoint, all changes that are simplificatory, or considered conditioned rather than isolative (2.2–4), should be excluded from the formula. There is no reason why the various simplifications, assimilations, dissimilations, metatheses, haplologies, etc. should not be regarded as occurring separately, word by word, according to

(a) the precise phonetic environment in the word and its usual contexts, and

(b) the use of the word, and degree of its use, in the system.

All such changes can be expected to occur in weak form. For example, in BM MS Sloane 3153, a South-East Midland text of the fifteenth century, 'which', 'while', 'who', 'what' are regularly spelt with *wh* but 'when' is regularly *wan*. The text was apparently not written in the region of an important *w-/wh-* isogloss, where such mixture might be expected: the voicing in *wan* would appear to have arisen independently somewhere not far from the place of writing, and had not at that time proceeded beyond that word. Certainly, the completion of such simplificatory changes is always possible. If an assimilation of /θt/ to /tt/ takes place in a large number of common contexts, the sequence /θt/ is likely to be excluded from the structure of the language. Or the completion could be social in origin: there must be many English-speaking communities today where the pronunciations /hw/ or /ʍ/, though well enough known, would be regarded as affected. But conditioned changes are always liable to remain sporadic or incomplete, as may be seen especially clearly from R. Posner's monograph on *Consonantal Dissimilation in the Romance Languages*.[1] She points out that it is especially common in long technical or borrowed words 'with little danger to comprehension, as they are not likely to be mistaken for other words'; and she finds that phonemes that have a high functional yield and are well integrated in the system are less liable to dissimilation, that dentals and velars are less liable to the change than labials, and fricatives less than plosives.

The boundary between these and isolative changes proper is by no means clear. At one end of the scale, we have changes that are so dependent on minute variations in conditioning that they can be reduced to no rule, and must be stated in 'weak' form. At the other end, there are changes like that of intervocalic /t/ to /d/ which (apart from the initially narrowing condition that it must be intervocalic) is usually complete except for the possibility of extrasystemic influences. A possible criterion for distinguishing is that a language system may well preserve its full complement of CVC sequences and yet

[1] Posner pp. 84, 100, 205ff.

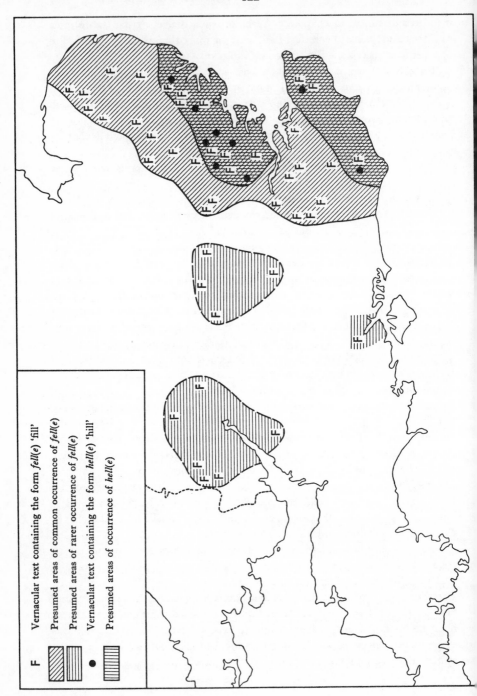

tolerate much redistribution through dissimilation of the consonants within them 'for convenience', because the dissimilated consonants are not in immediate contact; but changes in sequences like VCCV or VCV, where the consonants are in immediate contact with the conditioning features, will more probably be completed. But even so, there remain borderline changes like vowel-harmony and mutation where immediate contact cannot be taken for granted and yet rules, albeit with a number of exceptions, can be stated.

We must probably accept that the boundary between conditioned and isolative changes is a gradual one,[1] and that conditioned changes often occur sporadically and in a distribution which, though capable of description, would be so complex as no longer to constitute a 'rule'. However, even if restricted to isolative changes, the neogrammarian formula has long been regarded as impracticable by linguistic geographers, who have countered it with the equally extreme formula 'every word has its own history'. Some examples from South-Eastern ME will demonstrate this point of view. The change of OE/y/ to [e] took place not later than the late OE period, and by the early ME period original /y/ and /ɛ/ may be assumed to have merged under the latter. Yet in the case of individual words, functional factors could interfere. As is shown in Map 7, the *e*-area for *hell(e)* in the meaning 'hill' is much smaller than that for *fell(e)* in the meaning 'fill', and in the remaining area *hull(e)* and *hill(e)* have been selected (and have spread from adjacent areas) to avoid homonymic clash with *hell(e)* 'hell'. For this particular feature, Dan Michel's *Ayenbyte of Inwit* shows no exceptions, and it might therefore be argued that this is always the case with 'pure' texts from the central area of a change. But even that argument will not hold. If we examine in the same text the results of another change equally typical of east Kent, the so-called 'Second Fronting' of OE /æ/ to /ɛ/, we find that *yaf*, *yeaf* 'gave' and *zat* (beside *zet*) 'sat' contrast with the expected *e* in other forms (e.g. *bed* 'prayed', *brec* 'broke', *spek* 'spoke', *voryet* 'forgot'). This may be because *zet* 'sat' is liable to confusion with *zet* 'sets' (3rd sg. pres.), and *yef* is the normal form for 'if'; but whatever the reason, by 1340 in the 'pure Kentish' of Canterbury, forms from dialects to the north and west had been selected for these words.

Nevertheless, it would be an oversimplification to conclude that an isolative sound-change may *always* have as many different boundaries as the individual words that it affects. There is another factor that is usually not sufficiently considered in this controversy, and which will enable us to define how exceptionless (when viewed intrasystemically) an isolative change can be expected to be: the relation of the innovating phonemic system to those adjacent. Firstly, a distinction must be drawn according to whether the dialect in which the change has taken place possesses a phoneme with which unshifted forms (or forms that have undergone a different development elsewhere)

[1] Cf. pp. 20f and 25–7 above.

could be identified. Thus in the case of the South-Eastern merger of /y/ and /ɛ/ quoted above, the S.E. dialects possessed /ɪ/, and therefore the neighbouring form *hill* could spread into part of the S.E. area and replace *hell*. But conversely, when /æ/ and /ɑ/ merged in all dialects of early ME except those of the South-West Midlands, there can have been no exceptions resulting from a reverse spread of /æ/ back from the S.W. Midland area, since the area of change no longer possessed a phoneme with which the /æ/ could be identified.

Secondly, a change in the relationship between neighbouring phonemic systems, even much later in their history, can lead to a situation where an originally exceptionless sound-change eventually shows exceptions. The change of Southern ME /aː/ to /ɔː/ was initially complete, except in border areas (cf. below), because there did not remain at that time a Southern /aː/ which could provide a basis for the reverse spread of Northern forms with /aː/. Later, a Southern /aː/ came into existence, and its reflex (especially as augmented by merger with ME /aɪ/) could be identified with the Northern reflexes of OE and ON /aː/, with resulting forms like *hale* (cf. *whole*), *raid* (cf. *road*), *scale* (cf. ME and later dialect *scole, skole, scoal*). Similarly, where the continental model for a form has remained unchanged, it may be readopted through learned channels (cf. p. 96) and replace the shifted form. This is the most probable explanation of the present pronunciation of *Rome*, which was usually /ruːm/ in the sixteenth and seventeenth centuries.

Thirdly, the system of a border area may often combine both shifted and unshifted phonemes in its inventory (cf. p. 98f), agreeing with the innovating dialect for some words but with the conservative dialect for others; and this is relevant for a description of the change, since its boundaries will vary according to whether the border area is to be included or not. A classic case is the border area in N.E. Holland which shows shifted /yː/ in /hyːs/ 'house' but unshifted /uː/ in /muːs/ 'mouse'. On this Bloomfield remarks: 'the word *house* will occur much oftener than the word *mouse* in official speech ... *mouse* is more confined to homely and familiar situations';[1] i.e. the combination is to be explained as one of class- and/or register-variants. That this explanation is correct is borne out by an exact parallel in the dialects of Northern English: in the vicinity of the isogloss separating /uː/ and /aʊ/, certain border-systems in Yorkshire and Westmorland show a diphthong /əʊ/ or /ɛʊ/ in *house* but /uː/ in *mouse* and *louse*.[2]

The above examples show the main sources of interference for 'regular' sound-change in regional dialect. In urban societies, the range of possibilities for interference is greatly increased to include all the variations resulting from contact discussed in 6.5–6 above.

Elsewhere in this book it is urged that selection from two mechanically

---

[1] Bloomfield p. 330.   [2] Kolb pp. 256–7.

produced variants is likely to be motivated by functional or social factors. But, especially at the subphonemic level, there remains the possibility of 'arbitrary selection' (i.e. spread, extension, automatic imitation, or whatever else we choose to call it). The distribution of two existing variants may be successively altered in transmission from generation to generation, with or without residue of the recessive variant. For example, the change of earlier Italian /l/ to /j/ in the groups *fl-*, *bl-*, *pl-* (e.g. *florem>fiore*, cf. *bianco*, *fiamma*, *fiume*, *piace*, *piazza*) must represent extensions of palatalised [ʎ] from contexts where it had originally been conditioned (some Italian dialects preserve a distribution in which only *gl-*, *cl-* are affected, and this, in turn, may not represent the earliest distribution). Such a process can be intrasystemic,[1] and 'dialect mixture' is not a prerequisite.[2] But in urban societies, no boundary can be assumed between 'dialect mixture' and intrasystemic change; 'open networks' (pp. 89 and 118) automatically impose a whole series of overlaps which do not differ in principle from those treated as 'border areas' in dialect geography (cf. p. 128f below), and these overlaps may either accelerate or retard the spread of a variant. The probability of spread is increased in situations where young speakers are in contact with (*a*) those who use two variants, new and old, in an established conditioned variation, and (*b*) those who use the old variant only; confusion of these two distributions could then lead to a faster generalisation of the new variant. But in other, more complex cases, only small additions to the new variant may occur; the original conditioning is disturbed, but without disposal of the residue. A typical example at the phonemic level occurs in those types of English that distinguish both /ʊ/ and /ʌ/ in their systems, yet class *result, Ulster* under /ʊ/ not /ʌ/. Such an extension may be partly due to the following [ɫ], but a more likely reason is that, in some of the cases where /ʊ/ was originally conditioned by a preceding labial, it is also followed by /l/, as in *pull, full, bull, wolf*.

In view of such possibilities, it would seem that completely regular sound-changes can be expected only as rarities. The neogrammarian formula remains a theoretical possibility, with its greatest probability of realisation in the regional centre of origin for a given isolative change; in practice, exceptions are always to be expected.

(iii) *The process of isolative vowel-change*

It has been assumed above that, *in origin*, variants may be phonetic (e.g. stress variants, ch. 2), or acoustic (faulty recognition and/or reinterpretation in

---

[1] I.e. we assume (i) that [ʎ] was not borrowed or substratal, but was spontaneously conditioned, say, before front vowels, and (ii) that its spread was due to simple variations in its distribution and not to social factors like hypercorrection.
[2] Cf. Wang p. 16.

transmission), or due to social pressures (e.g. hyperforms), or any of these in combination; and that the selection and spread of these variants may depend on mere continuation of the same pressures, or on others such as those of function (ch. 3), or prestige (6.5). But two further questions are often raised: (*a*) whether such changes proceed by infinitesimal or discrete stages, and (*b*) whether they are conscious or unconscious. The view that only phonemic variations can be conscious has been disproved from the fact that many naïve speakers are aware of the differences between subphonemic variants, especially if they are socially significant.[1] It is true that phonemic variation is always more likely to be conscious (though it need not be), but there can be no strict correlation of the answers to these two questions. If they are considered separately, it would appear that both alternatives in each question are possible. At one extreme, an obviously discrete stage is to be seen in the redistribution of words from one phoneme to another, i.e. the selection of one phoneme rather than another for given words (cf. above, p. 123f); and equally obvious is the selection of discrete variants (whether phonemic or not) as status-markers. At the other extreme, there is the undoubted *existence* of minute allophonic differences; there is the case of the person who leaves home to live in a different community for a time, and, when told on return that he has 'changed his accent' is surprised and possibly even offended, yet the actual changes in phonetic quality may be very slight. Acoustic evidence bears this out (3.2); spectrograms show minute variations in the indications they give for expected formants, and there is no precise point at which it can be said that a distinctive feature has appeared or disappeared. We have seen, too, that there is diatopic evidence for the grading of infinitesimal variants on a continuum, and that, on other grounds, such grading should be 'translated' to the diachronic axis.

But quite apart from this probability that both discrete and infinitesimal stages exist, there are difficulties in the assumption that only the former are responsible for vowel-change. The reason why this view is popular is that change by discrete stages is the type that is best open to observation in modern dialect research.[2] But the fact remains that it will account only for the *spread* of variants, not for their origin. Discrete variants are, on the whole, intelligible only because they are known, i.e. they presuppose in the hearer some knowledge of the discrete variants existing in dialects other than his own. But this could not apply to the genesis of a new discrete stage. Familiarity with that is explicable only in a restricted area, and only then if it was reached via a series of small gradual stages. Naturally, this initial aggregation of small stages escapes the observer's notice, but that is no reason for denying the possibility

---

[1] Weinreich (1968) 131; Ladd (1965) 101.
[2] Cf. R. P. Stockwell, 'Mirrors in the History of English Pronunciation', in Lass 228–43, and references there quoted.

that every discrete variant is of this origin. Thereafter it may spread (possibly without further change) either by unconscious imitation or by the process of conscious selection so familiar to sociolinguists. For example, the hyperform /ɛʊ/ as in 'Oh, hello!' (cf. 6.6, p. 107) could hardly have first occurred, unless by deliberate or humorous distortion, without any intervening stages between it and /əʊ/; but, once developed (in however small a group), it could be suddenly adopted for social reasons by users of other variants.

We may conclude, then, that both infinitesimal and discrete stages may contribute to a vowel change; but that (*a*) the initiation of a vowel change by a discrete stage must, if it occurs at all, be extremely rare and probably limited to highly idiosyncratic speakers in positions of prestige and (*b*) it is fruitless to attempt to label a given stage as 'conscious' or 'unconscious', since the imitation of a variant may be conscious in one speaker but unconscious in the next.

(iv) *Regrouping and restructuring of grammatical systems*

The problem that was posed in 5.5 (p. 83) is to be explained by the heterogeneity of subcodes and registers within a system. As we saw there, it was a refusal to recognise this that led the Horn–Lehnert school to insist – wrongly – that the coexistence of zero and inflected forms in a single system must prove that loss of /-ə/ or /-(ə)n/ takes place for functional reasons only. In fact, the coexistence comes first, and selection and redistribution into a minor system is dependent on it. Variants carrying register-distinctions in one group are transmitted to other groups in altered distribution, until eventually they combine and, by the normal process of differentiation, form a new minor system in a single register (cf. (i) above, pp. 117–19). Thus whereas speakers in one group might use zero-forms in colloquial register but inflected forms in formal register, another group (or perhaps the next generation) might combine both in the same paradigm in formal register.

Hence if /-(ə)n/ or /-ə/ survives in the plural of one declension but not of another, or as a distinctive marker of one tense but not of another (5.5), that is no reason for denying that the loss, where it took place, was mechanical in origin. The mechanical changes involving such simplifications are of the 'weak' or 'discontinuous' type; they arise in different areas and contexts, and, as has been shown for /ə/ in Modern French, first in colloquial registers (irrespective of class), or in lower-class dialect (irrespective of register).[1] They are then available for selection as the system requires, and, if they are combined in an opposition, this involves no more than the redistribution to a single register of forms that are changed in one register but unchanged in another.[2] Conversely, the neogrammarian formula involving a general loss by

[1] Pulgram (1961).
[2] It should be clear from the above that the concept of 'morphologically-conditioned

sound-change and subsequent reintroductions by analogy is also inaccurate. Analogy is an important factor in restructuring, but the process is of redistribution of existing forms rather than their reintroduction. To explain a completely restructured paradigm, we need not assume that all the new selections took place at the same stage; the redistributions of the two forms in a new minor system change many times until *either* a systemic optimum is reached, *or* the older form is wholly ousted (cf. p. 117 above). By the same token, still more stages of redistribution may be needed for a paradigm containing a number of oppositions. Such a series of redistributions must be assumed for the changes in the noun and adjective declensions from Germanic to Chaucerian English, and from Vulgar Latin to the modern Romance languages, especially for a complete reversal like that from Old French *murs* (nom. sg. and acc. plur.), *mur* (acc. sg. and nom. plur.) to the later *mur* (sg.), *murs* (plur.).

The main factors in grammatical restructuring may now be summarised. New allomorphs and fresh extensions of their functions continually arise in the spoken chain (ch. 2 and 4), varying according to register and subcode (ch. 6). By chance or selection, they co-occur in new combinations, where by differentiation they form new oppositions (minor systems); these are then available for realignment to suit changing requirements in the major system. As in the case of both phonology and lexis, there are both push- and drag-chain pressures; upsets of balance may occur, and require systemic regulation (for detailed examples, see ch. 8).

The essential role taken in this process by differentiation of variants into new oppositions can be underestimated. Professor Malkiel regards the great variety of special subsystems in border-areas as due to 'secondary factors of causation' which are not on a par with primary or major factors like substratum influence or structural adjustment.[1] This may be true of isolated instances in small border villages, but the principle cannot be restricted to these; it applies to all spheres of contact, e.g. between standard language and dialect, between subcodes and registers of one or more systems. The example already quoted from Caxton (p. 118) may be transitional when viewed in the long term, but it applied to large numbers of Southern English dialect speakers in the fifteenth century. Even strictly regional 'border areas' can be wide, as may be seen from the forms for the verb 'be' in the early Germanic dialects. To the north of the Anglo-Saxon tribes on the Continent, the *es-* root predominated (ON *em*, Goth. *im*), but to their south the *beu-* root (Old Saxon *bium, biun*, OFris. *ben, bin, bim*, OHG *bin*). Old English alone, by virtue of its

phonological rules' (King p. 124) is a misleading oversimplification, which deprives us of our ability to explain why mechanically induced morphological ambiguities ever occur at all (cf. 5.5, p. 82 above).

[1] Malkiel (1967) 243–4.

antecedents' geographical position on the continent, possessed both forms, and for the whole of the OE period they formed an opposition in which *beu*-forms were used for the future and consuetudinal present tenses, *es-* forms otherwise.[1]

The difference, therefore, is only one of degree, not of principle: at one extreme, such differentiations are merely transitional in time or space, and result purely from the availability of the two forms; but at the other extreme, they may occur in central prestige dialects and supply an essential link in the processes of redistribution and restructuring.

(v) *The relation of spreading features to systems*

Since the reasons for the spread of individual features from system to system vary according to whether they are functional, mechanical or extralinguistic, it follows that not all spreads are in the same direction. In a small continuum of dialect systems ABCD, it would be possible for features typical of each to spread in some such way as shown in fig. 7. The later system of D thus

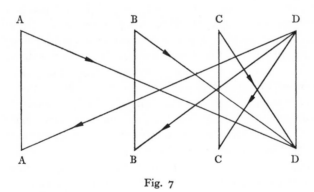

Fig. 7

contains features that belonged separately to A, B, C, while a single feature that originally belonged to D only has spread in the other direction to A, B, C. Furthermore, it is possible to envisage more extreme cases where, through migration of whole communities, later A represents earlier D rather than earlier A. As regards each system, this is to admit some justification in W. S. Allen's well-known stricture that there is no such thing as 'becoming' in

---

[1] This system may have received support from the same distribution of the parallel forms in Celtic, but that alone would not account for the survival of both forms in Old English prior to contact with Celtic. Cf. J. R. R. Tolkien, 'English and Welsh' in *Angles and Britons: O'Donnell Lectures* (Cardiff, 1963) 30–2.

language:[1] no single system can claim to be the exact reflex of any one preceding system. And the fluidity does not stop there; even if we have the evidence to 'describe' certain systems in the past, modern sociolinguistic research has shown that such descriptions are only convenient generalisations and abstractions of something that was more heterogeneous, for (*a*) they cannot cover the full range of registers,[2] and (*b*) they take no account of those members of each community who, under extrasystemic influences, already use features that could form part of a succeeding system.

The danger of assuming that pressures existing in cognate systems are necessarily equal was shown in 5.6. For both this and the other reasons just given, the limitations of our evidence must be recognised. If it is sufficient to show various directions of change, we may continue to distinguish systems at A, B, C, D. But if it is not, that need not mean total defeat; it means merely that we must generalise still further and trace only the history of the larger system of which A, B, C, D are, in turn, the heterogeneous members.

6.8   Relation of contact to other factors

It follows from 6.3–7 that contact, whether between styles or systems, can have two main effects: (*a*) it may hasten or retard a change, or (*b*) it may present a choice of development and operate as a deciding factor in selection; but it does not, in general, appear to conflict with the principles of intrasystemic linguistic development, whether functional or mechanical, outlined earlier. There are apparent cases of conflict, but these usually turn out to be of an ephemeral and transitory kind that can be shown from later developments to have been examples of retardation. To be sure of this, we need to know the *direction* of a change; but the direction of restructurings and other functional changes is usually clear, and, as was shown in chapters 2 and 4, the direction of most mechanical changes is equally so.

The more obvious of such cases of conflict between social and intralinguistic factors are of changes taking place in the present; in these, although the evidence is extensive, we have to judge without the advantage of hindsight. An example is the apparent reversal of an 'irreversible' change, to be seen in the present restoration of postvocalic /r/ as a prestige-marker in parts of the United States. As Le Page has pointed out,[3] it is unlikely that this would have happened if the spelling were not available as a model. When supported by strong social pressures, such a model becomes virtually prescriptive, and could be regarded as forming a bridge, as it were, back to the period before the loss of /r/. That is to say, for the present the combination of social pressure

[1] Allen (1953).
[2] As aptly put by Weinreich (1968) 101, 'nativelike command of heterogeneous structures is not a matter of multi-dialectalism or "mere" performance, but is part of unilingual linguistic competence'.
[3] Le Page p. 203.

and tradition succeeds in wholly retarding a mechanical change. But the pendulum can still swing back in its favour in the future.

An example from the past, therefore, may prove more illuminating. The modern English (RP) phoneme /ɑ:/ as in *bath* and *hard* goes back to a number of sources of allophones which arose from the seventeenth century onwards, notably lengthened variants of ME /a/ before fricatives, as in *after, staff, grass, bath*, and before /r/, as in *hard, arm, car, cart*. The phonemicisation presumably took place in the eighteenth century as a result of loss of postvocalic /r/, which left a large functional load to be borne by the quality or length of the vowel alone – some twenty pairs of the type *had ~ hard, cat ~ cart, match ~ march, ban ~ barn, back ~ bark*. But there were two further factors that greatly complicated this process. Firstly, in the position before nasals there was, in the seventeenth and eighteenth centuries, great variation between /ɔ:/, /e:/ and /a/ (the last including the newer [ɑ:]): words like *strange, ancient*, and *chamber* existed in all three variants, while words like *dance, lance, demand, daunt, haunt, launch* existed with two (/ɔ/ and /a/).[1] Secondly, /-r/ remained in some dialects, and in these no new phoneme /ɑ:/ arose: in so far as it existed in them, it was borrowed from the dialects where the loss of /r/ had taken place; but, conversely, a reintroduction of /a/ could take place in the other direction. It is probably for this reason that continual swings in fashions of preference for /a/ and /ɑ:/ took place in the late eighteenth and early nineteenth centuries. That these swings were of social significance appears from contemporary evidence: on the one hand, J. Walker (1791)[2] says that /ɑ:/ had formerly been common in words like *grant, dance, grass, last*, but that it had for some years 'been advancing to the short sound of the letter, as heard in *hand, land, grand*, etc.', and that the use of /ɑ:/ in *after, answer, basket, plant, mast* 'borders very closely on vulgarity'. On the other hand, both Kenrick (1773) and Batchelor (1809) refer to the use of /a/ in words like *lass, palm, past, dance* as 'mincing' and 'affected'.[3] It would appear from these pieces of evidence that, soon after the phonemicisation of /ɑ:/, there was the expected polarisation of /a/ and /ɑ:/ and the further integration of /ɑ:/ through the transfer to it of the longer allophones of /a/. The result was a swing towards /ɑ:/ (especially among speakers who did not recognise the phonemic distinction) that came to be regarded as vulgar; but the reaction to /a/, when overdone, was castigated as affected.

These swings in distribution bear little relation to the eventual selections, which seem to have depended partly on phonetic factors like the preference for /e:/ before nasal + voiced consonant, as in *strange* and *chamber*, and partly

---

[1] For the seventeenth century see Dobson (1957) §§ 62, 104, and 239.
[2] *A Critical Pronouncing Dictionary*. See Jespersen (1909) I 305–6.
[3] W. Kenrick, *A New Dictionary of the English Language*; T. Batchelor, *Orthoepical Analysis of the English Language*. Cf. Jespersen (1909) I 305; McKnight 454.

on the influence of French models: it is noticeable that /ɑ:/ was selected in words with obvious French counterparts like *dance, chance, example, demand, advantage* whereas in *taunt, paunch, tawny, lawn, fawn* the older /ɔ:/ was preserved, probably because the connection with French was less obvious.[1] But the significant fact is that throughout these processes of selection, and among the many different distributions that are found, the only examples of /ɑ:/ that are constant in all writers[2] who admit the sound are of the type *art, arm, part*, i.e. the only context in which its use was functionally determined. Although the distribution is more stable today than in the eighteenth century, interference from (and hypercorrection in) dialects lacking the distinction has continued ever since, as may be seen from the variation still accepted in words like *giraffe, plastic, transfer*. In sum, dialectal variation fostered by social cleavage has meant a continual blurring of the distributional boundary between these two phonemes, but the existence and phonemic status of /ɑ:/ has never been in doubt. Its origins were mechanical and functional, and interference due to social factors has been merely incidental. If considered in isolation, such interference might be regarded as important in its own right; but, viewed historically over a period of two centuries, it has contributed no more than some complications and retardations of a normal mechanical and functional change.

A corresponding acceleration of these changes is seen at its most obvious in the way that mere contact of different systems continually makes new phonetic, grammatical, and lexical variants available; but social factors may also work in this direction by supporting the polarisation of variants (6.6). It has been suggested[3] that changes gather momentum when the upper classes polarise differences to maintain their value as prestige-markers, the process continuing when the other classes, in their turn, narrow the differences by imitation; and Bright and Ramanujan have confirmed, from a study of class-dialects in India, that the more conscious (i.e. socially motivated) changes take place first in the upper class.[4] However, polarisation can also result from affectation at points lower in the social scale, and still find ultimate acceptance by the whole community. A possible example is in seventeenth-century London English, where the raising of the reflex of ME /a:/ from [æ:] to [e:], whether by discrete or infinitesimal replacements, took place at a faster rate than is to be presumed for the other stages of the Great Vowel Shift (except, possibly, the replacement of the reflex of ME /ɛ:/ by /i:/ in the

---

[1] Cf. Jespersen (1909) I 111.
[2] Cf. the references to Buchanan, Perry, Kenrick, Walker, Wright, and Murray in McKnight 453–4, and Jespersen (1909) I 305–7.
[3] J. L. Fischer, *Word* 14 (1958) 47–56, with reference there quoted to Joos, *Language* 28 (1952) 222–31.
[4] W. Bright and A. K. Ramanujan 'Sociolinguistic Variation and Language Change', in Lunt 1107–13.

seventeenth and eighteenth centuries, for which see 7.3). That this raising may have been accelerated by social factors is suggested by Alexander Gill's well-known remark (1619) that in his time certain affected women speakers ('Mopsae') were already using [e:].[1] In this case, therefore, an affected and advanced pronunciation which appears to have been of vulgar rather than upper class origin provided the model for the sound used by a majority of the community eighty years later.

But social factors need not be regarded as accelerating only mechanical changes like the raising just mentioned. They may also, in addition, accelerate the selection of variants required for restoring equilibrium. Thus the replacement of late eighteenth-century French /wɛ/ by /wa/ (6.6, p. 107) could be considered in the light of the suggestion made in 3.7–8 (pp. 42–4), that the selection of more sonorous variants for one phoneme compensates for the loss of sonority entailed by the raising of other phonemes. The same might be suggested for present-day English, when features of the so-called 'Midland flat accent' are replacing those of RP in the younger generation: [a] or [ɑ] instead of [æ] as in *that*, [ɑɪ] instead of [aɪ] as in *time* both supply a greater proportion of lower and more retracted phonemes, and similarly with the replacement of [ɛʊ] by [æʊ] or [ʌʊ] in *own*, *don't*. Above (p. 107) it was suggested that, in the origin of such replacements, the functional and social factors cannot be distinguished from each other. But it is at least arguable that their spread beyond the present younger generation and acceptance by older speakers is due to their greater functional viability, and is not a mere copying of fashion.

Finally, there is the acceleration of the normal processes of change which takes place under the special conditions of contact resulting from migration or invasion (6.3). Under these conditions, the level of redundancy is raised, and with it the proportion of stressed forms in phonology and of marked forms in grammar; shift and merger become more probable, but quicker remedies are found for the pressure points of homonymy and polysemy. This applies to migrations within the area of a single language, and is seen in a mild form in the differences of development between conservative peripheral areas and innovating central areas. But it is seen more clearly in the comparison of cognate languages, as for example within both the Romance and the Germanic groups of languages: in both, the most isolated areas show the lowest rate of change (Sardinian, Icelandic) and similarly in both, the two areas to show the highest rate of change are those that have absorbed conquering invaders speaking a branch of Indo-European long separated and therefore virtually non-cognate: Northern France, conquered by the Franks; and England, conquered by the Normans.

Extremes in the process of change and remedy are found in pidgin and

[1] See Dobson (1957) I 145.

creolised languages. In Jamaican Creole, originally under the influence of Twi or some related language, English /ɔ:/ and /ɑ:/ merged under /a:/, but the merger was partly compensated for by the retention of palatalised consonants, as seen in an opposition like /ga:dn/ 'Gordon' ~ /gja:dn/ 'garden'.[1]

1 I owe this example to R. B. Le Page.

7.1   Introductory

An attempt has been made in the foregoing chapters to show

(i) that there is a certain degree of predictability in the changes of intra-systemic origin that can take place: on the one hand, a continual 'inaccuracy' both in physiological production and in mental selection, which lowers the levels of information-content and redundancy and would, if not continuously remedied, lead to a 'blunting' or devaluation of the substance; and on the other, systemic regulation which automatically replaces lost information-content and, although certain limited areas of ambiguity are present in all systems, restores the overall level of redundancy;

(ii) that the precise direction taken in these normal processes of change may be wholly controlled by extralinguistic factors, or by extrasystemic factors that are ultimately of extralinguistic origin; and

(iii) that the rate of change, whether of intrasystemic or other origin, depends on the degree of exposure to extrasystemic contact.

To arrive at these conclusions, the subsystems of language have in the main been studied separately above. Such separate approaches are partly determined by the nature of the subsystems, but they are not sufficient in themselves. Amidst all the valuable specialist research on the subsystems, there is a danger of forgetting that substance – the spoken or written chain – is not a straightforward sum of its constituent parts, any more than a language system is the exact total of its subsystems. Both substance and system are entities in their own right, and therefore the study of their development requires a unified theory of change – a body of principles that will enable us to see changing subsystems as interdependent and interacting parts of a whole.

Special difficulty arises from the fact that, both in the search for a general theory and in the specialist study of subsystems, different schools have dogmatically insisted on their own favourite principle and excluded others, so that the over-rigid application of different principles has either yielded con-flicting results or led nowhere at all. This 'all or nothing fallacy' (cf. 1.2, p. 3) has been especially prominent in the long disagreement between two main groups of linguists, the first composed of 'traditionalists' and 'mechanists', the second of 'functionalists' and 'structuralists'.[1] Yet both hypotheses are valid (ch. 2–5); what has been lacking is a theory of diachronic linguistics that will accommodate both.

The predominant neogrammarian view was based simply on the twin mechanisms of sound-change and analogy. As put succinctly by Sturtevant:[2] 'Phonetic laws are regular but produce irregularities. Analogic creation is irregular but produces regularity.' But this is an oversimplification: analogy should not be identified with systemic regulation. In the latter process, analogical forms are often used, but analogical changes should be regarded as 'levelling' rather than regulating. As we have seen in chapters 4 and 5, levelling may often proceed further than the system requires, so that the effect of even analogical changes may be further regulation. Neither sound-change (ch. 2) nor analogy (ch. 4) can be regarded as providing any more than the raw material of change; the *process* of change, from its initiation to its acceptance in a system, is considerably more complex than this (ch. 3 and 5), and it has been one of the main criticisms of the traditional view that it fails to relate idiolect to change in system.[3] It is therefore not surprising that those linguists who have continued to regard sound-change and analogy as the only relevant intrasystemic factors should have been dubbed 'mechanists'.[4]

The factors proposed by earlier supporters of the functional view appear at first sight more promising. For example Horn (1921)[5] and Lehnert (1957)[6] supported the dichotomy of *Zwecktätigkeit* (expediency, utility) and *Ausdruckstätigkeit* (expressiveness). But they characterised the former as 'destructive' and yet the cause of uniformity and regularity, and the latter as creative and the cause of amplification, discrepancy, and irregularity. There are evident contradictions here, such as that discrepancy and irregularity can also be brought about by 'expediency'. Horn and Lehnert were working with an outmoded notion of sound change (pp. 81–3, 120–3) and they applied their principles dogmatically and in unacceptable form (pp. 127–9).

The functional view has since been stated more clearly by Martinet (1962):[7] 'the structure of language is nothing but the unstable balance between the needs of communication, which require more numerous and more specific units, and man's inertia, which favours less numerous, less specific, and more frequently occurring units'.

---

[1] Cf. Robson p. 154, Spence pp. 1–5, Hoenigswald (1957) 581–2. There is a partial (but only partial) parallel in the current controversy on 'competence' and 'performance' theories of change; but since the views associated with 'competence' are not accepted here, it has seemed preferable to avoid the use of the term.
[2] Sturtevant (1947) 109.   [3] Weinreich (1968) 104–19.
[4] An example is the statement by Hockett (1958) 389; 'the causes of sound-change cannot be found within the system of habits we call language'.
[5] Horn (1921) 139.
[6] M. Lehnert, *Zeitschrift für Anglistik und Amerikanistik* 5 (1957) 43–56, and references there quoted.   [7] Martinet (1962) 139.

This parallels what was said above in chapter 3 concerning form- and function-directed utterance. But whether it can form the basis for historical study is more open to doubt. Bloomfield[1] was of the opinion that 'general effectiveness . . . unfortunately quite escapes the linguist's control'; and although present-day researchers like Labov[2] have made accurate distinctions between careful and casual speech in informants, it would probably be difficult to carry out a controlled experiment in which informants were graded for the effectiveness of their spontaneous grammatical and lexical selections, since there would be no means of ensuring that informants were stylistically comparable (e.g. that one was 'committed' to the subject, another not). Even if this were possible, however, there remains the difficulty that what is creatively, expressively, or functionally motivated in one speaker may be socially motivated in another, and purely imitative in a third. And this difficulty increases at the diachronic dimension since what is selected for expressive needs may include not only the emphatic variants that would be analysed as such for that *état de langue*, but also variants originally developed as a result of expediency and economy but newly readapted for emphatic purpose. Conversely, emphatic variants may be readapted through use in relaxed style, in a process that could be shown diagrammatically as in fig. 8.

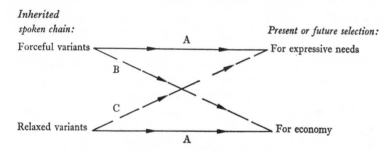

Fig. 8. Readaptation of variants
Note: Lines A,A show the two normal processes; lines B,C show the two different kinds of adaptation resulting, e.g. from the mixing of register-variants

In the specialised field of etymology, this has been long recognised. For example, the ME reflexes of OE *ic* are *ich* (strongly stressed) and *y*, *i* (weakly stressed). The former is gradually replaced by the latter, and from this originally unstressed form arises the new stressed form /i:/, the ancestor of MnE /aɪ/. (This process may take place continually on a far wider scale, if, as was suggested in chapter 3, it was relaxed variants that were selected for parts of the Great Vowel Shift, and, in their new function as stressed forms, redressed the balance of sonority.)

[1] Bloomfield (1935) 402.   [2] Cf. p. 104 above.

For the same reasons, the distinctions between 'conscious' and 'unconscious' or between motivated and unmotivated cannot be used as a framework, since neither are relevant at the level of idiolect and spoken chain. At the level of system, certainly, the distinction between motivated and unmotivated becomes crucial, and for that reason, if for no other, the framework must distinguish the two levels.

To sum up, neither view, mechanist or functional, provides a basis that will accommodate simultaneously the following problems of intrasystemic development:

(*a*) the distinction between the idiolectal origins of change and its ultimate acceptance in the system;

(*b*) the switching of functions for given forms between earlier and later systems, as described above;

(*c*) the assessment of mechanical and systemic factors;

(*d*) the interpenetration of subsystems.

7.2   A framework

We have seen that one feature common to all linguistic change (as indeed to all language) is the *process of selection*; and the solution proposed here is that this process provides an essential link in the apparatus of change. Every change is, at least in its beginnings, present in the variants of the spoken chain; it is the process of continuous selection that ensures its imitation, spread, and ultimate acceptance into one or more systems. The selection takes place both at the level of idiolect (and interlocutor) and at the level of system proper; and it may consist of a preference for a commoner variant rather than a rare one, or vice versa.

For the purpose of studying this process of selection, the difference between the physiological and psychological origins of variants in a single idiolect is here assumed to be irrelevant. Even at the level of idiolect, there are many borderline cases that cannot be definitely assigned to one or the other (ch. 2); but since an arbitrary variant of physiological origins may, while still entirely *parole*-based, gather motivation as it is imitated (p. 137 above) it follows that *all* sources of variation must be classed together. The term 'mechanical', therefore, is here understood to include all the sources of variation in the spoken chain discussed in chapters 2 and 4, together with all new variants entering it from elsewhere (ch. 6), irrespective of whether they are produced physiologically, psychologically, or (secondarily) by spread from other systems (cf. 1.4, p. 8).

The framework must accommodate the following range of situations. All changes entail a combination of mechanical (in the sense defined above) and functional factors, though either may predominate. At one extreme, there is the situation where new minor systems in border areas come into being purely because of the availability of the variants (p. 116); and at the other extreme, the situation where an originally rare and areally restricted variant spreads to fill a gap in the systems of a large area (pp. 114–16). These two types stand at opposite extremes of the whole scale of diversity of intrasystemic change, and others are intermediate; but irrespective of the position of each change in this scale, the process remains constant, and there is no fluctuation in the matter of selection and levels: all changes that are systemically relevant (i.e. they affect *langue* and not merely *parole*) take place on *both* levels, the spoken chain and the system. These levels exist throughout in their own right: the spoken chain by virtue of continuous contact via form-directed utterance between different but mutually intelligible groups; the system, in its smallest and least important manifestations, as used by two interlocutors, but gaining in importance according to the number of groups that conform to it.

In its barest essentials, then, the framework consists of the two levels, spoken chain and system, linked by the process of selection; and the relative potency of mechanical, functional, and extralinguistic factors is to be judged according to the evidence for the pressures in each level: the pressures referred to in chapters 3 and 5 as push-chain operate in the first instance at the level of spoken chain, and consist of majority-variants that provide the obvious selection, whereas those referred to as drag-chain operate at the level of system, and are more likely to affect minority-variants in the spoken chain.

The basis for such a theory, as we might have expected, lies in the second of Saussure's great antitheses. We have already argued that the first, between diachrony and synchrony, can be adapted as regards forms and etymology (ch. 2), and that due caution must be observed in tracing change from one system to another (ch. 6). A corresponding adaptation can be made, for historical purposes, of Saussure's antithesis of *parole* and *langue*. For these, the terms *spoken chain* and *system* are preferred here, especially since *langue* suggests a homogeneity that would not fit the requirements of chapter 6. At a roughly synchronic level, the minimum definitions are:

Spoken chain: the total utterances of a given group or community over a limited period, whether fully intelligible or not;

System: the total of accepted and intelligible norms, established by oppositions, in the same group and period.

But the diachronic implications are more complex. To enlarge on the introductory description given above, the spoken chain contains the whole range of potential alterations and innovations that can be regarded as internal during the period chosen: phonetic variants of all types, including accidental or rare allophones (ch. 2), grammatical and lexical extensions (ch. 4), neologisms, witty and devised collocations, slang, foreign words, calques, and so on. Two special ingredients to note are (*a*) non-distinctive suprasegmental features that have no counterparts in the system but are a fruitful source of internally induced variation in segmental forms, and (*b*) new forms (whether in phonology, grammar, or lexis) from neighbouring dialects or further afield that have just entered, or enter during the chosen period, as a result of contact, and represent the extrasystemic intake.

In a community of any size, the system includes the dialects of all groups, and the register distinctions applicable either to the main system or to its subcodes.

The mechanism will operate as follows. The variants occurring in the spoken chain may follow one of three courses.

(i) They may have no effect on the system, i.e. they are rejected. This applies particularly to mistakes, unsuccessful coinages and other occasional phenomena that occur mainly at the level of one pair of interlocutors only; they may spread temporarily to minor groups, and then die out. The place of vogue words could be regarded as peripheral, i.e. intermediate between this and category (iii) below. But it is not only trivial variants that may be rejected by a system. Even if they occur in quantity as a result of extrasystemic contact, they may conflict so radically with the existing system that they are still rejected.

(ii) They may be selected and marshalled into sets of oppositions according to current requirements of the system for the maintenance of equilibrium and of the level of redundancy. This may occur in two ways: (*a*) the variants expounding the three main subsystems of phonology, grammar and lexis are selected *within* those subsystems, resulting, for example, in grammatical or lexical restructuring; or (*b*) lexical variants are 'shunted' to fill slots in grammar (ch. 4 and 5).

(iii) They may occur in such quantity that the selection of other minority-variants is no longer in question. They are *imposed* on the system, and the system is thereby altered. As we have seen in chapter 6, the ultimate factors here are likely to be extralinguistic and extrasystemic, but they may operate either (*a*) directly, from the spread of new forms from one system to another, or (*b*) indirectly, through their acceleration of the normal (mechanical) processes of intrasystemic change.[1]

A diagrammatic representation of the above mechanism is attempted in fig. 9. For purely synchronic purposes, parallel or crossing lines would suffice to represent spoken chain and system, but they are here represented by circles in order to show interrelation and interpenetration. The arrows therefore

---

[1] In pidginisation, the spoken chains of both contributing languages have to be taken into account, and there is reinterpretation of phonemes and meanings to an extent far exceeding that outlined in chapters 2 and 4. Although the mechanisms in (i), (ii) and (iii) above continue to function, they are subordinated in importance to the process of coalescence of two wholly unlike systems (cf. pp. 93, 98).

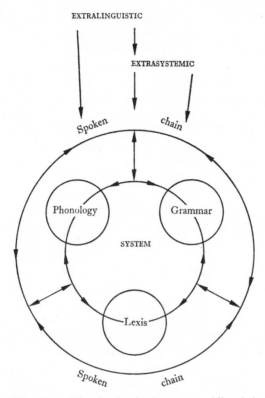

Fig. 9. Directions of (inter)action in the process of linguistic change

denote not only transfers from one subsystem to another, but also influences and pressures between subsystems and (with appropriate 'translation' from exponent to function where relevant) between the two levels. Furthermore, if the subsystems are not completely integrated in the total system, then interrelation will include not only reciprocal influences, but also conflicts, as for example between the phonemic system and phonaesthemes (cf. pp. 150–3). The result is a diagram which, though still strictly speaking 'synchronic', is dynamic: the arrows denote what is happening, has just happened, or is just about to happen. For a fully diachronic diagram, a further dimension would be needed to include a time scale. This is not strictly necessary for our purpose, but could be achieved by substituting tubes for circles and taking the length of the tubes to represent the lapse of time.

The assumption that all changes take place at both levels – spoken chain and system – leaves no place for doctrinaire insistence on mechanical or functional factors only. Between possibilities (ii) and (iii) there is a wide scope for either agreement or conflict between the two levels. A possible case of near-agreement is the eventual selection of variants in /uː/ in *poor, boor, moor* but of /ɔː/ in *floor, door*. In the spoken chain, there would be a greater frequency of /uː/-variants after a labial, and at the level of system, the /uː/-variants avoided homonymic clash (cf. *pour, pore, bore, more*). In such a case it would be misleading to argue that one reason is more likely than, or precludes, the other; each applies on its own level.

A more complex example, in which the two levels do not wholly agree, may be seen in the treatment of monosyllables in *-ind* (*bind, find, hind, behind, rind, blind, wind, kind, mind*). The modern dialect map shows /ɪ/ north of the Humber (except in *kind, mind*) but mainly /aɪ, ɔɪ/, etc. south of it.[1] The Northern /ɪ/ would no doubt lend marginal support to any /ɪ/-variants further south, but it will not explain why the commonest words to have /ɪ/ in the developing standard of the sixteenth and seventeenth centuries were *bind, find,* and *wind*.[2] At the level of spoken chain, there appears to have been a survival of certain paradigmatic or derivational variants in the south: just as the common Southern ME *stonde/stant* is shown by its vowel alternation to have existed in long and short forms, so /iː/ and /ɪ/ must have alternated in *binde/bint, finde/fint, wind/windy*. But whereas in transparent compounds like *grindstone* there would always be pressure to replace a shortened form by the long vowel of the simplex, such pressures would be more evenly balanced in the case of *bind, find, wind*. At the level of system, *wind* and *kind* are the only words of the group that are liable to homonymic or polysemic pressures. Although the clash of *wind* sb. and vb./*wind* vb. 'turn' is mainly between noun and verb, some confusion would arise in the many compounds and derivatives of *wind* sb.; and it certainly existed in the verb *wind* used of sounding a wind-instrument (past tense *winded* and *wound*, cf. OED s.v. *wind* v.2 II 3). There is in this case, therefore, some evidence of functional pressure for the adoption of /ɪ/. But the absence of differentiation between *kind* sb. and adj. may be due simply to lack of variation in the spoken chain; for earlier, when the S.E. form *kend* was common, there was still a strong semantic link between *kind* 'nature' and *kind* 'natural'. In these cases again, therefore, it would be wrong to accord priority to either level. The spoken chain has an autonomous development, and, if it does not provide all the variants required by the system, the resulting selections may appear to be an arbitrary compromise.

Nevertheless, the principle of two levels linked by selection is no mere compromise solution. It provides the only framework that will enable us to compare texts or systems of different periods from the same area and to take into account simultaneously (*a*) the possibility of spread from neighbouring systems, or from other sources like the standard language, and (*b*) a choice between variants arising within the system itself, and, especially where sub-

[1] Kolb p. 237.   [2] Dobson (1957) 479.

systems conflict, the particular pressures that condition the actual choice made. For example, if the reflexes of OE /y/ in Modern English are compared with the forms used in London English of *c.* 1400, there are far more 'exceptions' to the almost regular *i, y* of that period, and they may be accounted for as follows:

(i) Conditioned phonetic variants: *blush, rush, thrush, clutch, crutch, much, merry, bury.*

(ii) Avoidance of homonymy: *left* (cf. *lift*) and perhaps *dull* (cf. *dill, dell*) and *hemlock* (cf. *him*: apart from *hymn*, there are no common words commencing with /hɪm/).

(iii) Taboo: avoidance of /ɪ/ in *shut, shuttle.*

(iv) Phonaesthetic reasons: *knell* (cf. *bell*), *dent* (cf. *indent*).[1]

Of the above, (i) is presumably to be regarded as mechanical in origin, the rest as systemic. But further conclusions may sometimes be drawn from a detailed knowledge of the history of individual words: the history of *much*, listed in (i) above, shows a long conflict between the variants *much(e)* and *mich(e)*, and we may suspect, from its collocations, that the final selection was of a vowel that would contrast with, rather than match, that of the word *little.*

Similarly, the numerous exceptions to the ME change of *-er-* to *-ar-* may be classified as follows:

(i) learned channels of transmission: the bulk of the examples with French and Latin counterparts, e.g. *universal, certain, service, concern,* (cf. 6.4, p. 96);

(ii) avoidance of homonymy: *pert* (cf. *part*), *yearn* (cf. *yarn*), *herd, heard* (cf. *hard*); possibly *earth* (cf. *hearth*), *perch* (cf. *parch*);

(iii) avoidance of polysemy: *person* (cf. *parson*), *vermin* (cf. *varmint*);

(iv) phonaesthetic influence: *swerve* (cf. *swirl*);

(v) derivation: *dearth* (cf. *dear*);

(vi) prevalence of long variants in the spoken chain, especially when initial and/or preceding *n* or *l*: *earl, early, earn, earnest, earth* (cf. (ii) above), *learn, stern, fern, yearn* (cf. (ii) above), *kernel.*

In short, the approach must be all-inclusive, and cover every possibility from migrations and phonetic conditioning to homonymy and taboo. Such all-inclusive approaches have been proposed before, e.g. in 1948 E. Öhmann[2] listed the following seven factors in addition to sound-change: functional imbalance, emphasis, sound-symbolism, onomatopoeia, euphemism, taboo, and homonymy. They have been criticised on two main grounds:[3] firstly 'that investigators simply choose as they please from a list of such

---

[1] This leaves a residue of only *cudgel, fledge,* and *shed,* and even these might be shown, by means of the type of phonaesthetic research exemplified later in this chapter, to belong to (iv).

[2] 'Über unregelmässige Lautentwicklung', *Neuphilologische Mitteilungen* XLVII (1948) 145–64.

[3] Cf. Ladd (1964) 650; Trim p. 19.

possibilities', and that the result is a 'hotchpotch of unsystematised explanations'; and secondly, that our documentation of variants from past periods is insufficient for the purpose. As regards the first objection, the theory proposed here is an attempt to systematise the relevant factors; in previous chapters, for example, Öhmann's factor of 'emphasis' has not been left isolated, but treated as an integral part of the mechanism of change in each subsystem; both the interrelation of factors and their relation to chain and system has been indicated, and the model proposed provides a place for each. The second objection is more serious: a linguistic diversity such as is apparent today could never be recalled from records of the past. Nevertheless, in dealing with past periods, we are operating from hindsight, and can manage with less than the rich array of data available to investigators of modern languages. It is true that there are gaps everywhere, and particularly in certain periods like the Germanic, pre-invasion, and pre-700 periods of English. For such periods only the broader outlines can be deduced. Nevertheless, from about 1300 onwards the records of dialect variation become more detailed (cf. maps 3, 5, 7). For Early Modern English, there is much orthoepist, phonetic and other evidence, and dialect forms can sometimes be deduced by extrapolation from Middle or Modern English. Furthermore, Early Modern English is a suitable period for the study of selection, for the rate of both variation and selection is higher in a growing standard language than in other dialects.

7.3 An extended example

Within this comprehensive scheme we proceed – as usual in empirically based science – by collecting as many significant correspondences as possible. The relationships thus established need not necessarily be causal: two related changes, one in phonology and another in grammar, might both be symptoms of a more radical cause. But even if the evidence does not allow us to determine whether the correspondence is of cause and effect or of parallel symptoms, the detection of the correspondence is still of value. It is true that conflicting interpretations of it may still occur, but these are often due to scholars who are committed to one school of thought rather than another, be it mechanical, functional, dialectological, or sociolinguistic. If an extensive problem like the English Great Vowel Shift is approached without such bias, combinations of all factors are to be expected, and it will not be surprising if the patterns for them deduced in chapters 2 to 6 are found to fit the evidence best, namely (i) variation (mechanical); (ii) triggering and/or acceleration (social and demographic); (iii) systemic regulation (functional).

Within recent decades, various functional reasons for the origin of the Great Vowel Shift have been proposed. For example, Trnka and Vachek have pointed out that short /ɪ/ and /ʊ/ must, at the start of the shift, have correlated with close /e:/ and /o:/ rather than with /i:/ and /u:/, and that the latter, being isolated, moved out of the system of vowels proper.[1] But, although such a break in correlation is presupposed by the whole shift, its origins must lie in a purely mechanical phonetic change that had taken place some time after the recognition of the original correlation in the established orthography. Professor Martinet has attempted a further support of the functional view by his theory that quantitative distinctions had, in the late ME period, been neutralised;[2] but there is clear rhyming and orthographic evidence that these distinctions survived throughout in closed monosyllables. Furthermore, there were no obvious asymmetries in the various vowel systems of Middle English; on the contrary, there was greater asymmetry during and after the shift than before it. The only significant innovation was the addition of /ɑ:/, and, as we shall see below, there are reasons for discounting this as an initiator of the shift.

In the spoken chain, on the other hand, there are weighty correspondences. Firstly, the start of the shift followed closely on the most significant prosodic change in the history of the language – the loss of final /ə/ – by which English became the most monosyllabic language in Western Europe; its rhythm was entirely changed, as is shown, among other things, by the drastic alterations to the existing tradition of verse-writing. Secondly, there were, in the high long vowels, parallel raisings and diphthongisations in the two southern areas of continental Germanic, namely Dutch as opposed to Frisian, and High German as opposed to Low German and Scandinavian. In English, also, the first changes were in the high vowels, and this casts doubt on the theory that the English shift was initiated by the emergence of /ɑ:/ or /a:/, since, furthermore, this phoneme already existed in the continental West Germanic languages. Thirdly, the shifts in all these languages tally with what might be expected from normal mechanical change (cf. ch. 2 and 3). The fact that they were more extensive in Southern English than in Northern English and Scots is parallel to the north–south distinction on the Continent, and suggests that in all three areas (Southern English, Dutch–Flemish, and High German) certain inherited suprasegmental features are likely to have been a predisposing factor. But the accelerated rate of change in these three areas is presumably to be explained by the factors suggested in chapter 6, namely higher cultural levels and greater necessity for contact with speakers of non-Germanic languages than in the corresponding more peripheral northern areas.[3] Once initiated, it could be further accelerated by social factors (cf. 6.8, p. 132f).

---

[1] J. Vachek in *Brno Studies in English* III, discussed by E. J. Dobson, *TPS* (1962) 130.
[2] Martinet (1955) 248–56.
[3] It is possible that the actual circumstances of initiation may have varied in each area. R. B. Le Page suggests to me that in England there would be good reasons for the

For the early stages of the change, therefore, functional factors amount to no more than the normal preservation of distances in simple shift, and – negatively – the termination of the original correlations of long and short vowels. In the case of the back vowels, this simple shift was continued and completed, via the stages /ɔ:/ > /o:/, /aʊ/ > /ɔ:/, /əʊ/ > /aʊ/, without systemic complication. But, for the later stages of the changes affecting front vowels, a process of systemic regulation can be detected. Its origins lie in the ME addition of /a:/ already referred to. If this sound had remained a back /ɑ:/ or a central /a:/ the circular shift of front vowels might also have continued without complication. But, presumably for the same mechanical and/or social reasons as for the shift of the high vowels, this /ɑ:/ was fronted and raised, thus encroaching on the low-front vowel area. That some degree of merger had, by the late sixteenth century, become inevitable is shown by the varying mergers of low-front vowel phonemes in different systems in the London area at this period. The commonest was of the reflexes of ME /a:/ and /aɪ/, as in *made, maid*; in others, there was apparently merger of the reflexes of ME /ɛ:/ and /aɪ/, as in *mead, maid*;[1] and in yet others, there was merger of all three. It has been one of the main problems of Early MnE phonology to decide how these mergers of the reflex of ME /ɛ:/ could have been reversed, so that in the eighteenth century *mead* rhymed with *meed*, and its pronunciation to rhyme with *made* or *maid* became obsolete. The generally accepted explanation is that a different system had spread to London from certain neighbouring dialects where both ME /ɛ:/ and /e:/ had long before merged under /e:/, and had subsequently been raised to /i:/ in the early stages of the shift.[2] Such interference from a wholly different system is the only feasible explanation for the adoption in London – possibly word by word – of /i:/ for only those exponents of the /e:/-phoneme that contained the reflex of ME /ɛ:/.

This example has recently been used by Weinreich, Labov, and Herzog[3] to show that such a process occurs through heterogeneity and coexistence of two systems in the same area (i.e. primarily a sociological explanation). But further consideration of the evidence suggests that, although achieved via a state of heterogeneity, it was functionally motivated. There were, in the late seventeenth century, *two* main systems in the London area (i and ii below) which were both distinct from the third system (iii) that was to provide the model for redistribution. System i (with appropriate phonetic adjustment for the sixteenth century) is that which is borne out by the majority of sixteenth-century orthoepists and seventeenth-century phoneticians. System ii is, for

aristocracy of the late fourteenth and early fifteenth centuries to adopt affected forms of speech as a means of 'role-distancing' from the lower classes, from whom they had hitherto been differentiated by speaking French.

[1] Dobson (1957) § 228.
[2] See Dobson (1957) § 108 and references there quoted.
[3] Weinreich (1968), especially 147.

	I	II	III
meed	iː	iː	iː
mead	eː		
made		eː	eː
maid	ɛː		

the sixteenth century, based mainly on the evidence of rhymes and puns, though in the late seventeenth century it is increasingly vouched for by homophone lists as well as rhymes. The difference between I and II was probably one of social class, and that would account for the orthoepists' and phoneticians' support for I. Nevertheless, there must have been a continual transfer of speakers from I (the commoner system in the sixteenth century) to II (the commoner at the end of the seventeenth century); for, in spite of the evidence for I provided by Cooper as late as 1685,[1] the fact that only II, not I, survived into the eighteenth century as a rival to III is sufficient proof that this transfer must have taken place.

The reason for the redistribution to III then becomes clear. System II, in which all three phonemes had merged, was viable only for so long as it was used by a smaller proportion of London's population. As soon as it was spoken by a majority, the functional load on /eː/ became too great, and hence the redistribution of part of that load to /iː/ on the model of system III – a system which had been known long before in London (as rhymes testify), but which had never made headway until now.

It might appear at first sight that system III was functionally no more viable than II. The many homonyms in /iː/ entailed by III are often regarded as an indication that this change must have been primarily *non*-systemic in character. But a more relevant fact is ignored: had the change *not* taken place, the number of homonyms in /eː/ would have been much greater, as may be judged from the accompanying lists. The centre column of List A gives thirty-eight forms which, as may be deduced from comparison with the two outer columns, would have become homonyms in either event (whether at /eː/ or /iː/); in B are listed thirty-four forms in which the selection of /iː/ avoided homonymic clash with other forms containing /eː/, while List C gives the far smaller total of ten forms in which the selection of /iː/ actually resulted in homonymic clash.

The view that homonymic clash does not operate except between words of the same form-class was questioned above (5.2), but it is relevant to note that

[1] Dobson (1957) § 115 and note 5.

if that criterion is insisted on here, the case becomes still stronger, since many forms in List A then become significant instead of merely neutral; e.g. forms like *bean, beat, meat* would have clashed at /e:/ with words of the same form-class, *bane, bait/bate, mate*, whereas at /i:/ only *been, beet, meet* are in question. As a guide, an asterisk is added in the lists to those cases in which, on grounds of form-class, the functional yield was increased by the change (41), and a dagger to those in which it was decreased (7).

List A[1]

been v. (p.p.)	bean n.*	bane n.
beer n.	bear v. ⎫	
bier n.	bear n. ⎭	bare, a., v.
beet n.	beat v.*	⎧ bate v., n.
		⎩ bait v., n.
cheep n.	cheap a.	chape n.
deer n.	dear a.	dare v.
feet n. pl.	feat n., a.*	fate n.
flee v.	flea n.	flay v.
gleed n.	⎧ glead n. ⎫	glade n.
	⎩ glede n. ⎭	
Greece n.	grease, n., v.*	grace n., v.
grieve v.	greave n.*	grave n., a.
heel n.	heal v.*	⎧ hale a.
		⎩ hail n., v.
here adv.	hear v.	⎧ hare n.
		⎩ hair n.
lee n.	lea n.*	lay n., a., v.
leed n.	lead v.*	⎧ lade v.
		⎩ laid v. (pa. t.)
leek n.	leak n., v.	lake n.
meed n.	mead n.(*)	⎧ maid n.
		⎩ made v. (pa. t.)
meet a., v.	⎧ meat n.* ⎫	mate n., v.
	⎩ mete v. ⎭	
piece n., v.	peace n.	pace n., v.
peel n., v.	peal n., v.	⎧ pail n.
		⎩ pale a.
peer n., v. ⎫	pear n.	⎧ pare v.
pier n. ⎭		⎩ pair n., v.
reel n.	real a.	rail n., v.
reeve n.	reave v.*	rave v.
see v., n.	sea n.	say v.
seel v. ⎫	seal n., v.	⎧ sail n., v.
ceil v. ⎭		⎩ sale n.
seem v.	seam n.	same a.
seen v. (p.p.)	sean n.	sane a.
sheer a.	shear v.*	share v., n.
steel n., v.	steal v.†	stale a.
teem v.	team n.	tame v., a.

---

[1] The lists contain only words relevant for the eighteenth century; words of late dialect origin like *tee, raid* are omitted.

tier n.　　　{ tear n.　　}　　tare n.
　　　　　　{ tear v., n. }

week n.　　　weak a.　　　　wake v., n.
wheel n., v. }　　　　　　　{ wail n., v.
weel n.　　 }　weal n.　　　 { whale n.
　　　　　　　　　　　　　　{ wane v.
ween v.　　　wean v., a.*　　{ wain n.

weir n.　　　wear v.　　　　ware n., a.

List B

beak n., v.*	bake v.	neal v.*	nail v., n.
beast n.	baste v.	neap n., a.*	nape n.
deal n., v.*	dale n.	pea n.*	pay n., v.
dean n. ⎫ *	{ Dane n.	peat n.*	pate n.
dene n. ⎭	{ deign v.	plea n.*	play n., v.
ear n.*	{ air n.	plead v.	played v. (pa. t.)
	{ heir n.	pleat n.*	plate n.
eat v.	{ eight num.	reap v.*	rape v.
	{ ate v. (pa. t.)	rear v., a.*	rare a.
fear v., n.*	{ fare v., n.	seat n., v.*	sate v.
	{ fair a., n.	sneak n., v.*	snake n.
fleam n.*	flame n.	spear n., v.*	spare v., a.
heat n., v.*	hate n., v.	teal n.*	{ tail n.
lean v., a.	{ lane n.		{ tale n.
	{ lain v. (p.p.)	treat n., v.*	trait n.
lease n., v.*	lace n., v.	veal n.*	{ vale n.
leave n., v.*	lave v.		{ veil n.
meal n.*	{ male n.	weary a.*	wary a.
	{ mail n.	weave v.*	{ wave v., n.
mean v., n., a.*	{ mane n.		{ waive v.
	{ main n., a.	wheat n.*	{ wait v., n.
mere n., a.*	mare n.		{ weight n.

List C

beech n.	beach n.†	need v., n.	knead v.†
breech n.	breach n.†	peek v.	peak n.
creek n.	creak v.	queen n.	quean n.†
lief a.	leaf n.	reed n.	{ read v.
leech n.	leach n., v.†		{ rede v., n.†

Apart from the four main exceptions (*great, break, steak, yea*, which are discussed below), the redistribution of this group from /eː/ to /iː/ was almost complete, i.e. although a choice was available, there must have been a swing towards preference of the model provided by III that extended to most of the words in question. However, in the case of words ending in /r/, there were strong mechanical influences supporting selection of the lower variant. The two opposing factors, mechanical and functional, were thus more evenly balanced, and the resulting selections are of additional interest: for all such words in List A except *shear* (i.e. *bear, tear, wear, pear*) /eː/, or a still lower variant /ɛː/, was retained, with the noteworthy differentiation between /iː/ in *tear* 'lacrima' but /eː, ɛː/ in *tear* 'rend, rent'; but for words in List B where no words in /iː/ had previously existed (*ear, fear, rear, mere, spear*) /iː/ was selected, and the same applies to *shear* in List A, for the chances of conflict with *share* were obviously greater than with *sheer*.

The redistribution of the reflex of ME /ɛː/ has parallels – some only partial – in other English dialects, and is by no means restricted to London or Standard English. But the evidence for the processes of change in other dialects is sketchy and restricted. The changes in Northern English and Scots, though less extensive than in the South and mainly restricted to fronting and raising, seem to have started earlier than those in the South, and this, again, suggests some chronological connection with the loss of unstressed syllables (also earlier in the North); but, if so, initiation and extent of change are not necessarily connected. As regards extent, it is noteworthy that those modern dialects that show less raising also show less merger and subsequent systemic regulation, and that, in general, a majority of dialects show less merger than those of the South-East (the following table gives the main variants only).

	West-morland	W.R. Yorks.	Central Yorks.	Lancs. and S. Yorks.	Lincs.	S.W. and S. Midl.
geese	iː	əɪ	əɪ	iː	iː	iː
reach	ɪə	ɪə	ɪə	ɛɪ	ɪə	eː, eə
spade	ea	ɪa				
tail	eː	eː	ɛə	eː	ɛə	aɪ

Some of these differences in development are no doubt due to local phonetic or systemic variations inherited at the start of the shift. Nevertheless, the comparison suggests that in the London area there were both greater mechanical and social pressures, and a wider range of systemic solutions available, than elsewhere.

There remain for discussion the four well-known exceptions in Standard English, *great, break, steak*, and *yea*. Since the final stage discussed above was a redistribution at phonemic level, such exceptions are to be expected and raise no phonetic problem (6.7, pp. 123–5). In the early eighteenth century there was, for each word in the class, a choice of the two pronunciations, /eː/ and /iː/; and Dr Johnson's reference to both as 'equally defensible by authority'[1] could be interpreted as denoting an absence of social preference for one type or the other. Yet the question 'Why just these four words?' is a reasonable one, and deserves an answer. In the case of *yea*, there are straightforward

[1] *Plan of a Dictionary of the English Language* (1747) 13; cf. Wyld (1921) 212, and (1923) 62.

functional reasons: firstly, it would clash with *ye* at /i:/ (though *ye* was admittedly archaic by this period); secondly, at /e:/ a rhyme with *nay* must by now have been well established, and more frequent than the other (equally possible) habit of contrasting the vowels. But the position with *great, break, steak* is the opposite. On functional grounds, the choice of the attested variants /gri:t, bri:k, sti:k/ would be expected, since their clash with *grate, brake, stake* is, in sum, more serious than the alternative clash with *greet, breek,* and *steek* (the last two have long been Northern only). The countering factor must therefore have been a weighty one, and of a kind other than the strictly functional. That it could have been phonaesthetic is suggested by evidence from not long after the time when /e:/ in these words had attained a clear majority-preference, namely Walker's observation in 1791 that he found /gre:t/ and /bre:k/ more expressive.[1] There is a temptation to dismiss this observation as a subjective ex post facto judgment, but to do so would be unjustified since it is, even today, open to objective verification. The eighteenth-century phonaesthetic values of /-i:k/ and /-e:k/ depended mainly on the monosyllables then current which ended in these sounds, and the OED provides ample evidence of the words and meanings in question:

1. /-i:k/:

(*a*) Verbs denoting the making of noise, usually high-pitched: *creak, speak, squeak, shriek, screak.*

(*b*) Verbs denoting covert action: *peek, seek, sneak* and to some extent *leak* and *reek.*

(*c*) Nouns denoting narrow objects: *beak, creek, peak, streak, meak* 'narrow tool'.

(*d*) 'Derogatory' adjectives or nouns: *bleak, freak, weak, sneak, sleek, gleek* 'gibe', *pique* (earlier *peek, peak*), and perhaps *meek.*

Not classified: *eek, leek, cheek, Greek, week, teak, tweak, wreak.*

2. /-e:k/ (Mn /-eik/):

(*a*) Verbs denoting overt action, without any basic implication of noise: *bake, make, quake, rake, shake, slake, stake, take, wake.*

(*b*) Nouns denoting ordinary objects or animates: *brake, cake, drake, hake, rake, snake, stake,* and perhaps *flake.*

Not classified: *ache* v., *lake, sake, crake* (Northern), *fake* (nineteenth century).

Although there was a choice of /e:/ or /i:/ for words containing the reflex of ME /ɛ:/, it is probable that /i:/ had been accepted into London English for most of the words in the group fairly early in the century, and it is therefore reasonable to assume (as has been done above) that such words were at least beginning to contribute to the phonaesthetic values current when the variants /bre:k/ and /ste:k/ gained ground later. The reason why /e:/ was selected in

[1] Cf. Jespersen (1909) 1 338f.

F

these two words is therefore apparent: the meanings of *break* contrast strongly with 1*a* and *b* but agree with 2*a*, and those of *steak*, similarly, fit 2*b* better than 1*c* and *d*.

If the same procedure is applied to *great*, the following groupings result:

1. /-i:t/ in many cases suggests

(*a*) smallness, daintiness, politeness, dexterity: *cleat, feat* (a. 'dexterous'; n. 'trick'), *fleet* (a. 'nimble'; n. 'creek'), *greet, meet* 'fitting', *neat, pleat*,[1] *sweet, teat, treat*, and perhaps also *seat* n. and *meet* v.

(*b*) natural substances or produce: *beet, gleet, peat, sleet, wheat*, and perhaps *meat*.

Not classified: *feet, fleet* (of ships), *leet, sheet, street; beat, bleat, cheat, eat, heat, neat* n.

2. /-e:t/ (/-eit/) suggests the opposite – size, expanse, tangibility, grossness: *bait, bate* 'strife', *crate, eight, fate, freight, gate, grate, hate, pate, plate, prate, rate, sate, skate, slate, state, straight, weight* (and also, if expanse in time-relation is included, *late, date, wait*).

Not classified: *strait, trait, mate; spate* (Northern till nineteenth century).[2]

Here again, the meanings of *great* are diametrically opposed to those predominant in 1*a*, but closely match those of 2. In this case it might be objected that, of the words listed above, *beat, heat*, and perhaps *meat*, must also have had eighteenth-century variants in /e:/, and, since their meanings approach those of 2, they might have been expected to survive in that form; but these words have already been covered by the functional explanation given above (pp. 146–9), and it is interesting to note that, when two factors are found to have conflicted thus, the various resulting forms still admit of precise explanation. *Beat, heat*, and *meat* would all have coincided, at /e:/, with other words of the same form-classes, whereas the selection of /i:/ averted such a clash in each case:

(i) the verb *beat* would have clashed with the two verbs *bate* and *bait*, but at /i:/ only with the noun *beet* (according to the OED the verb *beet* had become obsolete in literary English before 1500; but its continued obsolescence in other systems is probably significant);

---

[1] The usual eighteenth-century form was *plait* (OED), and the phonaesthetic effect of the /i:/-variant must have been less at that period. The reassertion of /i:/ in this word provides a good example of the combined working of phonaesthetic and functional influences (cf. *plate*, n.).

[2] It is not certain how far the distinction between /i:t/ and /e:t/ extends to polysyllables, since compounding may often change and even reverse the meaning of the simplex. *Complete, conceit* 'fancy', 'trick', *discreet, discrete, receipt* and *replete* fit their class reasonably well; *deceit* and *counterfeit* (in which the preference for /i:/ developed late) may well have joined *cheat* to form a subgroup implying misused dexterity; and a further possible connection might be traced between *repeat* and *bleat*. But there remain many others, such as *relate, delete, defeat* which seem neither to partake of, nor to contribute to, the more obvious phonaesthetic properties of their structures

(ii) *heat* would have clashed with *hate*, but at /i:/ there was no form to occasion a clash;

(iii) the nouns *meat* and *mate* would have clashed, whereas at /i:/ there is less clash with either the verb or the adjective *meet*.

In these cases, therefore, the functional factor outweighed the phonaesthetic. But in the case of *great* (adj.) and *grate* (noun and verb) there was no clash at the level of form-class, and, since the phonaesthetic factor was especially strong here, it far outweighed the weaker functional one.

It is in dealing with such a complex as this that the 'all-or-nothing' fallacy appears at its most misleading. It would inhibit us from recognising the two conflicting pressures, from weighing their relative potencies, and from disentangling their various seams of influence.

8 Dimensions of study

8.1 Introductory

Although an attempt was made above to show that all linguistic change can be accommodated within a single framework, this is not to deny that great variety of change can exist within it. Pressures towards change can be strong or weak (5.5, p. 80), and for this reason alone, some changes can be expected to take place over a limited period (say, fifty years), whereas others may be more protracted and last for anything up to a millennium. Still further variations follow from the complexity of conflicting pressures.

Secondly, the scholar's viewpoint will to some extent depend on where he decides to make the 'cut' from the total history. In lexis, many cases of selection form part of a continual process of loss and replacement (with accompanying resolution of ambiguities), and for this process it is often impracticable or unnecessary to make any 'cut' at all.[1] In other cases, he may be guided by objective reasons (e.g. the absence of any apparent prelude or sequel, in a well-documented period of the language) to the points he chooses for the start or end of a change. The nature of the evidence (or lack of it) may limit the study of a change either in time or scope, so that it turns out to be restricted, say, to a single subsystem over a long period, or to all subsystems over a shorter period.

In addition to this problem, there is a continual danger of adopting a subjective viewpoint to define extent of change. Labels like 'inherent tendencies', 'trends', and 'drifts' have frequently been used in the past to describe a series of changes that took place over long periods, but it is not always obvious from the evidence that the series must be explained as due to some

---

[1] The history of adjustments in English spelling since *c.* 1400 has been largely of this type. Firstly the intake of symbols has been of the same haphazard and arbitrary nature as parts of the lexical intake; e.g. the digraph *ie*, which is partly due to introduction in French words like *chief, piece* and partly from South-Eastern dialect orthographies, as in *thief, lief*, was not introduced with any consistency in the fifteenth century, and, functionally, was rendered largely superfluous when *ea* was introduced in the sixteenth century, i.e. its use results purely from availability. Secondly, the differentiations introduced by printers have been parallel – though at a more artificial level – to the normal processes of semantic differentiation, or, where recondite spellings were adopted, to the processes of functional selection; but the process has been a gradual accretion, as may be seen from some of the systemically uneconomical improvisations that have become accepted, e.g. *whole* (cf. *hole*), *ghost* (cf. *gost* 'goest'), *tongue* (cf. *tongs*, but also the sixteenth-century spelling *tung* 'tongue').

continuous factor of this kind. It is suggested that because human communication is usually purposeful, therefore the changes in it must be the result of some overall purpose.[1] But, although it is probably true that the environmentally inherited bases of articulation may bring about a series of related phonetic changes that give the appearance of a 'tendency', this does not mean that every such series is to be explained as due to the same single and unidirectional pressure. On the contrary, we must start from the assumptions that (*a*) the range of actual variation is extremely wide, and (*b*) systemic regulation is an essentially *ad hoc* process. If the result appears to show a trend or tendency over a long period, this need mean only that the same pressures, though weak in each minor system, have existed continuously on a wide front of minor systems. It may then appear that each small innovation or regulation 'prepares the way' for further ones in the same direction, but it does not do so in any strictly teleological sense; each is essentially *ad hoc*, and determined by the pressures existing in the given *état de langue*.

8.2   *Ad hoc* nature of systemic regulation

This may be demonstrated by details from the largest grammatical restructuring known in the history of most European languages – the so-called change from synthetic to analytic structure. In English, it comprised the loss of a majority of the original inflectional endings, the replacement of certain pronominal forms, and the growth of a fixed word order, and of new oppositions to express a number of marginal grammatical categories, such as definite/indefinite (articles), animate/inanimate (pronominal system), aspect and modality (verbal system). It is true that most of these changes appear gradually in the texts, with a kernel of the more radical transitions in those of the ME period; but the fluctuating *ad hoc* nature of extension and regulation during this period can be seen from some typical minor developments:

(i) *Case and gender*. In the late Old English and early Middle English periods, the syncretism of inflectional endings resulted in a gradual regrouping and simplification of noun declensions and, to a lesser extent, of the declensions of preceding attributive words (demonstratives, adjectives). Since the complex system of grammatical gender depended on the survival of distinct inflections (as in Latin) or of preceding articles (as in French), it lost paradigmatic support. The best known concomitant of this is the extension of the phonetically heaviest inflections -*es* and -*as* for the marking of genitive case and plural number in almost all nouns, irrespective of gender. But it is often overlooked that in texts from the Anglian area this realignment was carried further. Two other phonetically heavy inflections, -*ne* (acc. sg. masc.) and -*re* (dat. sg. fem.)

[1] Vachek p. 18.

had frequent currency in the spoken chain, and, whereas in Southern texts they occasionally remained as archaic survivals of grammatical gender that happened also to mark case, in Anglian texts they were realigned, as case markers only, for use with pre-modifiers of nouns of originally different gender, e.g. (see fig. 10) *ðerh allne woruld* (Durham Ritual). That such collocations cannot indicate 'gender change' is shown by predictable variation within the same paradigms, e.g. *on þone mynstre* but *to þære mynstre* (Peterborough Chronicle), *hæfden muchelne care* but *mid muchelere care* (Laȝamon A).[1] If these extensions had continued, they would have provided a remodelled paradigm for pre-modifiers, with distinctive inflectional endings throughout.

Original distribution of gender and case		
	Masc.	Fem.	Neut.
Accusative	-ne ────────▶		────────▶
Genitive	-es ──────▶	◀──────	-es
Dative	◀────── -re	────────▶	

Fig. 10. Incipient restructuring in early Middle English of originally ambivalent case- and gender-forms
Arrows mark the spread of forms in case-function only

But meanwhile a different type of regulation was taking place on a wider front: the prevalence of endingless forms, to some extent in verbs as well as in nouns and adjectives, resulted in the regular use of the fixed word-order *Subject – Predicate – Complement*, and the earlier solution, via a remodelled paradigm for pre-modifiers, was thus rendered superfluous. Such a conflict of solutions suggests that both were *ad hoc* and that no teleological drive is involved; the solution that had wider application, in a limited succession of *états de langue*, prevailed.

(ii) *Pronominal system*. Similar conflicts are to be seen in the development of various pronominal subsystems (demonstrative and deictic modifiers, relative and indefinite pronouns). Here again, as with gender and case, there was some shifting of the same forms between different functions, so that they have to be considered together. A new system of determiners resulted from the realignment of the various forms of the OE demonstratives *se*, *seo*, *þæt*, and

---

[1] See C. Jones, *Grammatical Gender in Late Old English and Early Middle English* (B.Litt. thesis, Glasgow, 1964), and *ES* 48 (1967) 97–111 and 289–305.

þes, þeos, þis to the pattern þe/þis–þise/þat–þo(s); and as a result of systemic pressure to complete that pattern, the use of nouns without determiners decreased, and the indefinite article a(n) was differentiated from *one*. At the same time the relative þe was replaced by þat (cf. 5.6, p. 86), in spite of the fact that this particle (apart from its stressed demonstrative use) already performed numerous other functions as a conjunction and clause connective, e.g. causal, final, consecutive, temporal. It was not till later in Middle English that part of the relative function of þat was taken over by the new marked forms *which, who*; at this point, overt expression of the marginal category animate/inanimate was achieved, and has since been stabilised in usage. The point of interest here is that, quite early in the processes just described, temporary marking of the same distinction had existed in various dialects, in two different ways: (*a*) in late Old Northumbrian (the *Lindisfarne Gospels*) the originally masculine and feminine forms of determiners are used to modify animates, while the originally neuter forms are used for inanimates; (*b*) in Midland texts in early Middle English, there is a distinction between the relative pronouns þe and þat whereby þe is used when the antecedent is animate, while þat is used mainly (with some further distinctions in distribution according to text) when the antecedent is inanimate.[1] Yet, when compared with the main changes in system referred to above, these special minor systems are seen to have been transitional only, and at least partly dependent on the forms available at the time; their existence conflicted with greater systemic pressures working in a different direction, which were to delay the introduction of a distinction between animate and inanimate till some centuries later (cf. 5.6).

8.3 Long-term change

For the above examples, it could be argued that it is only the *rejected* solutions that were *ad hoc*, and that the larger patterns of change that were accepted over longer periods are still to be regarded as forming part of an overall plan or 'purpose'. To complete the argument advanced above (8.2), it is necessary to show next that the difference is merely one of scale, and that the processes and pressures operating in long-term change are essentially the same. As an example we may take the gradual elimination of /x/ and /ɣ/ from English.

The beginning of this change is common to all Germanic languages, and consists of a simplificatory mechanical change (loss of friction) from [x] to [h] when in initial position. But subsequent developments varied greatly in different branches of Germanic, and show that the assumption of some basic or continuous tendency towards weak articulation of these consonants is unjustified. The elimination was quickest in early Norse, mainly as a result

[1] McIntosh (1947–8).

of a large group of mechanical consonant simplifications which were not limited to /x/, e.g. */axto/ > *átta* (cf. */genk/ > *gekk*), /x/ occurring later only marginally, as in *sagt, dags*, and initial *hv-* (> dialectal /kv-/). In High German, on the other hand, /x/ survived because its distribution was reinforced by words like *suohhen* 'seek' with medial /x/ from /k/ by the Second Consonant Shift; and in Dutch, the survival as a fricative (even in initial position) of Gmc. /ɣ/ has similarly supported the survival of /x/ (with eventual merger of the two). In Old English itself, the fact that [x] and [h] were apparently treated as a single phoneme and both written as *h* in the standard orthographies cannot be held to show that the remaining [x] was close to [h] phonetically, for there are a number of texts where the two are separated, [x] being expressed by *c, ch*, or by the *g*-rune as in *fegtaþ* on the Franks Casket, and by the *eoh*-rune on the Ruthwell and Urswick inscriptions.[1]

The change of initial [x] to [h], therefore, must be taken as applying to its own era only; it has no relevance for subsequent changes to the remaining [x], or to /ɣ/, except in so far as the distribution thus set up was a changed one which would form part of the balance in any later changes in distribution. The next changes were again mechanical in origin: the front allophones of /ɣ/ joined /j/ by split and merger (3.6, p. 40), intervocalic /x/ was lost (Corpus Gloss *tahae*, West Saxon *tā* 'toe'), and, by devoicing of /ɣ/, the opposition of final /ɣ/ and /x/ was neutralised (*sloh* and *slog* 'struck').

The first sign that these consonants are no longer fully integrated appears in late OE. [h] and [x] must by now have separated, so that in initial position there was no /x–ɣ/ opposition; /ɣ/ had [g] allophones in medial and final positions (e.g. *þing, singan, dogga*), but had lost part of its fricative distribution through the merger of front allophones with /j/. In the distributions then existing, there were no oppositions of voice in the fricative series /f, θ, x, s/, but they existed in the plosive series /p, b, t, d, k/ with a gap opposite /k/ that was only marginally filled by the [g]- allophone of /ɣ/. There would therefore be systemic pressure to remedy the restricted distribution of [g]. The late OE change of initial [ɣ] to [g] (as in *god, guma, græs*) is thus the first change in the process that can be regarded as primarily systemic. But it was not 'predestined'. The balance in its favour had probably been tipped by the merger of [ǵ] and /j/, which is shown to have been mechanical by the parallel split of /k/ to /k/ and /tʃ/. This is suggested by comparison with Low Franconian, where no such palatalisations took place, and initial /ɣ/ remained in the fricative series, appearing as either [x] or [ɣ] in modern Dutch and Flemish.

By the beginning of the ME period, /x, ɣ/ were decidedly deficient in distribution: /x/ occurred only medially before /t/ or finally, as in *briht*

[1] A. Campbell, *Old English Grammar* § 57.3; B. Dickins and A. S. C. Ross, *The Dream of the Rood* p. 8 n.

'bright', *inoh* 'enough', or, more rarely, as a long consonant (*lauhwen* 'laugh'), and /ɣ/ only intervocalically or after *l* and *r*, as in *dahen, daʒes* 'days', *folʒen* 'follow'. They were thus in complementary distribution; a great variety of symbols is used for them (ʒ, *h, ʒh, g, gh, ch*) but consistent ME texts use the same symbol for both, and this suggests that they merged during the ME period. There was no possibility that they could join the new series of voiced and voiceless fricatives (/f, v, θ, ð, s, z/) but they could have survived as a single phoneme of deficient distribution.

Meanwhile, the new system of Middle English diphthongs was arising, in the earliest instances from the late OE combination of front vowel + /j/, as in *dæg* > *dai*, later from combination of vowel + /w/ and /ɣ/, e.g. *deaw* > *dew*, *dragan* > *drawe(n)*. Factors to be considered here are:

(i) the diphthongs /ɑɪ, ɑʊ, ɔʊ, oʊ, ɛʊ, eʊ/ all arose from variants of mechanical origin with vocalisation of [j, w, ɣ];

(ii) with the disappearance of the Old English diphthongs, there was space for the new diphthongs in the system;

(iii) most of them were reinforced by words from Old French containing diphthongs that could be identified with them, and, indeed, the existence of bilingualism throughout the early Middle English period suggests that the systemic change itself could have been partly of foreign origin;

(iv) shortly after their establishment from these two sources, they were amplified from others in the early thirteenth century, notably by the development of glides before [x], as in *tauʒte, brouʒte*.

To treat all these factors as merely incidental to the poor integration of /x/ would be out of proportion; it is the latter that must be regarded as incidental. The narrower view, that [ɣ] happened merely to be replaced by /w/ (as in *folwen*) because of poor integration at a time when these wider changes were in train, is less satisfactory. However, the last changes leading to the complete elimination of /x/ are evidently of this straightforward regulatory type: before /t/, as in *right, brought, daughter*, it was lost by simplificatory change, and also finally, in words like *high* and *bough*, through replacement by originally disyllabic forms; and elsewhere in final position it was replaced by /f/, e.g. *enough, cough*.

The controversy over whether this last change was by gradual or discrete stages has been considerable,[1] but needlessly so. All the views apply at their proper levels, and, as argued in chapters 6 and 7, the following combination may be suggested: (*a*) widespread existence in the spoken chain of a labialised variant [xʷ],[2] and sporadic development, by infinitesimal stages, to [ɸ];

---

[1] Dieth p. 290f.

[2] This is a conditioned change of an assimilatory type (2.3). The labialisation arises in final position when lip-closure is anticipated before a pause (a more obvious case is *nope* 'no').

(*b*) systemic pressure for replacement of a rare voiceless fricative phoneme by a common one; (*c*) replacement, in its limited areas of occurrence, of [ɸ] by /f/, and, elsewhere, the straightforward replacement of [x] or [xʷ] by /f/ by spread as a discrete stage. /x/ survives as a marginal phoneme in Scots, and, while we need not go as far as Trnka[1] in calling it a foreign phonological feature, it seems likely that its survival there in deficient distribution is due to support from Gaelic.

The above account has attempted to show that the series of changes leading to the elimination of original /x/ and /ɣ/ were of different types and origins. In some, restriction of one or other of these phonemes is central, in others it is merely incidental. In German and Dutch, other pressures interfered and led to the opposite result. Certainly, in English and Norse, some consistency can be traced, but it is by no means clear that it should be characterised as 'a manifestation of a purposeful activity of the language community'.[2] The consistency follows naturally from the normal processes of mechanical change and systemic regulation. When an established pattern loses support, initially from non-systemic causes, the systemic regulation happens to consist of continued change in the same direction. But this is pure coincidence; each stage of change is *ad hoc*, and merely reflects the decreased lack of support for the pattern amongst all other pressures existing in the *état de langue* in which the stage appears.

8.4   Patterns of growth and replacement

As with the loss of older patterns, so with the growth of new ones, and the replacement of one pattern by another. The beginnings of a pattern may exist through sheer coincidence, and the earliest accretions to it may be equally haphazard, but if there is a place for it in the system, it may gather support. Some examples of growth of minor patterns were mentioned in chapters 3 and 5 in the discussion of phonaesthemes, but the same process may be seen in wider spheres of grammar and lexis. Noticeable in the Middle and Early Modern periods is the start of a new pattern of quantitative gradation in the verb, reminiscent of, though unconnected with, the original Indo-European system which had been eliminated in Primitive Germanic by the shift of stress. Its origins were purely mechanical: the /dd/ that arose in the preterites of weak verbs (OE *lǣdan, lǣdde*) and the /t/ that had developed in those with stems ending in a voiceless consonant (OE *cēpan, cēpte*) both led to shortening of the root vowel. There was thus in Middle English a small nucleus of verbs with a quantitative distinction of tense that had developed by phonetic accident – those that yielded (with loss of /-ə/) the modern *lead–led, keep–kept, meet–met, hide–hid, feed–fed, bleed–bled*, etc. This was then extended, as a

[1] In Abercrombie (1964) 186.   [2] Vachek p. 18.

formative principle, to two other types of verb. Firstly, there were a number of strong verbs in which the qualitative distinctions on which vowel-gradation depends had been eliminated or lessened by sound-change (cf. pp. 170ff below): in class VII (OE ē – ē(o)) *sleep, weep* and *leap*, and in class II (OE ēo – ēa) *creep, flee, cleave* 'split' and *shoot*. These joined the weak conjugation, and eventually preterites with short vowel became predominant, though *cleave* and *flee* do not belong to the original phonetic grouping. The pattern was also extended to a number of weak verbs with root ending in a voiced consonant, so that e.g. *deme(n)* 'deem' and *reue(n)* 'reave' occurred with both types of preterite, viz. *demed* and *dempt(e)*, *reued(e)* and *raft(e)*, *reft(e)*. In these verbs, a further distinction appears. The selection of one or other preterite form in later English seems to have depended to some extent on the lexical aspect of the verb as well as on tense. If a terminate or point-action meaning was required for a majority of its occurrences in the preterite, the short vowel was preferred, whereas in the fewer cases where state or duration of action predominated, the long vowel was preserved. Thus *dealt, knelt, felt, heard, leant, left, reft, lost, shod, said*, and probably also *dreamt* and *meant*, compared with *seemed, deemed, teemed, healed, feared, reared, believed*, and *craved*.[1] Again, the basis for these extensions must have been the accident that, in some verbs where a short vowel had been developed phonetically, it was phonaesthetically suited for the expression of point-action (e.g. *met, hid, sped, leapt, swept, shot*).

It is not surprising that this pattern was never completed, for there are so many verbs that constantly occur in both types of meaning and context that extensive changes of form (e.g. doublets for many verbs) would have been needed. The possibility is shown by the history of the verb *deem*: its meanings 'judge', 'sentence', 'condemn' all became obsolete around 1600, and it can hardly be coincidence that *dempt* went out of use shortly after, while *deemed* was preferred for the surviving meanings 'think', 'consider'; similar distinctions attach to the surviving pairs *chided* and *chid, pleaded* and *pled*. But there were strong opposing pressures: some early short forms for primarily durative verbs were well established (e.g. *bled, kept, slept*), and a short variant was less likely to be selected for derivative verbs like *gleam* and *seal* where the long form was reinforced by that of the noun. That some preference for short variants in the preterite has continued throughout is shown by *light–lit*, which was still regarded as vulgar in the eighteenth century,[2] and the modern dialects supply further examples belonging to the point-action or terminate category: *save–seft, heat–het, cheat–chet, reach–rech, beat–bet* (it seems prob-

---

[1] *Crave* is originally a class II weak verb, but class II verbs were not excluded from the other development: cf. *reft* and *lost*. That *seethed*, not **sed(de)*, was the formation used for the past tense of *seethe* is also relevant here.

[2] Jespersen (1909–) VI 46.

able that the standard form would have been *bet*, not *beat*, were it not for the clash with the preterite *bet* 'wagered', for which cf. below).[1] It is shown also, in a more negative way, by the fact that, for verbs of this meaning with root ending in /d, t/, disyllabic variants have been rejected in spite of formal coincidence with the present: the contrasts appear by comparison of (i) the 'invariables' *burst, cast, cost, cut, hit, hurt, put, rid, set, shed, shut, spread, thrust*, and (ii) the disyllabic forms *shredded, dreaded, sweated, roasted, treated*, and (iii) formal distinction between point-action and durative/iterative in the doublets *bet* and *betted, knit* and *knitted, wet* and *wetted*.[2]

In the developing standard language, selections of short forms were likely to be made in periods when the choice of variants exceeded that of other periods. This applies to the sixteenth century, when – for reasons explained below (p. 171) – variants for the preterite increased and were in competition, among them further short forms in the strong verbs of class I, e.g. *write–writ, rise–ris, glide–glid*. These were derived from the original past plural or past participle, but also matched the already existing weak type *hide/hid*. Here again, the ultimate selection shows some separation of point-action and durative verbs: *bite/bit* and *slide/slid* joined the point-action group, and are distinguished from the other verbs of the same class, the majority of which are primarily durative (*abide–abode, drive–drove, ride–rode, stride–strode, thrive–throve/thrived, write–wrote*, and cf. *glide–glided/glode, writhe–writhed*). It is noteworthy that *strike–struck* and *shine–shone* have shortened preterites of other origin, and, apart from (*a)rise* – (*a)rose* (which is fairly evenly distributed over both meanings), this leaves only *smite, rive*, and perhaps *shrive* as exceptions to the pattern in this class of verbs.

However sporadic and incomplete, this development in certain preterite forms must be considered as part of a wider change, for the selection of short or long variants according to meaning can also be traced in the present and infinitive forms of many verbs. It is seen most clearly in verbs that originally belonged to the same class and had comparable phonetic structures: *knead* (OE *cnedan*) but *tread* (OE *tredan*); *make, quake* (OE *macian, cwacian*) but *crack* (OE *cracian*); *scrape* (OE *scrapian*) but *lap* (OE *lapian*). The short forms are often attributed to separate verbs with 'expressive gemination', whether evidenced in Old or Middle English, or merely inferred from continental cognates, e.g. *slit* is from ME *slitte*, 'obscurely related to OE *slītan*' (OED);

---

[1] Wright (1905) §§ 425, 428.
[2] The existence of such aspectual distinctions in modern written English is convincingly demonstrated by Quirk (1970). He adopts a partly different criterion – the endings *-ed* and *-t* in the preterite and past part. of the verbs *burn, dream, kneel, lean, leap, learn, smell, spill*, and *spoil*; and he shows, by means of rigorous 'forced-choice' selection tests, that *-t* co-occurs more often with point-action, *-ed* with durative aspect. As Quirk rightly observes, the greatest support for forms in *-t* arises – for both phonetic and functional reasons – in the past participle.

sup (OE *sūpan*) appears with gemination in ONhb. *suppa*, but the short vowel could have originated in the past participle, as also probably in the case of *shove* (OE *scūfan*) and *suck* (OE *sūcan*). Other sources are (i) a different type of analogy, as in *lock* (OE *lūcan*), influenced by the noun *lock* as well as the OE p.p. *locen*, (ii) a different verb of similar form, as seen in the replacement of OE *bēodan* by *biddan*, or (iii) later shortenings of mechanical origin, especially before /-d, -t/. But whatever the origin, it is the replacement of the older long forms by shorter forms that is remarkable; one need only compare OED entries like *gripe* and *grip*, *slite* and *slit*, *dreep* and *drip*, *crake* and *crack*, *lape* and *lap*, *louk* and *lock* to see the process that has been at work.

Within each separate phonaestheme, the distinction was reinforced by numerous new formations. To take only one, the verbs *clap*, *flap*, *rap*, *slap*, *swap*, and *wap* are all first evidenced in the fourteenth century; some have cognates, but the OED regards them all as 'probably onomatopoeic in origin'. Similarly, the pattern seems to have played some part in the more general processes of lexical replacement: in point-action contexts, the older *slay*, *smite*, *strike* have been partly replaced by *hit* (ON *hitta*), and similarly *snithe* and *carve* (OE *sniðan*, *ceorfan* and compounds) have given place to *cut* (ME *kutte*, *kitte*, *kette* of obscure origin). Naturally, the present meaning sometimes conflicts with the distinction, but this need not mean that the verb is a wholly unexplained exception. For example, the selection of *stick* in preference to *steek* does not agree with its present meaning 'adhere', but that selection was made when the predominant meaning of the verb was still 'stab'; its semantic extension to 'adhere' took place later, when the homonymic clash of *cleave* 'adhere' and *cleave* 'split' had increased and caused a vacant slot (cf. 8.6, p. 170 below).

To return now to the problem of assessment: is this wide, though incomplete, development to be dismissed as merely arbitrary, or was there a place in the system for it, that fostered its growth? Within the total system, the distinctions it marks are admittedly secondary; but that is no reason for considering it only in isolation, and it can in fact be shown to belong to a much larger pattern of replacement. In Old English, the distinction between punctual and durative was one of a number that were expounded, in a wholly different way, by the transparent word-forming system of prefixation. This system could also express completive and intensive functions, and the proportions of each varied from verb to verb. Examples are *sittan* 'sit' – *gesittan* 'sit down', *hieran* 'obey' – *gehieran* 'hear', *brecan* 'break' – *abrecan* 'smash, destroy', *slean* 'strike' – *ofslean* 'kill', *bærnan* 'burn' – *forbærnan* 'burn up', *ceorfan* 'carve' – *toceorfan* 'cut (up)'. The obsolescence of this system is a major example of the combined working of push- and drag-chain processes of replacement. The loss of verbal prefixes was due partly to their lack of stress but, in the North and Midlands, the immediate model for the loss was provided by Old Norse (the Germanic system of prefixation had been lost early in Norse as a result of radical changes in rhythm; cf. 5.6, p. 84f). Those with greater phonetic substance (*to-, for-*) remained productive till Chaucer's time, but the rest, even where they survived, underwent considerable weakening of information-content (cf. *abide, awake*); and in the case of the commonest (OE *ge-*, ME *y-*) extension and grammaticisation appear to have contributed to this weakening (cf. 4.4, p. 59f). This drag-chain pressure was supported by a push-chain pressure – the availability of new words from Norse and French which could take the place of the prefixed verb in each pair, e.g. OE *þencan – aþencan* replaced by *think – devise*. It was usually the more 'expressive' functions of the prefixed verb (whether intensive, completive, or punctual) that were taken over by the new words, e.g. *rive, sling, thrust* (from Norse) and *rob, catch* 'seize', *destroy* (from French) replaced OE forms that would usually have been prefixed. The opposite, as seen in OE *winnan – gewinnan* replaced by *strive* (from French) – *win* (OE *gewinnan*), was rarer. But whichever member was replaced, once the correlations of a number of pairs had been disrupted in this way, the drag-chain pressures were in turn increased: the formative pattern for the Old English system of prefixation waned, and a gap was left in the lexical system as a whole. The importance of drag-chain influences is shown by the fact that versions of some earlier Middle English works, whether because of their dialect or date, do not always show replacements for the prefixes, e.g. *breke, berne, hew* where the version that is probably nearer the original has *tobreke, forberne, tohew*.[1] Usually, however, such comparisons show that the prefixes were being gradually replaced from various sources, of which the following are the more prominent:

(i) Adverbs like *away, down, out, up* had been used in Old English to reinforce prefixed verbs in special contexts, but in early Middle English the combination verb + adverb becomes much commoner, and one adverb, *up*, gradually takes on a purely completive function. This sense was at first incidental in phrases like *fill up, build up, grow up*, but it was extended to verbs where the direction 'upwards' was not inappropriate (*eat/drink/burn/ waken up*: these coincide with Norse usage). Finally, with verbs like *break* and *cut*, it becomes a pure and otherwise colourless completive. In Middle English literature it is commonest in alliterative poetry, e.g. with *bind, burn, dry, fasten, knit, waken, wipe*, in the *Destruction of Troy*; but its use in medical and cookery recipes suggests that it was becoming commoner still in colloquial register (examples occur with the verbs *fry, seethe, heal, temper, season* and *colour*).[2]

---

[1] Examples of such differences are to be found in the different manuscripts of *Laȝamon* and *King Horn*.
[2] E.g. in the BM MSS Sloane 442 and 3160, Harley 1735, Add. 18216, in MS Bodley 177, and in the Royal Library Stockholm MS x 90.

(ii) There is a noticeable increase in the use of fixed phrases as completives or intensives, as *hew to pieces, burn to ashes, rend to clouts, ding to dust, clean forget,* as well as a more general increase in the use of adverbs like *wel, fast(e).*

(iii) For point-action, there is the great increase in new verbs of both foreign and native origin, especially those with short vowels in the infinitive, like *put, push, crush, shunt* (cf. *cut, hit, kill, slap,* etc. discussed above).

It is in this context that the revival of quantitative gradation, described above, must be considered. It was merely *one* of the consequences of the disruption of Germanic processes of word-formation. There was no one-for-one correspondence in the types of replacement, which were of diverse origins. Their heterogeneity, as well as the time-lag in their appearance, once again emphasises the makeshift nature of expedients adopted for regulation. But seen in their perspective as replacements, they confirm the view, suggested above, that chance patterns of arbitrary origins may extend to fill a place that exists for them in the system.

8.5 Predominance of extralinguistic factor

In contrast to the processes of gradual obsolescence and growth that have just been discussed, the effects of extralinguistic influences may often appear with greater suddenness. For studying past periods of the language, the researcher's main task will be to find a convincing correlation between the linguistic and historical evidences.

A typical example is provided by the early history of the London dialect. The earliest evidence is restricted, consisting as it does of street-names in twelfth-century Latin documents, but, so far as it goes, it is a strong indication of an Essex-type dialect (e.g. *Fan* 'fen', *Strat(e)* 'street'). This is supported by the first piece of continuous text (the sole surviving example from the thirteenth century) – the English Proclamation of Henry III from 1258,[1] in which the forms *ʒew* 'you' *þan/þo ilche* 'the same', *ænde* 'end', *oa-* spellings as reflexes of OE *ā*, and the distinction between the reflexes of late OE *ǣ* (*ilærde, æhc, ræde-*) and *ēa* (*healden, deadliche, ʒeare*) all point in the same direction. But other forms in this text suggest that the London dialect should not, even at this early period, be regarded as divided into two distinct types;[2] the presence, in the same text, of *beoþ* 'are' (not *bieþ*), *heo* 'they' (not *hy*) and *kuneriche,* suggests that this dialect had some correspondence with those of Middlesex and Surrey as well as with that of Essex, though whether through

---

[1] Forms quoted are from the PRO text. Those of the Bodleian text are less outstanding, but suggest the same general conclusion.

[2] For this view see Wyld (1927) 140ff, and B. A. Mackenzie, *The Early London Dialect* (Oxford, 1928). It is invalidated by their acceptance of the *Lambeth Homilies* (a West Midland text) as evidence for their 'Middlesex type'.

standardisation or merely as a concomitant of its geographical position is harder to determine.

It has long been recognised[1] that the London dialect changed in character from a Southern to a more Midland dialect between 1258 and the late fourteenth-century stage to be seen in the next localised documents and in the language of Chaucer; and in view of the lapse of some 130 years this is not wholly surprising. What is surprising is the nature of the intervening evidence. It consists of a group of texts which, on both linguistic and more general grounds, must be considered as very probable evidence for the London dialect. According to the lesser differences in the language of the scribes, the texts may be divided as follows:

1. The main hand in the Auchinleck MS.[2]
2. The Early English Prose Psalter in BM Add. MS 17376.[3]
3. BM MS Harley 5085: *The Mirror* (Sermons).[4]
4. Glasgow Hunterian MS 250 of the same work.[5]
5. Three manuscripts in the hand of a single scribe: Magdalene College Cambridge, Pepys 2498,[6] Bodl. Laud Misc. 622[6] and BM Harley 874.[4]
6. Hand 3 of the Auchinleck MS.[7]
7. MS St John's College Cambridge 256.[4]

All these texts are written in a reasonably consistent orthography, and there is no reason for doubting their reliability for dialect purposes. From the accompanying table (which lists the Chaucerian forms for comparison) it can be seen that they contain a combination of features not found elsewhere in Middle English, and yet there are sufficient differences between them to show that they are not all of precisely the same origin. One form in particular, *þat i(l)che*, provides a link with the Proclamation of Henry III, and otherwise the combination is again an amalgam that cannot easily be fitted elsewhere than the London region: e.g. *þerwhiles þat* 'while' is otherwise mainly Kentish, *þat i(l)che* mainly Essex or East Anglian. The amalgam is extended in different texts, e.g. (1) combines Kentish *hye* 'she' with non-Kentish forms like *wald* 'would', *warld* 'world'; and all the texts contain at least traces of the Essex

---

[1] L. Morsbach, *Ursprung der neuenglischen Schriftsprache* (Heilbronn, 1888) 161; Luick § 36; Wyld (1921) 50–3.

[2] Hand 1 in the nomenclature of A. J. Bliss, *Speculum* XXVI (1951) 652–8.

[3] Ed. K. D. Bülbring, EETS OS 97.

[4] Microfilm, Edinburgh University Library.

[5] The first twelve sermons have been edited by T. G. Duncan (Oxford University B.Litt. thesis, 1965).

[6] Large published portions are available in *The Pepysian Gospel Harmony*, ed. M. Goates, EETS OS 157; *The Recluse*, ed. J. Påhlsson, Lund, 1918; *Kyng Alisaunder*, ed. G. V. Smithers, EETS OS 227.

[7] The principal works in this hand are *The Seven Sages, Floris and Blauncheflur, Sir Degare*, and *The Assumption of the Virgin*.

Some outstanding features of pre-Chaucerian fourteenth-century texts, probably written in the London area, compared with corresponding Chaucerian forms

Chaucer	1 Auchinleck MS, main hand	2 Early English Prose Psalter	3 BM MS The Mirror	4 Glasgow MS The Mirror	5 Three MSS in one hand	6 Auchinleck MS, hand 3	7 St John's College MS
thilke, that ilk	þat ich	þat ich	þat ich(e)	þat ilke (? þat iche)	þat ilch(e)	þat ilche (ich)	þat iche
nat (noght)	nouȝt, no	nouȝt	nouȝt	nouȝt	nouȝth, no	nowt	nouȝt
old(e)	eld, old	eld	eld(e)	eld, old	elde	eld(e)	elde
-yng)	-and (-ende, inde)	-and (-aund, -end, -yng)	-ande (-inge)	-and(e)	-ande, -ynge (-ende)	-and (-ende, ind)	-ande
dide	dede	dide (dede)	did (dede)	dede (did)	dude	dede (dide)	dede
saugh	seiȝe, seyȝe	seiȝ (saiȝ)	seiȝe	seiȝ(e)	seiȝ	segh(ȝ)	seȝ, sei
they	þai, hye	hij	hij	hij, he (þei, pay, þai)	hij	þai (hi, þei)	hij (þei, pay)
tho(u)gh	þei	þeȝ	þeiȝe	þeiȝe (þouȝ)	þeiȝ	þai, þei (þough, þouȝ)	þow, þei
eche	ich(a)	ich(a) (vch)	ich(e)	ech, ich	vche	ech(e) (-a)	ech(a)
muche(l), moche	miche(l)	michel (mechel)	michel, -il	michel, muchel	mychel	moche(l), muche	moche(l), miche(l)
wol(e), wil(le)	wil	wil	wil	wil	wil	wil(le)	wil(le), wol(le)
whil	(þer)while(s)	þerwhyles þat	þerwhiles (þat)	whiles þat, whil(e) þat	(þer) whiles, while	(þer) while	þerwhiles, wil(es)
ageyns, ayeyns	oȝain(es), oȝains	oȝain(s)	oȝein(e)(s)	aȝe(i)n(es), oȝain(es)	aȝeins	aȝen	aȝain(s) (oȝein)
neither	noiþer	noiþer	noþer	no(i)þer, noyþer	noiþer	neiþer, noþer	neyþer
sholde	schuld (schold)	shuld	schuld(e)	schuld (schul, schud)	schulde	(s)scholde (sschulde)	scholde
world	warld (werld, world)	worl(e)d (werld)	world, werld	world	werlde	werld	werld, world (worlde)
after	after	efter	efter	efter, after	after	after	after
thurgh	thurth	þurȝ	þoru	þurth(ȝ), þurȝt(h), þurȝ(h)	þorowȝ	þourgh	þorw

and early London *ā* as in *lade* 'lead'. In view of the great variety of their contents, both secular and religious, the inevitable conclusion is that they represent an incipient standard of the London region.[1]

But this conclusion is forced on us in spite of the problems that remain. Firstly, certain forms in these texts are unexpected when considered both geographically and in relation to what precedes and follows them. The most outstanding is *-and(e)*, the main form for the present participle in all the texts (beside rarer *-ind(e)*, *-ende*, *-ynge*), and this contrasts with *-inde* in the Proclamation and *-ynge* in Chaucer; a majority show *werld* or *warld* 'world' as their main form, and *michel*, *schuld*, and *ich* 'each', rather than the expected *moche(l)/muche(l)*, *scholde* and *ech*. This combination of unexpected features did not exist in any area immediately adjoining London; the nearest area where such a combination was regular was Norfolk, and to a lesser extent Suffolk.[2]

Secondly, the dating of these texts on palaeographical grounds ranges from 1330 to 1380, and this suggests that the change during the period between 1258 and the Chaucerian English of 1380 onwards was by no means a gradual one: there must have been East Anglian influences in the intervening period, and the effects of these continue to appear in the texts right up to *c.* 1380, when they are suddenly replaced by the type of language found in Chaucerian MSS and contemporary documents. This replacement consists to a small extent of forms common in the South or South-East (e.g. *nat* 'not', *sholde*) but to a much larger extent of typically Midland forms (*old(e)*, *dide*, *saugh*, *whil*, *ageyns/ayeyns*, *neither*) or of forms common to both the Midlands and the South (*þilke*, *-yng*, *eche*, *muche(l)/moche(l)*, *wol(e)*, *world*). This spread of Midland features to London appears to have continued into the fifteenth century: when London English was adopted (*c.* 1430) instead of French and Latin for the purposes of official business, further replacements appear in the great quantity of government documents now written in English (the more outstanding are tabulated below). Some of these were originally Northern (*gaf*, *theyre*), but they had spread southwards as far as the North Midlands; they were in process of spreading still further south, and there-

---

[1] Although none of the texts are localised on non-linguistic grounds, there are some lesser indications of this type that bear out the general conclusion, e.g. it has been convincingly argued that the Auchinleck MS is the first surviving example of commercial book-production from the ME period (L. H. Loomis, *PMLA* LVII (1942) 595–627). There is also further linguistic evidence that a number of the works themselves were of London authorship (G. V. Smithers, EETS OS 237, 40–52).

[2] The theory that *-ande* in London texts is from an 'indigenous' Essex development is not supported by the evidence. It does not occur in earlier Essex texts, and its sporadic occurrence in later ones is more probably due to a spread southwards from Norfolk and Suffolk, i.e. it has the same origin as that here assumed for *-ande* in London texts.

A further and more specific pointer to East Anglian influence is the occurrence of forms like *perk* 'dark' and *nouel* 'navel' in the main hand of the Auchinleck MS.

Chaucer	1430 onwards	Chaucer	1430 onwards
yaf	gaf	hir(e)	theyre, þeir(e), þair(e), her
nat	not	thise	thes(e)
bot	but	thurgh	thorough, þorow(e)
swich(e)	such(e)	sholde	shulde

fore probably belong to the same Midland influence on London. Its immediate source would appear to have been the Central Midlands, for it shows no trace of any of the more peripheral peculiarities of the West Midlands or of East Anglia. A further relevant point is that, although some of the features may have reached London by normal southward shifts of isogloss, more of them appear first in London as isolated enclaves, due presumably to immigration or commercial contact (cf. maps 1, 2 and 5 on pp. 70 and 102).

To sum up the linguistic evidence: the London dialect was originally of an Essex type, but also contained features in common with Kent, Surrey and Middlesex; in the early and mid-fourteenth century, it assumed a marked East Anglian colouring, but at the end of the fourteenth century this was largely eradicated by an influx of Central Midland features.

The historical evidence bears out this hypothesis in a remarkable way. Firstly, the original connection with Essex is confirmed by the early diocesan boundaries. Secondly, in Domesday book, Norfolk and North Suffolk are the most densely populated areas, and are known from names in taxation-lists to have provided most of the migrants to London in the earlier ME period.[1] But thirdly, in the mid-fourteenth century there was a change in proportion: the populations of Leicestershire, Northamptonshire, and Bedfordshire had increased, and the immigrations to London from the latter two counties now equalled those from East Anglia.[2] The dating of this last change in particular agrees well with the corresponding but abrupt change in the surviving texts from the late fourteenth century.

Such a correlation of linguistic and historical evidences provides the only possible solution for sequences of abrupt replacements that are evidently non-functional in origin: the changes from *-inde* to *-ande* and then to *-ynge*, or from *schulde* to *s(c)holde* and then back to *s(c)hulde* were doubtless complex at the level of register or of contact between immigrant and indigenous groups (cf. ch. 6), but the chronology shows that the immediate cause of their presence in London was extralinguistic. This is not to deny that the normal

[1] E. Ekwall, *Two Early London Subsidy Rolls* (Lund, 1951).
[2] Ekwall, *Studies on the Population of Medieval London* (Stockholm, 1956); H. C. Darby, *Historical Geography of England before 1800* (Cambridge, 1936) 232.

intralinguistic processes of selection continued throughout. There were cogent systemic factors favouring the selection of certain forms like *they*, *though*, and present participle *-ing* in the speech of both immigrants and native Londoners, and the fact that London was in advance of the rest of the South-Eastern area in adopting them can be regarded as a normal development in a 'type B' situation (cf. 6.3, p. 92f). In addition, there is the wider factor of functional utility – a preference for the most widely and readily intelligible dialect or dialect feature (cf. 6.6, p. 108f). It is this factor that may explain why East Anglian influence on the London dialect ceased after the mid-fourteenth century, although immigration from there continued. The Norfolk dialect was peripheral and unsuited for the role of *lingua franca*, whereas the Central Midland dialect fulfilled, to a greater extent than other Midland dialects, Higden's claim that the 'Mercian' dialects were the most widely understood in the country. To that extent, therefore, the spread of features of a central dialect to the more peripheral capital city could be regarded as functional in origin. But the suddenness of the changes and their obvious dependence on immigration shows that the extralinguistic factor was the decisive one.

8.6   Interpenetration

Finally, a well-documented period of *any* length can be selected and studied for interpenetration of various factors, both extra- and intralinguistic. For our present purpose, sixteenth-century English will serve as an example. It might be supposed that pure (circular) shift would not normally affect morphological distinctions. But, besides the fact that the Great Vowel Shift was accompanied by some degree of merger, the system of vowel-gradation in the strong verb is one that would inevitably be disturbed by shift alone, depending as it does on a general distinction between front vowels for present state or action and back vowels for past. The original opposition of /e/ and /o/ that had existed in Indo-European had been successively altered by sound-change in the Germanic, OE and ME periods, and, especially in some classes of verb, had already proved inadequate. Of the verbs of class II, Wright remarks 'there is not a single N[ew] E[nglish] verb which has preserved what would have been the regularly developed parts'.[1] It is not hard to see why class II verbs should stand out in this way: by the ME period, the original Indo-European gradation /eu~ou/ had altered, via OE /eːo~ɛːɑ/, to /eː~ɛː/, and the result was that most verbs in this class were transferred to the weak conjugation (cf. 8.4, p. 161); for the two main exceptions, *freeze* and *cleave*,[2]

---

[1] Wright (1924) § 344.

[2] This refers mainly to the verb meaning 'split', though *cleave* 'adhere' was confused with it from the fourteenth century onwards. See OED s. vv., and Dobson (1957) I 56; and cf. p. 163 above.

the ME preterites *fre(e)s* and *cleef, cleue* were gradually replaced by *frose, frore, cloue* with *o* which, as the handbooks have it, had been 'levelled from the preterite plural and past participle'.[1] In the fifteenth and sixteenth centuries there are signs that the opposition /ɛ∼ɑ/ in class III verbs is no longer adequate: in the verbs *delve, help* and *melt*, preterites in *o* (*holp, molt*) and weak forms were increasingly selected, and the latter ultimately preferred; and in the verbs *bark, carve, smart, starve, warp* (ME *kerve(n), smerte(n)*, etc.) the change from /ɛr/ to /ɑr/ in the infinitive meant that even *o*-forms were less viable than weak forms.

The change from strong to weak conjugation is usually regarded as a natural extension by analogy from the larger to the smaller group of verbs, and this is no doubt true as regards the *origin* of the weak variants; but it is noticeable that the rate of their *adoption* is closely related to the adequacy of vocalic contrasts in various classes of verbs at different periods. Similarly, the occurrence of /ɔ/ in the past tense was, in origin, an extension from the past participle and occurred automatically in some parts of the spoken chain; but its adoption must be due to the fact that it provided a better contrast to the /ɛ/ of the present stem than the /ɑ/ that it replaced. Both, then, are rather to be regarded as cases of interpenetration of the phonological and grammatical systems.

The fresh growth of an /ɛ∼ɔ/ gradational pattern in Early Modern English is suggested by a development outside the verbal system – the rise of the opposition *these–those* in the newly established standard English of the mid-fifteenth century onwards. Its distinction of 'immediate' ∼ 'distant' is closely parallel to that of 'present' ∼ 'past' in the verb, yet it was not developed by any regular or straightforward process: *þees, thes(e)* was preferred to the original S.E. form *þise*, and *þos, those* was a later importation from the Central Midlands, to form a system which, even as late as Joseph Wright's[2] day, did not belong to any genuine English dialect other than the standard language. Yet, at the same time as this development, in the system of the strong verb, the loss of final inflectional /-ə/ produced the situation where the distinction between present and past was increasingly carried by the root-vowels alone. It is probably no coincidence, therefore, that in the sixteenth century, when the Great Vowel Shift was in train of altering the balance of gradational oppositions still further, we are confronted with a far greater variety and profusion of new 'analogical' forms in the strong verb than previously. There is other evidence, too, to suggest that the verb system during this period was in a state of imbalance. The main stages and results of this may be described as follows:

(i) In verbs of classes IV and V (*bear, break, shear, speak, steal, tear, tread, wear, weave*), the commoner variants of the preterite were lengthened (late

---

[1] Wright (1924) § 345.　　　[2] Wright (1905) 279.

ME *bar(e)*, *brak(e)*, etc.), and their vowel /a:/ or /æ:/ was in process of being raised to /ɛ:/ in many dialects. It was therefore either close to, or coincided with, the root-vowel /ɛ:/ of the present, as today in *bare*, the archaic preterite of *bear*. These verbs now followed the same development as that of *freeze– froze*: gradually through the century, at different times for each verb, preterite variants in /ɔ/ were selected and preferred, e.g. *stale* was replaced by *stole* early in the century, later *bare* by *bore*, and later still *brake* by *broke*.

This process of systemic regulation is of an expected type, and not in need of further explanation. But, as an innovation, it could be complicated by any of the extralinguistic factors mentioned in chapter 6. The change had repercussions on another part of the verbal system, and these are sufficient to show that, in the same way as in the examples quoted in 8.2 above, it was an *ad hoc* change, which restored the balance in some classes of the strong verb but disrupted that of another class.

(ii) In class I verbs (e.g. *write*, *drive*) the inherited contrast was /əɪ~ɔ:/, the reflexes of ME /i:~ɔ:/. It was a contrast of a different type from that of classes III, IV, and V, but still adequate. The problem is that in the sixteenth century, in addition to the historical preterites *wrote*, *drove*, the new variants *wrate*, *drave* occur frequently, but appear for about a hundred years only, giving place to the original forms at the beginning of the seventeenth century. Their origin cannot be justified etymologically, for there is no evidence that they are Northern forms; and it can hardly be functional either, since, whether pronounced [æ:] or [ɛ:], they provided a less effective opposition to the vowel of the infinitive, /əɪ/, than did the original /ɔ:/. The usual explanation is that they are analogical extensions from the type *bare*, *brake* in classes IV and V, but this does not seem likely at the very period when that type was being replaced by *bore*, *broke* (see fig. 11 for a summary diagram of the usual explanation).

The explanation of this apparent contradiction is probably to be found in social repercussions of the original innovation in classes IV and V, for which see (i) above. Investigation has shown that the type *wrate*, *drave* is typical of printed literature, whereas *wrote*, *drove* are commoner in letters and manu- scripts.[1] This provides us with a clue about the status of *a*- and *o*-preterites irrespective of their verbal class; it is reasonable to assume that preterites of the type *bore*, *broke* were an innovation that entered the language first in dialect and colloquial register, and that they were socially stigmatised forms; but, since their motivation was functional, they nevertheless gradually gained ground. As a reaction, many speakers would either preserve or aim at the conservative forms *bare* and *brake*; and further, they would tend to avoid all *o*-preterites including the historically developed *wrote*, *drove* of class I, and to substitute the hypercorrect forms *wrate*, *drave*. These hypercorrections,

[1] Price pp. 11–35.

together with other expedients like *writ* (cf. p. 162 above), replaced the original forms in formal register for a limited period. Finally, when the innovation *bore, broke* was accepted into formal register, there was no longer any cause for perpetuating the hypercorrect forms *wrate, drave*; they were replaced by the original *wrote, drove*, which were accepted back into formal register simultaneously with the newly accepted *bore, broke*. As a corollary, the very existence of such hypercorrect forms can be used as evidence that the type *bore, broke* must previously have been far commoner in sixteenth-century colloquial use than our written records might otherwise lead us to suppose.

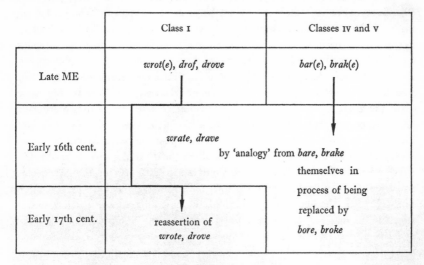

	Class I	Classes IV and V
Late ME	*wrot(e), drof, drove*	*bar(e), brak(e)*
Early 16th cent.	*wrate, drave*	by 'analogy' from *bare, brake* themselves in process of being replaced by *bore, broke*
Early 17th cent.	reassertion of *wrote, drove*	

Fig. 11.

(iii) The above are not the only symptoms of instability in the sixteenth-century verbal system. We would expect, in such a period, a greater use of marked forms, and in this context another noticeable feature of the sixteenth-century verb – which would appear problematic when considered in isolation – falls into place. The history of the *do*-periphrasis differs from those of all the other periphrases of the English verb, e.g. with *have, be, shall, will, may*: whereas these latter have resulted from an almost imperceptibly gradual growth since OE times, the *do*-periphrasis does not appear till the thirteenth century, and was, even in the fifteenth century, only a peripheral category in the grammatical system. There was then a sudden increase, and it reached a peak in the period 1535–1625, thereafter decreasing to its more restricted MnE uses in negative and interrogative clauses. Its use in these latter shows a fairly steady growth, but it was by no means obligatory in them at the end of the sixteenth century (e.g. *goest thou, he goeth not* were still common), while in affirmative clauses it was, according to the grammars and handbooks,[1] in free variation with the simple verb forms for the expression of tense. From this we might surmise that it was fulfilling the function of a marked form to remedy current instability. This surmise is confirmed by the special contexts in which it occurs more frequently: (*a*) it is often used with those strong verbs that presented the ambiguities of conjugation referred to in (i) and (ii) above; especially noticeable is the verb *eat*, which had the same form /ɛ:t/ for both present and preterite in the sixteenth century (cf. the exclusive use of *did eat* in the 1611 Gospels); (*b*) likewise, with weak verbs which since that period, in more stable systems, have been accepted as invariable (*cast, put, set*);[2] (*c*) as a signal of verbality, it was used to introduce many of the neologisms from Latin like *imitate* or *illuminate*, which had not yet been fully assimilated to the grammatical system (e.g. *do imitate, did imitate* in Sidney's *Apologie for Poetrie*); (*d*) in the long complex sentences of many Elizabethan writers, where considerable ambiguity could arise from the borrowing of stylistic features not suited to an analytic language, *do, doth, did* could often act as extra grammatical markers, especially to denote a return to the main clause after the interruption of a subordinate clause.[3] Such varied uses are a good indication that the *do*-periphrasis had the status of a marked form.

(iv) The originally Northern ending of the third singular present indicative, -(*e*)*s*, had spread southwards to the Central Midlands during the ME period, and thereafter, in certain registers only (colloquial, poetic) to the rest of the country.[4] But the written standard of the mid-fifteenth century was conservative in this respect and retained -*eth*, the early printers followed suit, and the normal written form in most sixteenth-century texts except poetic remained -*eth*. Then, in the last decade of the century, -(*e*)*s* was suddenly accepted into prose. It occurs on the whole more commonly in monosyllables except where the root ends with /s, z, tʃ, dʒ, ʃ/ (many texts differentiate between, e.g., *runs, lives* and *riseth, preacheth*), whereas in disyllabic verbs -*eth* is still preferred (*intendeth, employeth, attaineth*). There is little uniformity in this transitional period, and the choice of each writer depends on a complex combination of phonetic, rhythmical, semantic, and stylistic factors. But a noticeable exception to the main distinction just mentioned is that -(*e*)*s* is also common with the polysyllabic verbs in -*ate*, and this suggests a reason for the sudden change. Previously, cumbersome forms like *illuminateth* had been avoided, and the periphrasis *doth illuminate* served as an expedient. But it is clear from the way that these words in -*ate* are used in Elizabethan drama that they were now no longer purely literary neologisms, but were also used

---

1 Sweet II 88; Curme p. 23; Ellegård p. 170, and references there made to Palsgrave, Bellot, and Mason.
2 Jespersen (1909) V 504–6; Dahl p. 88.
3 Dahl p. 92.
4 Norman Davis, 'A Paston Hand', *RES* n.s. 3 (1952) 219.

in colloquial registers. Though still predominantly literary, their phonetic form required, and received, the 'contraction' /-s/ when spoken, and they are therefore a probable source of entry for this ending, via formal spoken register, to the written language. And if this was the case, the replacement of -*eth* by -(*e*)*s* could be said to demonstrate a further type of interpenetration – that between lexis and grammar, resulting from the phonological form of new lexical intake.

The above correlation of some of the main changes in the sixteenth-century verb has thus shown interpenetration of all subsystems, complicated by the interference of social pressures. But the limits chosen for this period of study were arbitrary, and the account can be carried further to include later inter-actions and realignments. The situation in 1600 was that the *do*-periphrasis, a grammaticisation of originally lexical material, had been called into common use as a marked form in a variety of contexts, but, for many of these, other remedies were now being found: the new preterites in -*o*- were being accepted into formal register (the 1611 Bible is somewhat archaistic in this respect); the termination -*ed*, which had been avoided with verbs in -*ate* throughout the century, was now commonly used with them, and similarly, as described above, with the -(*e*)*s* ending for the third singular present indicative of such verbs; and, with growing standardisation, the variety of conjugational forms in verbs like *eat, strike* was being reduced. But the *do*-periphrasis, as a prominent inherited feature of the spoken chain, could not suddenly dis-appear; its use could decrease at a moderate rate, but not before, by the normal processes of differentiation from the simple forms, it had been diverted to-wards other functions and tested for its effectiveness in them. In one type of function, in negative and interrogative clauses, it was already becoming well established, occurring in forty to fifty per cent of instances. Here it was joining the normal pattern of auxiliary verbs in these clauses, e.g. *I do not go, do we go?*, parallel to *I cannot go, must we go?* There were now two possibilities: either (*a*) its use in these clauses could decrease, leaving English with the same distinction as in cognate languages between the order aux.+neg.+ lexical vb. (e.g. *I cannot go*) and the order lexical vb.+neg. (e.g. *I go not*), and the similar distinction between *can we go?* and *go we?*; or (*b*) its use could be extended so that *all* negative and interrogative clauses had the orders aux. (+neg.)+lexical vb. Of these (*b*) has evident functional advantages since it allows the use of a fixed word-order at clause level; but to say that its selection was a foregone conclusion (i.e. teleologically predetermined) will not explain why English differs from cognate languages in this respect. Rather (as else-where in this chapter) we must regard both stages as *ad hoc*: firstly its rise as a marked form *at group level* in a variety of contexts, and secondly its exten-sion to join the existing pattern of auxiliaries, as a functional advantage at clause level. It is at least arguable that the completion of the second stage,

G

however functionally desirable, could not have taken place if the periphrasis had not already been established on a much broader front, and as a result of factors less applicable in other Germanic languages, through the first stage.

Here again, as in the examples quoted in 8.2 above, there is some confirmation of the non-teleological nature of this development, from evidence of an abortive realignment of the same periphrasis. In the seventeenth century, just at the time when it had been deprived of some of its earlier functions (cf. p. 175 above), we find claims in seventeenth-century grammarians that *do* has an 'imperfect' sense, i.e. by virtue of mere availability it had been differentiated and realigned to an aspectual function. These claims have been questioned,[1] but an analysis of the well-known *do* and *did* of Pepys' *Diary* suggests that there is some truth in them. But in this case, the periphrasis was not joining an existing and growing pattern; instead, it was in competition with an older and better-integrated form expressing the same (or at least partly overlapping) functions – the gradually increasing form *be+-ing*, and its disappearance in this function is to be expected. Once again, therefore, we are reminded of the importance of a *combination* of conditioning factors operating simultaneously: the acceptance of a form into the system depends on the strength or weakness of support for it present in a given *état de langue*.[2]

---

[1] Ellegård p. 171.

[2] The emphatic affirmative use of *do* is not treated here, partly because the difference of stress to some extent separates it from the other functions, and partly because of the difficulty of assessing the degree of stress to be assigned to examples from written records of the past. But its origins appear to be secondary, and not directly connected with the original unstressed periphrasis. For example, it could be reached by an extension of the following type. The propword *do* has always existed in both stressed and unstressed forms, and the stressed form would be used naturally as a positive antonym to the negatived propword, e.g. *they dó* in answer to *they do not*. Then, with the increase of *do* in negative clauses generally, a parallel positive antonym would arise on this model, e.g. *they dó go* in answer to *they do not go*.

9 Conclusions

The basic causes of linguistic change have been variously defined in the past, some views being criticised as complex and amorphous, others as oversimplified. The arguments advanced in this book suggest that the entire phenomenon should be attributed to three causes:

(i) variation due to (*a*) inertia, and
    (*b*) differences of style;
(ii) systemic regulation;
(iii) contact.

This estimate does not include an obvious fourth cause – extralinguistic influences – except in so far as (i) and (iii) provide routes for their entry; but, if that is taken into account, there remains no room for scepticism: *every* change can be accounted for as due to one, or a combination, of the above.

If it is claimed that this view, like others, is an oversimplification, we may answer, firstly, that these three causes relate to the whole universe of human communication: (i) relates ultimately to the speaker as an individual, (ii) to the language system in abstract, and (iii) to both speakers and systems in contact. Secondly, if the scope of the three causes is examined, their possible workings and interactions are seen to be complex; yet, because of close parallels between systems, these are always referable to the main causes.

(i) The origin of change, variation, consists of departures from existing norms, and is manifested in differing but parallel ways in phonology, grammar, and lexis. In each the change decreases the distance that has hitherto served to differentiate either discrete forms or discrete functions and meanings. The result is 'devaluation' or loss of information-content, and, if the process is completed, the result is merger (phonology), syncretism (grammar), homonymy and polysemy (lexis). In phonology, in extreme cases, an excess of phonemes is concentrated in one articulatory area (with or without merger); in grammar and lexis, the parallel case is where the same forms eventually perform antonymous functions. The main difference is that in phonology the loss of distance is articulatory, whereas in grammar and lexis (in so far as coincidence of form does not result from phonological change) it is due to the selection of forms that are initially aberrant, irrespective of whether they arise from conscious motivation (e.g. creativity) or from inertia, and the result is extension of function or meaning that reduces differentiation in a way parallel to the effects of phonic shift.

For all subsystems, it is necessary to specify both inertia and stylistic variation, though there is a wide overlap in the effects of inertia and relaxed style. In phonology, many forms (especially those resulting from conditioned change, cf. 2.2–3) can be regarded as due to either or both; but for isolative change, forceful variants are of equal importance, and, in origin at least, cannot be accounted for by inertia (2.5). Similarly in grammar and lexis, the vagaries of selection (as seen, e.g., in exaggeration, understatement, metaphor, extension of marked forms) are in some cases due to stylistic variation and in others to inertia (ch. 4).

(ii) Systemic regulation, which comes about through selection of variants (7.2), consists of the restoration of the distances lost in (i), that is, it is a compensatory mechanism. It is seen typically in the circular shift of phonemes (3.7), in the gradual replacement of weakened grammatical forms by new marked forms from lexis (5.5), in the remedying of homonymy and polysemy (5.2–4), and, on a larger scale, in grammatical restructuring (6.7, 8.2, 8.6). It is essentially an *ad hoc* process, and, even where long-term or large-scale changes give the opposite impression, they can be shown to consist of a series of smaller changes each of which depended on the balance of pressures existing at the time (8.2–3, 8.6). In phonology, circular vocalic shift is partly determined by the limitations of the speech-organs (3.3), but also by the need to restore the sonority lost in raising (3.7); but complete circularity is not essential, and an equivalent result may ultimately be obtained by the selection of lowered variants from split, or from conditioned change (3.8). Similarly, merger of vowels is sometimes found to be compensated for by new consonantal distinctions (6.8).

(iii) Contact is a factor that is to some extent present in all changes. As a natural concomitant of communication, it appears at its most obvious in contact between individuals, in the resultant alterations and reinterpretations during transmission or imitation, and in the spread of changes generally, whether they are mechanical or functional, and whether at the level of idiolect or system. The spread may take place by either gradual or discrete stages: in phonology it is often by the latter, once the discrete variants have developed from either gradual or saltatory change (6.7, pp. 125–7, and 8.3, p. 159f). In grammar and lexis, gradual spread takes place typically by a series of stages in which minor systems combine the old and new forms in changing proportions (6.7, pp. 116-19). Such minor systems may then survive intact, or terminate in complete replacement of one member by the other, or contribute to restructuring (6.7, pp. 127–9).

Contact between systems greatly increases the number of variants available for selection; it accounts for the spread of features across language boundaries (6.4) and from one regional or class dialect to another (6.5), and for standardisation (6.5–6). In class dialects especially, the motive of prestige imitation gives rise to the further complications of hypercorrection and polarisation (6.6). More indirectly, contact accounts for the varying rates of intrasystemic change in different languages and dialects (6.8): these depend on the abruptness or smoothness of the contact, the degree of difference between the systems in contact, as well as on retarding factors like the existence of a written language, degree of literacy, and prescriptivity (6.6). But although high rates of change have occurred, especially in areas that have sustained invasions, or in periods when the degree of literacy was low, normal everyday contact between speakers of only slightly differing dialects is sufficient to trigger the typical processes of intrasystemic change: even in comparatively isolated systems with a low rate of change, there is always some evidence of change that has followed the usual patterns (e.g. in Modern Icelandic, the diphthongisations of long vowels, and the raising and fronting of /au/ to /øi/).

(iv) The sphere of those extralinguistic factors that affect a system directly is in some cases obvious (1.4, 6.1), but in others can be difficult to distinguish from that of intrasystemic factors (6.6, p. 107, and 6.8, p. 133). The effects of those that reach a system through extrasystemic contact are easier to define, but vary greatly: some, like invasion or other population shifts, provide the whole impetus for a change, dictate its nature, and determine the direction which the subsequent history of the system is to take (6.1, 8.5); others, like social cleavage, may interfere with normal intrasystemic processes by accelerating or retarding them, but appear to affect the eventual result less than is often thought (6.8); admittedly prestige imitation of idiosyncracies may produce untypical changes, but these are equally liable to systemic regulation (6.8).

Of the above four, (i) and (ii) are predictable within the general limits set out in chapters 2–5; (iii) is predictable only to the limited extent that it is not at the control of (iv); and (iv) is wholly unpredictable. The tasks of the historian of the language are, therefore,

(*a*) to attempt to distinguish (i) from (iv), though this may not be feasible if the required historical and demographic evidence is not available;

(*b*) to distinguish (i) from (ii), i.e. between those changes that are imposed on the system as a result of mechanical or extralinguistic pressures (push-chain process), and those that are due to pressure from the system itself (drag-chain process).

The latter task entails a consideration of all the variants known to have existed in the speech of a community and to have been available for selection at the time of a change. The variants ultimately to be selected for either push- or drag-chain processes are of the same origin; they are all selected in the same way, and their initial motivation (or lack of it) is not necessarily relevant to their acceptance (7.2). An eventual preference for a rare or obscure variant is not to be regarded as anomalous, or as contravening a rule; if it cannot be explained extralinguistically, the reason for it is a systemic one, whether central (e.g. risk of homonymy, inadequacy of unmarked form) or marginal (e.g. lack of integration, phonaesthetic attraction). In addition, for many changes it is necessary to examine the interpenetration of subsystems (7.2, 8.6), and to assess the relative weight of conflicting pressures (7.3).

The arguments that have been presented here in favour of the above theory will, it is hoped, answer recent statements such as that 'change occurs because the grammar of the language has changed, and the largely random effects of performance have nothing to do with it' or that 'grammars become simpler all the time, not less simple'.[1] The effects of performance are indeed (initially) random, but there could be no change without them; and simplification is indeed proceeding all the time, but it is always counterbalanced by the rise of new complexities.

The notion that a theory that is 'powerful' for some purposes is necessarily ideal for all is a dangerous one. Some recent writers claim that the whole of our knowledge of historical phonology will have to be reformulated in generative terms before any further progress can be made.[2] But to attempt such a task will be a luxury we can ill afford if it distracts us from other more urgent tasks that await us. Some idea of their scope will have been deduced from previous chapters; for example, there is a need for further detailed studies on the relation between social and linguistic changes, especially in phonology (6.5), and for much fuller histories of the phonaesthemes of every language that has a recorded history of some length (3.10). More glaring still is the absence of apparatus for studying the history of the lexis of all such languages. As was pointed out in 5.5, no solution to the problem of push- and drag-chains in lexis will be forthcoming until it is possible to study simultaneously *all* the forms involved in a complex series of semantic shifts and replacements. The required data exist in multivolume historical dictionaries like the OED, but they cannot be utilised because the presentation is alphabetical, not notional. The need is for a historical *thesaurus* which will bring together under single heads all the words, current or obsolete (and all the obsolete meanings of words still current) that have ever been used to express single and related notions.[3] The production of such a thesaurus is arduous. Every attested meaning, past and present, must be semantically analysed and classified, and this can be achieved only by conventional methods, not by computer. It is at present being attempted for English only, and, from experience so far gained, will be a lengthy task.[4]

---

[1] King pp. 15 and 216.   [2] E.g. R. P. Stockwell, Foreword to Lass (1969).
[3] Cf. Ullmann pp. 255–6, von Wartburg pp. 174–8.
[4] As already reported in *TPS* (1965) 40, this work is being carried out at the Department of English Language, University of Glasgow, which gratefully acknowledges help currently received for the purpose from the Leverhulme Trust. But it is no exaggeration to say that a task of this size could reasonably have been undertaken jointly by three large university departments, not by one small one as at present.

But although the historical study of lexis is as yet in its infancy, this is not due to any fault in our linguistic *theory*. It has been the main aim of this book to show that conflicting dogmas can be reconciled, that the problems arising from some previous theories can be solved, and that the residue can be rationalised into a comprehensive and workable theory of historical linguistics. A more pressing need is for further research – much of it laborious – from data that are freely available. Some of the evidence thus collated will no doubt be inconclusive, or will suggest to us no more than random redistributions; but other parts of it – and this is where the main interest of the subject lies – will provide us with the explanation for changes that are not random, but which reflect, in their own unique way, the lives, purposes and aspirations of the human beings that language serves.

Bibliography

Included here are all works quoted in abbreviated form in the footnotes, together with a few others central to the theme of the book; but certain more specialised references have been restricted to the footnotes only. For abbreviations of the titles of periodicals, see p. ix.

Abercrombie, D. *Elements of General Phonetics*. Edinburgh, 1967.
et al. (eds.). *In Honour of Daniel Jones*. London, 1964.
Allen, W. S. 'Relationship in Comparative Linguistics'. *TPS* 1953, 52–108.
'Some Problems of Palatalization in Greek'. *Lingua* 7 (1957–8) 113–33.
Bernstein, B. 'Aspects of Language and Language Learning in the Genesis of the Social Process'. In Hymes 1964, 251–63 (= 1964*a*).
'Social Class, Speech Systems and Psycho-Therapy'. *British Journal of Sociology* 15 (1964) 54–64 (= 1964*b*).
Bloomfield, L. *Language*. London, 1935.
Bradley, H. *The Making of English*. London, 1904. Revised edn by S. Potter, London, 1968.
Bréal, M. *Essai de sémantique: science des significations* (Paris, 1897). Translated under the title *Semantics: Studies in the Science of Meaning* by N. Cust, New York, 1900, reprinted 1964.
Bright, W. 'Social Dialect and Language History'. In Hymes 1964, 469–72.
(ed.). *Sociolinguistics: Proceedings of the UCLA Sociolinguistics Conference, 1964*. The Hague, 1966.
Campbell, A. *Old English Grammar*. Oxford, 1959.
Crystal, D. *Prosodic Systems and Intonation in English*. Cambridge, 1969.
and Quirk, R. *Systems of Prosodic and Paralinguistic Features in English*. The Hague, 1964.
Curme, G. O. *A Grammar of the English Language III: Syntax*. Boston, 1931.
Dahl, T. *Linguistic Studies in some Elizabethan Writings, II: The Auxiliary Do (Acta Jutlandica* 28, no. 1). Aarhus, 1956.
Dal, Ingerid. *Ursprung und Verwendung der altnordischen Expletivpartikel "of, um"* (Avhandlinger utgitt av Det Norske Videnskaps-Akademi, Hist.-fil. klasse, 1929, no. 5). Oslo, 1930.
Dieth, E. *Vademekum der Phonetik*. Berne, 1950.
Dobson, E. J. 'Early Modern Standard English'. *TPS* 1955, 25–54, and in Lass 1969, 419–39.
English Pronunciation 1500–1700. Oxford, 1957.
Duraffour, A. *Phénomènes généraux d'évolution phonétique dans les dialectes franco-provençaux d'après le parler de Vaux-en-Bugey, Ain*. Grenoble, 1932.
Ellegård, A. *The Auxiliary 'Do': The Establishment and Regulation of its Use in English* (Gothenburg Studies in English, 2). Stockholm, 1953.
Firth, J. R. *Speech* (London, 1930) and *The Tongues of Men* (London, 1937), both reprinted in one volume, London, 1964.

'The Use and Distribution of certain English Sounds'. *English Studies* 17 (1935), 8–18, reprinted in *Papers in Linguistics 1934–51*, Oxford, 1957, 34–46.

Fishman, J. A. (ed.), *Readings in the Sociology of Language*. The Hague, 1968.

Fouché, P. *Études de phonétique générale*. Paris, 1927.

Fourquet, J. *Les mutations consonantiques du germanique*. Paris, 1948.

Fridén, G. *Studies on the Tenses of the English Verb from Chaucer to Shakespeare*, Uppsala, 1948.

Frings, T. 'Germanisch ō und ē', *Beiträge zur Geschichte der deutschen Sprache und Literatur* 63 (1939) 1–116.

Gilliéron, J. and Roques, M. *Études de géographie linguistique*. Paris, 1912.

Gimson, A. C. *An Introduction to the Pronunciation of English*. London, 1962.

Grammont, M. *Traité de phonétique*. Paris, 1933.

Greenberg, J. H. *Language Universals*. The Hague, 1966.

'Synchronic and Diachronic Universals in Phonology'. *Language* 42 (1966) 508–17.

Gumperz, J. J. 'On the Ethnology of Linguistic Change'. In Bright 1966, 27–49.

Hall, R. A. 'Pidgin English and Linguistic Change'. *Lingua* 3 (1952) 138–46.

Introductory Linguistics. Philadelphia, 1964.

Halle, M. 'Phonology in Generative Grammar'. *Word* 18 (1962) 54–72. Reprinted in *The Structure of Language*, ed. J. A. Fodor and J. J. Katz, Englewood Cliffs, New Jersey, 1964.

Halliday, M. A. K., McIntosh, A. and Strevens, P. *The Linguistic Sciences and Language Teaching*. London, 1964.

Heffner, R. S. *General Phonetics*. Madison, 1949.

Hockett, C. F. *A Course in Modern Linguistics*. New York, 1958.

Hoenigswald, H. M. *Language Change and Linguistic Reconstruction*. Chicago, 1960. Review of Martinet 1955, *Language* 33 (1957) 575–83.

Horn, W. *Sprachkörper und Sprachfunktion* (Palaestra, 135). Leipzig, 1921.

and Lehnert, M. *Laut und Leben: Englische Lautgeschichte der neueren Zeit (1400–1950)*. Berlin, 1954.

Householder, F. W. 'On some recent claims in phonological theory'. *Journal of Linguistics* 1 (1965) 13–34.

Hymes, D. (ed.). *Language in Culture and Society*. New York, 1964.

Iordan, I. and Orr, J. *An Introduction to Romance Linguistics*. London, 1937.

Jacobsson, U. *Phonological Dialect Constituents in the Vocabulary of Standard English* (Lund Studies in English 31). Lund, 1962.

Jakobson, R. *Selected Writings I: Phonological Studies*. The Hague, 1962.

Jespersen, O. *A Modern English Grammar* I–VII. Heidelberg and Copenhagen, 1909–49.

Language, Its Nature, Development, and Origin. London, 1922.

Efficiency in Linguistic Change. Copenhagen, 1941.

King, R. D. *Historical Linguistics and Generative Grammar*. Englewood Cliffs, New Jersey, 1969.

Kivimaa, K. Þe *and* Þat *as Clause Connectives in Early Middle English* (Societas Scientiarum Fennica, Commentationes Humanarum Litterarum 39.1). Helsinki, 1966.

Kolb, E. *Linguistic Atlas of England: Phonological Atlas of the Northern Region*. Berne, 1966.

Kuhn, H. *Das Füllwort 'of, um' im altwestnordischen*. Göttingen, 1929.

Kurylowicz, J. *The Inflectional Categories of Indo-European*. Heidelberg, 1964.

Labov, W. 'Hypercorrection by the Lower Middle Class as a Factor in Linguistic Change'. In Bright 1966, 84–113 (= 1966a).

The Social Stratification of English in New York City. Washington, D.C., 1966
(= 1966*b*).

Ladd, C. A. 'The Nature of Sound-Change'. In Lunt 1964, 650–57.

'The Status of Sound-Laws'. *AL* 17 (1965) 91–110.

Ladefoged, P. *Three Areas of Experimental Phonetics.* London, 1967.

Lass, R. (ed.). *Approaches to English Historical Linguistics.* New York, 1969.

Laziczius, G. *Selected Writings,* ed. T. A. Sebeok. The Hague, 1966.

Leed, R. L. 'Distinctive Features and Analogy'. *Lingua* 26 (1970) 1–24.

Le Page, R. B. 'Problems of Description in Multilingual Communities'. *TPS* 1968, 189–211.

Luick, K. *Historische Grammatik der englischen Sprache.* Leipzig, 1914–.

Lunt, H. G. (ed.). *Proceedings of the Ninth International Congress of Linguists, Cambridge, Mass., 1962.* The Hague, 1964.

Lyons, J. *Introduction to Theoretical Linguistics.* Cambridge, 1968.

McIntosh, A. 'The Relative Pronouns *þe* and *þat* in Early Middle English'. *EAGS* 1 (1947–8) 73–87.

'The Analysis of Written Middle English'. *TPS* 1956, 26–55, and in Lass 1969, 35–57.

'A New Approach to Middle English Dialectology'. *ES* 44 (1963) 1–11, and in Lass 1969, 392–403.

and Samuels, M. L. 'Prolegomena to a Study of Mediaeval Anglo-Irish'. *Medium Ævum* 37 (1968) 1–11.

McKnight, G. H. *Modern English in the Making.* New York, 1928.

Malkiel, Y. 'Some Diachronic Implications of Fluid Speech Communities'. *American Anthropologist* 66 (1964) 177–86 (reprinted in *Essays on Linguistic Themes,* Oxford, 1968, 19–31).

'Linguistics as a Genetic Science'. *Language* 43 (1967) 223–45.

Marchand, H. *The Categories and Types of Present-Day English Word-Formation,* 2nd edn. Munich, 1969.

Martinet, A. *Économie des changements phonétiques.* Berne, 1955.

A Functional View of Language. Oxford, 1962.

Elements of General Linguistics (translated by E. Palmer from *Éléments de linguistique générale,* Paris, 1960). London, 1964.

Menner, R. J. 'The Conflict of Homonyms in English'. *Language* 12 (1936) 229–44.

'Multiple Meaning and Change of Meaning in English'. *Language* 21 (1945) 59–76.

Modéer, I. *Fornvästnordiska Verbstudier II* (Uppsala universitets årsskrift 1943). Uppsala, 1943.

Moulton, W. G. 'The Short Vowel Systems of Northern Switzerland'. *Word* 16 (1960) 155–82.

'Dialect Geography and the Concept of Phonological Space'. *Word* 18 (1962) 23–32.

Orr, J. *Words and Sounds in English and French.* Oxford, 1953.

Oxford English Dictionary, ed. A. H. Murray, H. Bradley, W. A. Craigie, and C. T. Onions. Oxford 1888–1933.

Paul, H. *Prinzipien der Sprachgeschichte.* Halle, 1880; 2nd edn, translated by H. A. Strong, London, 1888.

Posner, R. *Consonantal Dissimilation in the Romance Languages* (Publications of the Philological Society XIX). Oxford, 1961.

Price, H. T. *A History of Ablaut in the Strong Verbs from Caxton to the end of the Elizabethan Period* (Bonner Studien zur englischen Philologie 3). Bonn, 1910.

Pulgram, E. 'French /ə/: Statics and Dynamics of Linguistic Subcodes'. *Lingua* 10 (1961) 305–25.

'Trends and Predictions'. In *To Honor Roman Jakobson*, The Hague, 1967, vol. 11, 1634–49.

Quirk, R. 'Relative Clauses in Educated Spoken English'. *ES* 38 (1957) 97–109.

Essays on the English Language, Medieval and Modern. London, 1968.

'Aspect and Variant Inflection in English Verbs'. *Language* 46 (1970) 300–11.

Read, A. W. 'English Words with Constituent Elements having Independent Semantic Value'. In *Philologica: The Malone Anniversary Studies*, ed. T. A. Kirby and H. B. Woolf. Baltimore, 1949.

Robson, C. A. Review of Martinet 1955, *AL* 8 (1956) 151–7.

Samuels, M. L. 'The *ge*-prefix in the Old English Gloss to the Lindisfarne Gospels'. *TPS* 1949, 62-116.

'The Elder Edda and the Lindisfarne Gloss: a Syntactic Parallel'. *EAGS* 3 (1949–50) 37–41.

'The Suffixed Article in North Germanic'. *AL* 3 (1951) 23–37.

'Some Applications of Middle English Dialectology'. *ES* 44 (1963) 81–94, and in Lass 1969, 404–18.

'The Role of Functional Selection in the History of English'. *TPS* 1965, 15–40, and in Lass 1969, 352–44.

Sapir, E. *Language*. New York, 1921.

Saussure, F. de. *Cours de linguistique générale* (1916 and subsequent editions). English translation by Wade Baskin, London, 1960.

Schmitt, A. *Akzent und Diphthongierung*. Heidelberg, 1931.

Sievers, E. *Grundzüge der Phonetik*, 4th edn. Leipzig, 1894.

and Brunner, K., *Altenglische Grammatik*. Halle, 1942.

Sivertsen, E. *Cockney Phonology*. Oslo, 1960.

Spence, N. C. W. 'Towards a New Synthesis in Linguistics: The Work of Eugenio Coseriu'. *AL* 12 (1960) 1–34.

Stern, G. *Meaning and Change of Meaning*. Gothenburg, 1931.

Sturtevant, E. H. *Linguistic Change*. Chicago, 1917.

An Introduction to Linguistic Science. New Haven, 1947.

Sweet, H. *A New English Grammar*. Oxford, 1891–8.

Trager, G. L. 'Paralanguage: A First Approximation'. *Studies in Linguistics* 13 (1958) 1–12.

Trim, J. L. M. 'Historical, Descriptive and Dynamic Linguistics'. *Language and Speech* 2 (1959) 9–25.

Ullmann, S. *Semantics: An Introduction to the Science of Meaning*. London, 1962.

Vachek, J. 'Notes on the Phonological Development of the NE Pronoun *She*', *Sborník prací filosofické fakulty brněnské university*, III, Ser. A. (1954) 67–80.

'On Peripheral Phonemes of Modern English'. *Brno Studies in English* 4 (1964) 7–110.

Wang, W. S-Y. 'Competing Changes as Cause of Residue'. *Language* 45 (1969) 9–25.

von Wartburg, W. *Einführung in Problematik und Methodik der Sprachwissenschaft*. Tübingen, 1943; revised edition with the collaboration of S. Ullmann, translated from the French edition by Joyce M. H. Reid, Oxford, 1969.

Weinreich, U. *Languages in Contact*. New York, 1953.

Labov, W. and Herzog, M. I. 'Empirical Foundations for a Theory of Language Change'. In *Directions for Historical Linguistics*, ed. W. P. Lehmann and Y. Malkiel. Austin, 1968, 95–195.

Whorf, B. L. *Language, Thought and Reality: Selected Writings of Benjamin Lee Whorf*, ed. J. B. Carroll. New York, 1956.

Williams, E. R. *The Conflict of Homonyms in English* (Yale Studies in English 100). New Haven, 1944.

Wilmanns, W. *Deutsche Grammatik*. Strasburg, 1897–1909.

Wright, J. *The English Dialect Grammar*. Oxford, 1905.

and Wright, E. M. *Elementary Historical New English Grammar*. Oxford, 1924.

Wyld, H. C. *A History of Modern Colloquial English*, 2nd edn. London, 1921.

Studies in English Rhymes from Surrey to Pope. London, 1923.

A Short History of English, 3rd edn. London, 1927.

Index of persons

Abercrombie, D., 19
Allen, W. S., 32, 129

Batchelor, T., 131
Bellot, J., 174n
Berndt, R., 81
Bernstein, B., 97
Bliss, A. J., 166n
Bloomfield, L., 22, 47n, 117, 120, 124, 137
Bolinger, D. L., 47
Bradley, H., 50
Bréal, M., 64f
Bright, W., 110, 131
Buchanan, J., 132
Bullokar, W., 69
Butler, C., 174n

Campbell, A., 158
Capell, A., 50
Caxton, W., 118, 128
Chaucer, G., 166–9
Chomsky, N., 3, 29, 112f, 120
Chowdhury, M., 98
Cooper, C., 147
Coseriu, E., 11
Crystal, D., 24n
Curme, G. O., 174

Dahl, T., 174
Dal, I., 60n
Darby, H. C., 169
Davis, N., 116n, 174
De Vries, F. C., 72
Dickins, B., 158
Dieth, E., 21, 115, 159n
Dobson, E. J., 45n, 131, 133, 142n, 146f, 170n
Duncan, T. G., 166n
Duraffour, A., 23

Ekwall, E., 169
Ellegård, A., 174, 176
Elphinston, J., 36

Ferguson, C. A., 98

Firth, J. R., 12n, 16n, 46
Fischer, J. L., 42n, 132
Fouché, P., 22
Fourquet, J., 41n
Fowler, H. W., 110
Fridén, G., 51
Frings, T., 23
Fudge, E. C., 31n

Gauchat, L., 113n
Gill, A., 133
Gumperz, J. J., 89

Hall, R. A., 97n, 98n, 107
Halle, M., 29, 112f, 120
Halliday, M. A. K., 90n
Haudricourt, A., 98n
Heffner, R. S., 19
Heller, L. G., 43
Herman, S. R., 119
Hermann, E., 113n
Herzog, M. I., 146
Higden, R., 170
Hobbes, T., 54
Hockett, C. F., 9, 29n, 136n
Hoenigswald, H. M., 136n
Honikman, B., 19
Hopkins, G. M., 62
Horn, W., 81, 84, 127, 136
Householder, F. W., 29n

Jacobsson, U., 69
Jakobson, R., 2n
Jespersen, O., 3, 36, 50, 73, 77, 131n, 132n, 151n, 161, 174
Johnson, S., 150
Jones, C., 156
Jones, R. F., 94n
Joos, M., 132n

Kapteyn, J. M. N., 23
Kenrick, W., 131f
King, R. D., 17n, 55n, 127n, 180
Kivimaa, K., 86
Kohler, K. J., 99n
Kolb, E., 98f, 124, 142

187

Index of subjects

NOTE ON TERMINOLOGY. The terms *phonetic* and *phonemic* have been preferred; *phonic* is used as a neutral term applied to substance only, while *phonology* is intended as an inclusive term covering both etic and emic levels. *Drag-chain* is preferred to *drag-mechanism* since it has the advantage of including the connotation of chain-reactions within a system. The term *push-chain* may perhaps be criticised as illogical or contradictory, but is used as a convenient and reasonably well-established counterpart to *drag-chain*.

189